e.biz

For Jackie

e.biz

The anatomy of electronic business

Geoffrey Sampson

ELSEVIER
BUTTERWORTH
HEINEMANN

AMSTERDAM   BOSTON   HEIDELBERG   LONDON   NEW YORK   OXFORD
PARIS   SAN DIEGO   SAN FRANCISCO   SINGAPORE   SYDNEY   TOKYO

Butterworth-Heinemann
An imprint of Elsevier
Linacre House, Jordan Hill, Oxford OX2 8DP
200 Wheeler Road, Burlington, MA 01803

First Published 2004

British Library Cataloguing in Publication Data

A catalogue record for this book is available from the British Library

Library of Congress Cataloguing in Publication Data

A catalogue record for this book is available from the Library of Congress

ISBN 0 7506 58959

For information on all Butterworth-Heinemann publications visit
our website at www.bh.com

Typeset by Mouse Nous, Llanwrtyd Wells
Printed and bound in Great Britain by Martins the Printers Ltd, Berwick-upon-Tweed

Contents

Contents

Acknowledgements

I warmly thank the friends who helped to shape my understanding of e-business and offered detailed comment on part or all of this book in draft: Lee Braine (Accenture), Denis Johnston (I4B, formerly BT Labs), Jan Metzger (Technology Investment Banking, Deutsche Bank), Felicity van Rijn (BMW Group), and Stephen Sampson (consultant, formerly Sun Microsystems). They are not responsible for the views I express.

Thanks too to my students and colleagues at Sussex University, particularly Andy Balaam, John Carroll, Gerald Gazdar, Andy Holyer, Rudi Lutz (who invited me to teach this subject), and Kevin Tansley, to Huw McCarthy, and to A. L. Peel of Nottingham Business School.

I am grateful to VNU Business Publications for supplying the indispensable newspapers *Computing* and *IT Week*.

Notes on terminology

People who hear the term 'e-business' sometimes ask 'Is that the same as e-commerce?' It is broader. Commerce refers to the trading activities which take place at the interfaces between company and company or company and individuals. Business includes commerce, and it also includes all the internal arrangements which enable a company to transform its inputs into its outputs. Information technology – 'IT' as it is called for short – is bringing about large changes in both these areas, and both of them are covered in this book. When I use the term 'e-commerce', this will refer strictly to trading across organization boundaries.

It is often useful to contrast e-business with business as it was conducted before information technology changed business techniques. I call the latter 'conventional' business, as in 'conventional warfare'. Much successful business today is conventional in this sense.

Rather than tediously repeating 'he or she', I prefer to stay true to the long-standing grammatical convention that the masculine stands for either sex in the case of unknown or hypothetical individuals. The use of masculine terms throughout this book represents the choice of the author, and not the publisher.

The prefix http:// is understood and not shown explicitly when URLs are quoted in this book.

1

Introduction

Scope and assumptions

This book is written to help students of computer science and related subjects understand how their expertise is changing the nature of business.

The topic of the book is a recent development. Businesses have used computers for decades. But, for most of that time, broadly speaking they were using the machines to execute, more cheaply and/or faster, the same processes that were previously carried out manually. Now, computers are often changing the content of what businesses are doing – and, although there were isolated earlier cases, it is only since the late 1990s that this has been true to any great extent.

There are a lot of books about 'e-commerce' or 'e-business' available, many of them called into existence by the extraordinary dotcom bubble which burst in the year 2000. This book is rather different.

For one thing I have tried to make it more factual and less hype-laden than a lot of them are. For someone who has a business to run, it is not helpful to read slogans along the lines 'Either you're an e-business tomorrow or you're dead' – managers do not need to be told that they must come to terms with the IT revolution, the difficulty is finding successful ways of doing it. In any case, that sort of sloganizing has felt less persuasive since the year 2000, now that so many e-businesses founded with high hopes are themselves dead, and some of those which survive have been dropping the '.com' from their company names and changing their image from denizens of pure cyberspace to bricks-and-mortar organizations which make use of the internet.

More important, though, this book assumes a different pattern of background knowledge and interests on the reader's part. Most books about e-business are written for managers who know about business and economics but are baffled by the new technology. This book is written mainly for readers like my own students, who are at ease with the technical side of computing but may never have had occasion to think about business issues, other than as consumers. I hope that businesspeople who come across the book may find it enlightening and helpful, but there is certainly material here which, to them, will seem too obvious to spell out. To computer science students, basic economic or business concepts are not always self-evident. There is no reason why they should be.

Technical IT details will be avoided so far as possible. Computing students study them in other contexts. Other readers will often prefer not to learn about them at all.

The book will look at developments worldwide, but its perspective will be centred in Britain and Europe. Unlike most topics studied by computing students, in e-business geography matters. Business environments are very different in different parts of the globe.

Bubble and reality

Now is a good time to write this kind of book: the bursting of the dotcom bubble has cleared away much misunderstanding.

During that crazy period at the end of the 1990s, what the typical IT student really wanted to know about e-business was where to apply to get millions thrown into his lap for minimal effort on his part. People who controlled capital were so desperate not to miss out on an investment bonanza that things like that were actually happening. Daniel Levine asked the VC (venture capitalist) Guy Kawasaki about that mad time: 'There's a sense today that a few years ago all you had to do was sit down for a cup of coffee with a VC, jot down a business plan on the back of an envelope and you could walk out with a check for $30 million. Is that a myth?' [Kawasaki:] 'Well, it wasn't that easy. You also had to boot PowerPoint, but that's it. (laughs) ... Much of that myth is true.'[1]

Since the bubble burst and new-technology companies collapsed or saw their share prices fall to fractions of earlier values, some people have been swinging to the other extreme and concluding that e-business is a delusion. But this is as irrational as the earlier dotcom fever. Now that has subsided, we can see that there are many IT-fuelled developments happening in solid, successful businesses, though these are not always concentrated in the areas which were in the spotlight a few years ago.

The mere fact of numerous bankruptcies tells us nothing about the future of e-business: such things are usual with disruptive economic innovations. As David Manasian (2003) writes:

> In the 1870s America's railroad industry boomed in much the same way as the world's telecoms industry in the late 1990s, only to collapse in a similar heap of bankruptcies ... A few years later ... [railways] revived, changing American business for ever. ... In the first few years of the 20th century there were thousands of people tinkering with carmaking, most of whom went bust. A decade later only a handful survived, but the car was about to become the icon of progress.

This book is being written as commercialization of the internet approaches its tenth anniversary. (Some legal constraints on acceptable internet use were relaxed

---

1. 'One-on-one with Guy Kawasaki, CEO, Garage Technology Ventures', *San Francisco Business Times* 29 Mar 2002, taxpunko.notlong.com

in 1990, but significant commercial exploitation began only in late 1993–early 1994.) We have come through the early growing pains. Dimly, we may now discern the outline of longer-term trends.

B2C, B2B, B2G

People who talk about 'dotcoms' usually mean companies which sell to the public – though the URL suffix .com is not restricted to retailers. Even in that *B2C* (business to consumer) area, the bursting of the dotcom bubble has not meant a reduction of business activity. Far from it.

Online B2C sales in Britain rose by 53 per cent from 2000 to 2001, the blackest period for investors in the technology; from 2001 to 2002 they almost doubled, and then from the first half of 2002 to the same period in 2003 they did double. (By mid-2003 online shopping accounted for six per cent of all retail sales in Britain.) The engineer turned venture capitalist Andy Kessler has described the situation: 'Technology stocks are down, but technology itself has no clue whether we are in a bull or a bear market, boom or recession. It just marches ahead'.[2] The technology is going to be used one way or another, though plenty of people have lost money trying to foresee precisely how.

But in any case, B2C sales – *e-tailing* – is only part of the picture. When the World Wide Web first arrived, it is true that B2C was where the excitement lay. Partly, this was because the directness of communication between individual customers and retailers was genuinely the thing about the Web which represented its biggest single innovation from a business point of view. Largely, though, it was for the more superficial reason that B2C commerce is the aspect of business which is directly visible to people like journalists who help to form public opinion.

Any business is an operation which takes in various goods and services as inputs, and turns them into (normally more valuable) goods and/or services as outputs. Things bought by consumers represent the ends of long *value chains* which trace back ultimately to unprocessed raw materials; normally, many companies will have played successive parts in the process by which raw materials turn into consumer goods. B2C trading is the very last step in the series of transactions which deliver a manufactured good or service to a consumer, and it is preceded by a long series of *B2B* (business to business) transactions. One American estimate puts total B2B market size at ten times the size of the B2C market.

B2B trading via the internet did not become the stuff of media and investor feeding frenzy in the same way as e-tailing was; but the evidence seems to be that B2B is actually a more important aspect of e-business, not merely in terms of helping buyers and sellers to find each other, but in terms of allowing established business relationships to function more efficiently. Online B2B sales in Britain rose 36 per cent from 2000 to 2001, which is less than the B2C increase, but from a higher base: the value of online B2B sales in 2001 was almost double online B2C sales.

2. Quoted by Michael Lewis (2001: 146).

Some people distinguish a further category of *B2G* – business to government – trading; trading where government is the customer has features distinguishing it from both retailing and selling to private-sector organizations. Governments, at national and local level, are very important customers, and during the present economic downturn they are among the chief forces driving e-business forward.

Business process re-engineering

The impact of IT is not limited to the interfaces between companies and other companies or individuals – *e-commerce*. It is also affecting the internal processes by which companies do their work of transforming inputs into outputs. *Business process re-engineering* (BPR) has been a management buzzword since the mid-1990s, and often it refers to reorganizing business operations in ways that are not related to computing in particular. But one important area of BPR involves using IT to run businesses in ways that would not have been possible with manual methods: that is how the term BPR will be used in this book.

Business process re-engineering is even less publicly visible than B2B e-trading, let alone B2C e-tailing; and because it is not about things being sold, there is no straightforward way to quantify it and measure year-on-year change as one can with B2B and B2C trading. But many observers suggest that of these three aspects of e-business, B2C, B2B, and BPR, the most significant of all may be BPR.

Even for retailers, IT may achieve more in streamlining internal business processes than in selling to customers. While Tesco and some other British grocery chains are investing in online shopping systems, Safeway has chosen not to take that route: instead, it is focusing IT spending on innovative back-office and in-store systems. There will be plenty to say about BPR, as well as about e-commerce, in the chapters that follow.

The chief constraint on the development of e-business in practice is not stock market turbulence, but the simple fact that the software is often not all that good yet. Nowadays it is widely recognized that the first half-century of computing focused too much on technical wizardry, at the cost of failing to develop applications that make it genuinely easy for people to do useful tasks. The domain of *enterprise applications* – software to carry out specifically business-related functions – has a particularly poor reputation. More than half of business IT projects fail to deliver the intended business benefits and end up judged as failures.

But although there may be a long way to go, plenty of worthwhile things are already happening in e-business. The fact that there are failures as well as successes make the field more interesting. E-business is not a topic that is done and dusted. It continues to advance; people who get involved today can expect exciting developments in the years to come.

Aims of this book

There is no shortage of material worth learning about, then, despite the slump in new-technology investment. This book will not teach the reader how to become an instant millionaire; there never has been an algorithm for that. What the book does aim to do is to give the reader a sense of the trends, the technical possibilities, and the IT systems which are changing business now and which seem likely to matter in future.

A computer science graduate may find himself seeking to convince a venture capitalist to back a startup that he has dreamed up with a few friends; more likely, he will find himself working for a large company and seeking to persuade a senior manager of the potential of some company-internal e-business project. Either way, he will need to know what considerations are likely to weigh with those who make the decisions.

More likely still, in the early years of a computing graduate's career, he will find himself involved in e-business developments initiated by others. For a recruit in an established company, the pressures encourage focus on immediate, short-term issues. The recruit needs to get to know his colleagues and the company culture, and to find out about the task he is initially assigned. If he is lucky, the computing environment will be familiar from his degree course, but the project management methodology which the company has adopted for its software projects may well be quite unfamiliar.

Yet, to maximize the value of his contribution, the graduate will need to look beyond the immediate technical tasks, in order to grasp the overall rationale of the development of which those tasks are part. That is what this book aims to help him do. It gives him the vocabulary and the concepts he needs to hit the ground running, when he first becomes a player on the e-business stage. It sets up signposts to guide people who find themselves asking 'Where the **** are we?' as they are caught up in the e-business maelstrom.

Abandoning preconceptions

E-business is a topic which contrasts in flavour or ethos with the typical computer science student's intellectual background, and it will be as well to spell some of these differences out. This will involve an element of caricature in portraying the 'default' computer science student: not all students in this field are alike, any more than students in other fields. Still, there are traits which are relatively common among students of this subject, and they can make it difficult for computer scientists to come to terms with thinking about e-business.

So, to a rough approximation:

- *Computer science is twenty-year-olds in T-shirts.* Even after they move on from graduation into employment, computer people tend to retain the informality of youth, and tend perhaps to be slower than most to embrace the outlook of middle age. People directly involved with computer technology are usually young, whether because the work requires a mental agility that fades in later life or simply because the systems themselves are new. Computer science students know that middle-aged people exist, but they can sometimes seem to be just part of the furniture. But an e-commerce startup requires investors – venture capitalists in suits; and a company-internal e-business initiative needs backing by senior managers – men in suits again. And any business ultimately survives by serving consumers (either directly, in the case of a retailer, or via value chains down which its own output is ultimately transformed into consumer goods or services); consumers come in all ages, so on average they are middle-aged. The tastes and outlook of people much older than themselves loom larger in connection with e-business than they do elsewhere in a computing undergraduate's studies.

During the late-1990s bubble years, even sober investors briefly imagined that youth held all the answers. But it did not last. Quoting the Guy Kawasaki interview again, 'Three or four years ago people were looking for youth and romance, unencumbered by silly notions such as profitability ... Gray or no hair is good today. We've gone from pierced ears to bald heads.'

- *Computer science is statements like 'Arrays in C start at zero rather than one' –* truths that must be learned and accepted, with no room for debate or doubt. Business is just the opposite; like war, business is guesswork in a fog. Running a business is a matter of trying out best guesses about how to manage available resources so as to squeeze out most value from them in an ever-changing, unpredictable environment. The guesses are often wrong; managers must be constantly ready to change tack.

If people could know for sure the consequences of alternative managerial decisions, the activity we call 'business' would scarcely exist. All that society would need would be a kind of static administrative activity to oversee the fixed processes by which consumers would be optimally served. Business in real life is what the economist Joseph Schumpeter (1943) famously called a 'process of creative destruction'. Existing organizations and ways of doing things are for ever being swept aside through the discovery of more efficient methods, or things that are more worth doing. Bankruptcies are a specially dramatic case, but on a less dramatic scale it is happening constantly as systems are reorganized within companies that continue to survive.

IT has its analogue: anyone who spends many years in the computing world gets used to painfully-learned mastery of particular programming languages, operating systems, and so forth being obsoleted by newer and better replacements. But within any one technical system, all questions typically have cut and dried answers. This can make it frustrating for computing students to read discussions of e-business that say things like 'arguably, X' or 'many people think Y'. It can seem as though the writer has not done his job properly: 'don't tell us what might be so, tell us what *is* so'. When discussing business, that is often impossible. A writer who pretended that things were more certain than they are would not be a good writer but a poor one.

There is a further reason for occasional vagueness in a book on this topic: in the academic world 'truth lies open to all' (to quote a motto shared by several universities), but the business world is one where many things are secret. However, the City and Wall Street contain numerous *analysts* – business experts who make their living by compiling data and predictions about company activities and performance; part of an analyst's job is to draw inferences about areas that companies might prefer not to discuss. At the level of an introductory textbook, commercial confidentiality is not really a problem. The real reason why writing about business sometimes has to be vague is that, for many important questions, *nobody* knows the answers.

- *Computer science is 'You've been doing the same things for ever, but now our computers are going to change everything!'* Computers have caused what is probably the biggest single change in working methods of the last hundred years, but this can lead computing people to imagine naïvely that IT is the *only* important thing to have happened. Grant Norris and colleagues comment:

  > For many large, global companies, becoming an e-business is the fourth or fifth major organizational change they have undergone since the early 1980s. Many companies have gone through one or more rounds of business process reengineering (BPR); installation and major upgrades of an ERP system; upgrading legacy systems to be Y2K compliant; creating shared service centers; implementing just-in-time (JIT) manufacturing; automating the sales force; contract manufacturing; and the major challenges related to the introduction of Euro currency. (Norris et al. 2000: 119)

  Some of these developments, such as ERP (enterprise resource planning, see Chapter 7) are themselves IT-based, but others, for instance just-in-time manufacturing, have little or nothing to do with computers. (Manufacturing businesses traditionally held large inventories of products so that they could fill orders which arrived unpredictably, but inventory represents capital tied up unproductively. The trend over the last twenty years towards JIT has involved developing methods for predicting demand so that goods can be manufactured as needed and not before.) Part of learning about e-business is learning to allot IT its proper place, important but not overwhelmingly dominant, within the wider scheme of things.

- *In computer science, technology is king.* Computing students study many topics, but it is tacitly understood that the techie stuff is what really counts. The students most admired by their peers are the technical gurus. E-business uses technology, but the technical details are not what matters. To quote Grant Norris et al. again (p. 137), they describe the first 'large truth' about e-business as:

  > E-business is about strategy; it is not about technology.

  This point cannot be emphasized enough. The interesting, difficult issues in e-business are how to move businesses forward with the help of the new technology. Somebody needs to know the technical details, but most people involved with e-business, most of the time, can take those details as read – they will rarely be what decides the success or failure of an e-business initiative. E-business is business that happens to use IT; it is not a branch of IT that happens to be applied to business.

E-business is business

Since e-business is business, longstanding principles that apply to other aspects of business apply equally to it.

This axiom went temporarily out of fashion during the dotcom bubble. For a short while people believed that the internet had changed all the rules. The *Wall Street Journal* celebrated New Year's Day, 2000, with a special edition on the new economy, in which its Washington economics editor Thomas Petzinger announced the abolition of the laws of supply and demand, and the Santa Fe Institute economics professor W. Brian Arthur asserted that earnings were no longer a requirement for a successful company: 'If everyone thinks you're doing fine without earnings, why have them?'

Not many weeks later came the crash, and since then it has been hard to grasp how people could have said such things. The only rational justification for investing is expectation of future profit – earnings in excess of expenditure. As Stan Liebowitz puts it:

> In fact, the internet changes very few of the tried-and-true business strategies. Like other important technological advances, the internet will change many aspects of our lives. But the economic and business rules that worked in previous regimes will largely continue to work in the new regime. These rules of business endure because economic forces do not change – and cannot be changed by – mere changes in technology, no matter how much some of us might wish it were so. It is just our hubris at work when we start to think that our technology can change forces that are not of our conscious creation. (Liebowitz 2002: 1)

Although e-business itself is a very recent phenomenon, I shall sometimes refer to examples and ideas dating from much earlier periods. This is deliberate. If one hugs the ground too closely and does not look more than three or four years into the past, one has no basis for envisaging what might happen more than a few years into the future. E-business can only be well understood from the perspective of a larger sweep of economic history and theory.

In any case, a survey which was tied too exclusively to the temporary realities of the current scene would be tedious to read. Our main focus will be on the present, but it is by standing back sometimes to see present-day phenomena in historical and theoretical perspective that the study of e-business becomes interesting and intellectually rewarding.

I hope this book will convey some of that interest.

2

IT and the structure of the economy

The move to outsourcing

IT is not just changing the nature of goods and services, and changing the methods used to produce and sell them. It is changing the pattern of organizations doing the producing and selling. Companies seem to be getting smaller – Adam Wishart and Regula Bochsler (2002: 120) write about an age 'dominated by herds of tiny fleet-footed firms'. *Outsourcing* – 'buy, don't make' – has become a favoured strategy. What is going on here?

There are actually two separate things going on, only one of which has much to do with IT. One trend is what Americans (whose economy was traditionally far more self-contained than Britain's) call the 'hollowing out' of the US economy. The image is of an apple eaten away by wasps: from the outside, the fruit may look as whole as before, but behind the glossy skin there is now far less substance, as manufacturing operations are shifted overseas. The same is happening in Britain. Last time I bought shoes, I picked a pair from Clarks, the famous company based near my childhood home in Somerset, and was startled to see a MADE IN CHINA sticker on the sole. The friend who helped me choose them giggled with the saleslady at my naïvety – like many other British firms which used to make the things they sold, Clarks now licenses to companies elsewhere the right to brand goods with its logo, and the home company focuses on marketing and distribution.

Developments like this may mean that the firms involved employ fewer people. But this trend has little to do with IT. The impetus towards globalization comes from the fact that labour costs vary in different regions of the world. The progressive reductions in tariff barriers that have occurred by international agreement over the last half century, rising skill levels in the third world, and perhaps lower transport costs, have made it easier and more compelling for Western companies to take advantage of low third-world wage rates. Modern communication technology no doubt plays a part, but that is a minor consideration.

Disaggregation

The development we are concerned with is separate. Even when a set of interrelated industrial and commercial operations are still carried out wholly within Britain, it has become commoner for them to be executed by a number of smaller companies, each specializing in one narrow niche and interacting with one another contractually, rather than by a single large company. Administrative functions such as payroll or personnel are often now outsourced to specialist firms. And there is a trend towards *vertical disaggregation*. Normally there are very many successive steps in the process by which consumer goods are created, ultimately, from raw materials. It was never usual for one company to do everything from one extreme of the chain to the other, but in the new economy firms are taking responsibility for shorter segments of the chain.

Again there is a potential confusion. Any new company naturally starts small and hopes to grow, as it wins market share. In an area where new activities are being carried out by new organizations, it is inevitable that the organizations will tend to be small. But many commentators feel that there is something deeper going on. They believe that it is in the nature of Web commerce and e-business more generally to shrink company sizes permanently, not just in the obvious sense that automation means things being done by machines which previously had to be done by people, but in the sense that the same chains of operations will be divided among larger numbers of players occupying smaller niches.

This, incidentally, is part of the attraction of e-commerce for young people. It is not just that the Web is socially 'cool', and they are fascinated by the technology. Those things are important. But there is also the apparent promise that, in this field unlike most parts of the traditional economy, one can start something going on a shoestring which will have a fair chance of turning into a worthwhile piece in the economic jigsaw. Many of us would like to run our own show, rather than working at someone else's beck and call as an employee. The disaggregative property of e-business seems to be opening up a world in which a group of pals can start a company together and, with luck and hard work, can make a good living.

So why should IT have this type of impact on economic structure? And will the trend last?

As always where business is concerned, nobody can claim to know the answers beyond dispute. But there is an answer to the first of these questions which has convinced many observers; and, if this answer is correct, it seems to have an interesting consequence for the second question.

What to produce how?

To understand these answers, we need to stand back for a while from the new economy, and think about the fundamentals of how any society, traditional or modern, is organized from an economic point of view. We shall look at concepts that are elementary for businessmen or students of economics; but they are not routinely part of the education of computer science students, so I hope that readers who know about them will bear with us while they are explained.

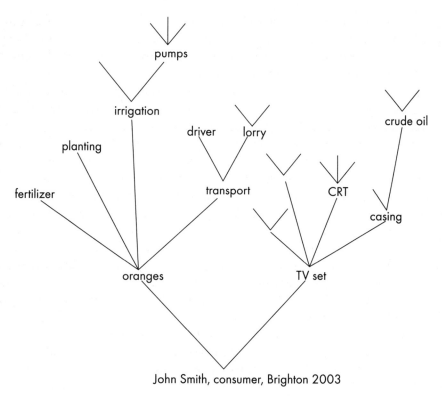

John Smith, consumer, Brighton 2003

Figure 2.1

Suppose one of my students sallies forth from his flat in Brighton this morning to do some shopping: let's say he buys oranges, and a TV set. Then he is placing himself at the apex of an immensely complex tree-shaped structure of specific economic operations. Drawing out the entire tree would be impractical, but Figure 2.1 suggests a small part of what it might look like.

For oranges to be harvested, they must have been planted. Fertilizer will have been applied, and they will have needed irrigation, using machinery manufactured from diverse input elements. To get the oranges to the Brighton supermarket, transport was needed: at the latest stage of the journey, a lorry – itself the result of a complex process of manufacture – driven by a driver who had received training for this work. The television comprises a cathode ray tube, made out of various materials, a plastic casing made ultimately from crude oil (which was sucked out of the ground using very complicated machinery); and so forth.

Because we are all thoroughly used to the fact that the things we want are waiting in shops to be bought, it is easy to overlook how astonishing this fact really is. The network of decisions and actions that have placed oranges and a TV set in Brighton shops this morning is unimaginably vast and ramified, and few people involved will have known about more than one small part of the pattern. The man who planted the orange trees had perhaps never heard of Brighton. There was certainly no central authority thinking along the lines 'In 2003 a student in

Brighton will be wanting oranges and a television, so we need to see about getting orange trees planted, a lorry built, …' Indeed the oranges, and probably the television, will have been produced in other countries, so no government had authority over both producers and consumer.

Notice in particular that the mass of decisions and actions are not determined by the nature of the materials and activities involved. At almost every step, there are many real choices to be made. Almost every *factor of production* (each type of input to one of the production processes) will be capable of many different uses: the lorry which transported oranges might have been used for different transport tasks, the man who drove it could have chosen to train for some other work. Perhaps the final stages of making the TV set involved assembling components that had no uses other than as parts of that sort of set, but this is not the typical situation: most input factors will have alternative potential uses, often a large range. And conversely, the outputs at the various stages could usually have been produced from different patterns of inputs. TV casings these days are normally plastic, but they could alternatively be made of metal or wood – in the early years of television, wooden casings were usual. The oranges might have reached Brighton by rail rather than road – and so on; again there will be fewer alternative input patterns at some stages than others, but mostly there will be alternatives.

So, if almost every input can be used to produce different outputs, almost every output can be produced from different patterns of inputs, and nobody is overseeing the system as a whole, how is it determined what in particular is produced how? Why does my student not find that, often, the things he would like to buy are unavailable, and why does the system not frequently produce far more of some things than anyone needs, so that the surpluses are wasted? The latter does happen sometimes – there are cases where farmers have to plough in a crop because it turns out not to be worth the cost of harvesting; but the wonder is why this is not a much more widespread phenomenon.

Supply and demand

The answers to those puzzles are the basic subject matter of economics. They are expressed in terms of the *price mechanism*.

For the individual consumer, prices are nasty things that stand in the way of enjoying all the goods and services he would like to have. For society as a whole, though, prices do an important job of work: they transmit just enough information throughout the economy to enable individuals, each of whom knows only one small corner of the economy in detail, to co-ordinate their actions so that as much value as possible is squeezed out of the resources available, and waste is kept to a minimum. Prices achieve this by reconciling *supply* and *demand*.

For any particular product – oranges, say – there exists a *supply schedule*: a graph something like Figure 2.2, in which the *x*-axis represents the quantity of fruit grown annually, and the *y*-axis represents the price at which the fruit are sold. The schedule runs S.W. to N.E.: the higher the price for oranges, the more will be produced, because owners of land and other production factors will increasingly find that it pays to divert these resources from their current use to the production

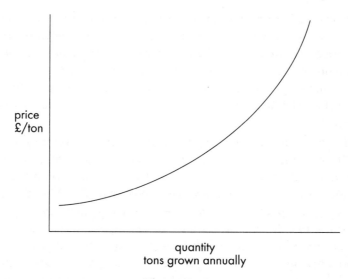

price
£/ton

quantity
tons grown annually

Figure 2.2

of oranges. The true line will probably not be nearly as smooth as I have drawn it. There might for instance be a price point where it becomes worth using some particular expensive fertilizer that greatly increases production, so the graph will kink upwards at that point. But the trend must be broadly S.W. to N.E.

Figure 2.3 shows the *demand schedule* for oranges: the total quantity that would be bought at different prices. This runs N.W. to S.E.: the cheaper oranges are, the more of them people will buy. When I was a child, oranges were an expensive imported luxury: it was a minor treat to be given one at Christmas or on a day out. Now they are relatively far cheaper, and people eat them routinely alongside local fruit such as apples.

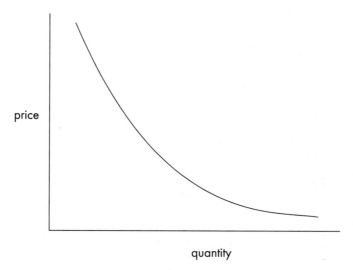

price

quantity

Figure 2.3

These graphs are both somewhat hypothetical: at a given period, the price for any particular thing is what it is, and we can observe how much is produced and sold at that price, but we have no direct way of checking what the corresponding quantities would be at every possible alternative price. So we usually cannot draw exact plots of supply or demand schedules. But we know at least this much about them: the supply schedule must run S.W. to N.E., while the demand schedule must run N.W. to S.E.

That being so, if the two lines are plotted on the same graph they must cross: see Figure 2.4. The crossing point fixes the price which oranges will actually fetch (and the quantity that will actually be produced). If someone tries producing oranges in a way that requires him to charge a price higher than P, say by using expensive fertilizer when the economy is capable of producing quantity Q of oranges by cheaper methods, then he will be left with his output on his hands; he will have to cut the price to get rid of them, and shift to growing something else, or to growing oranges more cheaply, in future. If people sell oranges for a lower price than P, consumers will want to buy more in total than it pays growers to produce at that lower price: disappointed customers will bid the price back up to P. P is the *equilibrium price* at which the same quantity is produced that customers are willing to buy, leaving no waste and no shoppers confronted with empty shelves.

This is an idealized picture – the system does not always work as smoothly as my discussion might suggest, but broadly speaking this is how prices are determined.

My example used oranges, a consumer good. But the same principles fix the prices of everything else, including items – say, railway goods waggons – that have no direct value to consumers, and are relevant only as inputs to processes high in the network which links raw materials at the top to consumption at the bottom.

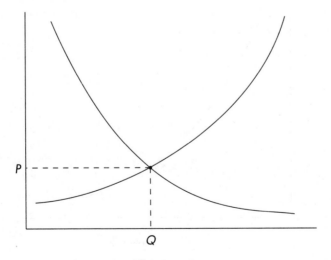

Figure 2.4

An invisible hand

The result is that prices constitute a *signalling system*, showing the controller of any factor of production how best to apply it. Someone who deals with one little corner of the economic world could never acquire, or cope with, all the detailed knowledge of his potential customers' businesses, their own customers' businesses, and so forth, that would show him why, ultimately, the production factor he is responsible for will end up yielding more value to consumers if he sells it to business A, who will make one use of it, than if he sells it to business B, who will use it in a different way. But he does not need to go into all that detail. The price system gives him just enough information to make decisions *as if* he had encyclopaedic knowledge. Business B will not buy at a price that makes it worth supplying them, because for the use they want to make of the given production factor they can substitute some cheaper alternative. Business A wants to use the same input for a process where there is no cheaper alternative; so they will pay the required price, and business A gets the good. Thus the multifarious resources available to society are distributed to the uses where they will produce most value for society.

Adam Smith, the father of economic thought, put it like this, in a passage that must have a high claim to a place among the top ten texts of all time that explain how the world works:

> As every individual ... endeavours ... to employ his capital [so] that its produce may be of the greatest value; every individual necessarily labours to render the annual revenue of the society as great as he can. ... he intends only his own gain, and he is in this, as in many other cases, led by an invisible hand to promote an end which was no part of his intention. (Smith [1776] 1976: vol. 1, p. 456)

An invisible hand! This is the economists' answer to the question how society determines what is produced how, with no overseeing authority. In terms familiar to computer scientists, an economy is a self-organizing system, and prices are the mechanism by which its organization is optimized.

In principle, this machinery can determine the price of human labour – what people earn – in the same way as any other factor of production. Obviously, many people feel that 'people are special' and that incomes ought not to be determined entirely by the same impersonal mechanisms that fix the prices of inanimate goods. In Britain and many other societies, the State acts in various ways to modify the pattern of incomes, in cash and kind, that would emerge from a pure market economy: medical services are financed by a progressive tax system, income support is provided for the poor, etc. Economists sometimes warn that policies like these, though they may be desirable, by interfering with the operation of the price mechanism entail hidden disadvantages that need to be balanced against the clear advantages. But that is the realm of politics rather than economics, and outside the purview of this book.

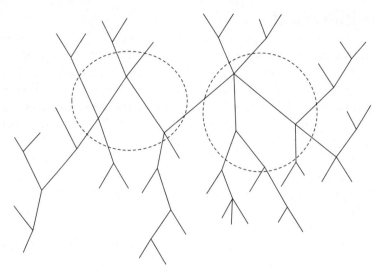

Figure 2.5

Coase's theory of the firm

So far, we have been considering classical economic theory – the common background for most economic discussion over the past two centuries. It has nothing directly to say about the size of firms, which was the topic that led us into examining economic basics. For that, we must come forward to a theory stated by Ronald Coase, winner of the 1991 economics Nobel Prize (and British by origin, though he taught at the University of Chicago). Coase's *theory of the firm* was first stated in a famous article published before the Second World War (Coase 1937).

Figure 2.5 schematically represents one small part of the network of economic transactions in a society: the nodes are individuals, the links between nodes are transfers of resources from one individual to another and agreements by one individual to do something for another. In a market economy, many of these links come into being through the system of freely-negotiated contracts on which the price mechanism depends. But, Coase points out, within this sea of contractual relationships there are islands (indicated by dotted lines) within which activities and use of resources are decided by managerial instructions rather than by negotiated contracts: the 'islands' are what we call firms or companies. As between individuals and/or firms, economic decisions are made freely in response to price signals. *Within* firms, decisions are imposed on employees by managers implementing plans. Why, Coase asks, should the 'islands' be the size they are, rather than much larger or smaller?

One way to think about this is to consider the logical extreme possibilities. What would economic life be like if, at one extreme, the whole of society formed one big island of command relationships?

This case is easy to think about: it is one aspect of the political ideal called socialism or communism. The reason why a market economy does not spontaneously adopt that form is that it requires a level of centralized planning of economic decisions which is thoroughly impractical. If I were writing twenty or thirty years ago, I might have needed to argue this point at length; until about 1980 many educated people believed that a socialist economy was a valid ideal, even if it had never been satisfactorily realized anywhere. Since then, it has been generally recognized that socialism is a system that simply cannot work: no planners could assemble enough detailed information about the implications of using all the separate factors of production in different ways to devise a reasonable blueprint specifying what to produce, how. We have to let such decisions be guided by the price signalling system, which is sensitive to more considerations than any planners could consciously take into account.

Historically, opposition to communism was fuelled largely by the wickedness of many 20th-century communist leaders. From an economic point of view, that is not the significant issue. Even if those leaders had been saints, the economic system they claimed to be implementing could not have served their populations adequately.

But in that case, why have firms at all? Why does the network of Figure 2.5 not consist wholly of freely-negotiated contracts between individuals, with no islands of command relationships?

This opposite extreme is harder to think about, because it has not traditionally been discussed even as a hypothetical ideal. But, with an effort, we can envisage a world in which all economic relationships are between individuals. As a university teacher, for instance, I might rent weekly slots in a lecture hall from someone who had borrowed the large sum of capital needed to create a university, and I would charge individual students a subscription fee for the right to attend. If one pursues this scenario very far, a science-fiction quality sets in – nobody, including Ronald Coase, has ever suggested it is a realistic possibility. But what is it that compels the economic sea to contain islands of command relationships, and why are they as big as they are, not much larger or much smaller? Before Coase, no-one had asked this question.

Transaction costs

Coase's answer is in terms of *transaction costs*: the costs of creating and maintaining the dense network of links between economic agents. Classical economics focused on the substance of transactions: a supermarket buys a load of oranges from a supplier for X pounds. But the money paid for the oranges is not the only cost paid to bring about this transaction.

Economic agents have search costs: they must put time and effort into locating suitable suppliers and potential customers. There are co-ordination costs: for instance, time has to be put into ensuring that the hour and location at which a supplier delivers oranges is an hour and location at which the supermarket can receive them. The process of negotiating contracts will often be time-consuming and therefore expensive; and operating the contracts once agreed involves costs of its own, for example, for sending out bills (for a telephone company, billing is the largest single cost in supplying a household with phone service). If things go wrong, larger costs will be incurred – in the worst case, a company has the expense of enforcing its contract in a law court.

These costs are very far from negligible. One estimate (Wallis and North 1988) suggests that transaction costs may account for about half the gross national product. So they must have a large influence on economic organization.

Now, Coase argues, although transactions between companies inevitably involve costs of these kinds, within a small company achieving the same arrangements is costless or nearly so. If a company employs its own driver, no-one asks 'What would you take to deliver this load to Brighton tomorrow?' and gets involved in dickering over price and comparing alternative quotes. The manager simply says 'Your job tomorrow is to deliver that load to Brighton'. Companies are a device for eliminating transaction costs; Coase sees that as their basic raison d'être.

But, as a small company gets larger, organizing arrangements internally becomes more complex and expensive. In a large firm which makes many deliveries and employs many drivers, internal searching becomes necessary: 'Who can we give this assignment to?' Internal politics begins to complicate the process of agreeing tasks: 'How can we persuade the Deliveries department to take on responsibility for recyclables?' The larger the segment of the total economic network comprised within a single firm, the higher its internal management costs will be, until eventually if the firm gets larger the extra transactions that are 'internalized' will be as expensive as if they were carried out on the open market, between separate firms. This is Coase's answer to the puzzle about 'island size'. Firms tend to expand until the marginal cost of internal managerial arrangements matches the cost of carrying out the corresponding transactions on the market.

If this is the crucial factor determining company size, then IT will change things: IT reduces transaction costs. Most obviously, the World Wide Web makes it far cheaper to search for potential transaction partners. Contracting costs, and co-ordination costs, may also be reduced; think for instance of automatic stock market trading, where buyers and sellers of a stock are matched, and sales executed at pre-approved prices, without human intervention. IT is giving us what people have taken to calling a *frictionless economy*.

If transaction costs in the market are lower, the break-even point at which company expansion causes internal management costs to equal them should be reached sooner. So, by the logic of Coase's argument, companies ought now to be smaller: which is where we came in. A prediction which follows from a theory put forward in the 1930s is being tested and apparently confirmed, more than sixty years later!

Coase and IT

Ronald Coase's 1937 article said nothing about computers; they had not been invented. The classic statement of the implications of Coase's theory for e-business was a far-sighted paper by Thomas Malone, JoAnne Yates, and Robert Benjamin (1987). Many well-informed commentators feel that Malone et al. have made their case. The IT revolution means that the trend towards smaller, niche companies is here to stay, and Coase's analysis is the correct explanation linking these two phenomena.

There is an alternative, negative view of Coase's theory that has been expressed by more than one author who ought to know better. Some writers say, in effect, 'Coase's theory predicted that firms should be the size they were; but the size of firms is now changing, so we see that Coase's theory must be wrong'. This seems embarrassingly naïve. Like most scientific theories, Coase's theory of the firm says that a factor X causes an effect Y. If X (transaction costs, in this case) has changed, naturally we expect Y (firm size) to change, and that doesn't refute the theory: it confirms it.

But there is a third possible point of view. The internet has reduced the costs of transactions on the market; but the internet is not the only aspect of IT to affect business operations, and other aspects might lead to different predictions.

Coase's 1937 article did not mention computers; the nearest thing he did mention was the telephone – at that period still a relatively novel business tool. Coase's prediction was that the telephone was destined to make firms *larger*: he saw the telephone as reducing the co-ordination costs of a firm's internal operations. If internal management costs are reduced while external transaction costs are unchanged, a firm can expand further before reaching the break-even point where the two are equal.

Sixty years on, it is not clear why Coase saw the telephone as affecting management costs but not external transaction costs. In those days trunk calls between different regions, although possible, were cumbersome affairs involving manual intervention by telephone operators, so perhaps in 1937 telephones seemed more significant as facilitators of within-company communication than as channels of communication between firms. That is a question of mainly historical interest.

But the analogous question about IT and present-day business is very relevant. We saw in Chapter 1 that the initial impact of computing technology on business related to the Web as a new medium for B2C and B2B commerce; but that the focus is shifting now towards business process re-engineering, using software such as the enterprise resource planning systems to be discussed in Chapter 7.

Internal BPR reduces a firm's management costs. So, what we are perhaps witnessing is a first wave of business computerization which impacted mainly on external transaction costs, and hence caused company sizes to shrink, followed now by a second wave that is impacting mainly on internal management costs, and which, by the same logic, will cause company sizes to grow again.

It is too soon to be sure. But a likely bet seems to be that the shift towards 'herds of tiny fleet-footed firms', which was such a feature of the turn of the millennium, could be short-lived. We may see a return to an economic landscape dominated as much as ever by big businesses. With the wave of mergers that became a feature of the scene in 2002 (for example, Hewlett-Packard/Compaq; IBM/Pricewaterhouse-Coopers Consulting; Logica/CMG), perhaps we are beginning to see this already.

The virtual organization

Even if firms do on the whole remain smaller than in the past, there is another way in which IT is allowing *effective* company size often to be larger than *formal* company size. Separate companies are collaborating as so-called *virtual organizations*.

In the mid-20th century, when firms tended to be larger, relationships between companies were relatively distant. They had to be: there was no e-mail or voicemail, documents or artwork were generated and exchanged via chains of clerical assistants and the postal service, not transmitted at electronic speed between the desktops of the staff immediately involved. Nowadays it is easier for legally separate organizations to collaborate in an intimate fashion.

'Virtual organization' has become a buzzword, and like other buzzwords it is used to mean different things. Peter Marshall, Judy McKay, and Janice Burn (2001) identify three different ways in which the phrase is used (and there are others):

1   a single organization which functions mainly online – what is called in this book an 'e-business';

2   a grouping of independent firms and/or individuals who collaborate so that in some respects they function as if they were a single organization;

3   some commentators named by Marshall et al. systematically blur the difference between (1) and (2) and write as if they amounted to much the same.

(1) and (2) are essentially unrelated ideas, so blurring them together makes no sense. Worse still, according to Marshall et al. some writers blur 'virtual' together with 'virtuous', as though doing things by computer is axiomatically preferable to conventional methods. That is obviously silly. But sense (2) does identify a distinctive phenomenon which is facilitated by IT and is more salient now than before the electronic revolution.

Virtual organizations (in the (2) sense – the only sense in which the phrase will be used in this book) are flexible alliances of companies or individuals, which come together to respond to business opportunities, then dissolve and rearrange themselves in other alliances as opportunities change. Marshall et al. describe various forms such alliances can take. One pattern is the *intermittent partnership*, where consultancy in a particular business area is offered under the umbrella of a trading name that allows individual consultants to be slotted in when commissions call for their special expertise, while at other times those individuals work independently. Another pattern is the *star alliance*: for instance, a car breakdown service may orchestrate the contributions of a battery distributor, a windscreen replacement service, and other functions as needed, without itself providing all the capital investment which these operations require. Other patterns again are possible. Not all the alliances discussed by Marshall et al. depend on IT, but the suggestion is that the rapid, data-rich communications facilitated by IT encourage this kind of flexible independence.

Arguably, this pattern of organization has advantages in a fast-changing business environment. Small companies can limit themselves to their core competences, where they have a competitive edge, while outsourcing functions where they have no special expertise to other companies which have; yet there is continuity – although the partners are not legally yoked together permanently, they are regular collaborators who know each other's strengths and co-operate on a basis of familiarity.

Furthermore, IT is facilitating new levels of collaboration between large, established companies. Company-internal *intranets* are being expanded into *extranets* linking companies with their trading partners. Feng Li and Howard Williams (2001) discuss a Japanese car manufacturer in Britain which is using IT to enable its suppliers to collaborate in developing a new car model. The car manufacturer provides CAD (computer-aided design) data on the specifications of a component and the space it has to fit into; the supplier designs the component, negotiating details with the manufacturer. All this is only possible with broadband electronic links allowing engineering drawings and other detailed data to be passed back and forth freely and rapidly, and it grows out of trust engendered by earlier, more routine IT-mediated collaboration: for instance, the car manufacturer has for several years given suppliers access to its production planning database, so that they can organize their own production so as to supply components on a just-in-time basis.

Designing a new car model would until recently have been seen as an enterprise-critical function that a manufacturer would not share with outside firms. The partner companies in this case are acting in a manner that does make them look rather like a single organization. In this case the partners were deepening an existing relationship, but it has also become common for companies large and small to appoint senior executives with the specific role of seeking new alliances with companies whose strengths are complementary.

Control versus trust

One consequence is that *trust* has to do a share of the work that used to be done by hierarchy and discipline in co-ordinating the activities of collaborating workgroups. Michael Capellas, chairman of then-independent Compaq, said in 2002: 'nobody can do it all. Successful companies will be the ones that are able to build up trusting partner relationships.'[1] An alliance of companies who join forces on a project will make a contract governing the main lines of their collaboration, but a legal contract can never prescribe all the detailed rules and practices which develop within a single organization; so, 'trust has to substitute for hierarchical and bureaucratic controls' (Lipnack and Stamps 1998). It is widely agreed that the business environment is tending to lay increased importance on trust as opposed to formal control. If true, this is a real and significant new development.

It is perhaps a surprising one, because in many areas of public life the movement over recent decades has been in the opposite direction. Thirty years ago, professionals such as doctors, schoolteachers, or academics were normally trusted to do the best job they could; nowadays, they are monitored and regulated at every turn. Company staff recruitment and contracting used to rely heavily on personal contacts, which tend to foster trust; nowadays, regulatory changes such as Equal Opportunities legislation mean that working relationships are more often with strangers. The social changes have been so pronounced that they were chosen as topic of the 2002 BBC *Reith Lectures*, in which Onora O'Neill argued that the abandonment of the trust principle in public life is creating intractable social difficulties (O'Neill 2002).

---

1. Quoted in *SAP INFO Quick Guide* 4/2002, cirquana.notlong.com, p. 29.

It is not easy to see how an increasing role for trust in business can be reconciled with the reality of decreasing trust in much of life. We shall find that trust is a recurring theme in the study of e-business.

An undamped economy

There is a further point to make about the 'frictionless economy'. We think of friction as a bad thing, and from the point of view of individual economic agents – consumers, or firms – lower transaction costs are a gain, at least in the short term. (If they enable rivals to outcompete a company, for that company the gain vanishes in the longer term.) But in the physical world friction has positive as well as negative aspects. Frictional mechanisms can be used for *damping* dynamic systems, ensuring that oscillations do not build up and get destructively out of control. In an economy, it may be that transaction costs have a similar beneficial effect on the system as a whole even though they are a drain on the resources of each individual player.

The past half-century has been a period of unusual economic stability, with waves of alternating expansion and recession much gentler than at earlier periods (see, for example, Woodall 2002). There are indications that the world is now moving into a time of greater economic volatility; if true, one reason would be the abolition of friction through IT. Economic agents everywhere can now instantly pile on to bandwagons or bale out of sinking ships, so the ups and downs of economic cycles feed off themselves and are magnified.

Other than a few speculators, we may all be losers if this proves correct.

Firms as tools

One idea to take away from this chapter is that firms are only tools – they are not ends in themselves, as individual human beings are. Most of us are glad to see effort going into keeping other people healthy, not because of the useful work which those people will do in future (if that were the sole reason, it might be best to kill everyone off at retirement!), but simply because they are fellow human beings with the same right as ourselves to make as much of their lives as they can. If you work for a company, you are encouraged to see the flourishing of that company similarly as a good thing in its own right. The economic system works best if employees do to some extent embrace their employers' interests as their own. But, standing back a pace and focusing on the social system as a whole, we see that companies are really no more than instruments which society has evolved to serve the needs and aspirations of the human beings who constitute society.

That means that a book like this needs to examine not only the e-business strategies by which companies can seek profits, but also the impact of e-business technology on individuals and on society.

A short book cannot cover every topic in detail, and these social issues will be secondary to the main theme. But even someone who thinks he is interested exclusively in how to use IT for profit would be wise to keep half an eye on the wider picture. He may not be interested in the social consequences of e-business;

but many voters are, and they are quite capable of causing government to change the rules of the game which companies have to play.

At present, governments and voters, as well as companies, are feeling their way uncertainly into the new world which IT is creating. A large issue for companies is how governments will decide to remodel the e-business environment, once they acquire the confidence to do so.

3

E-commerce strategies

A case study

It is time to make the discussion concrete. This chapter will examine one e-business in depth: Amazon.com.

Nobody suggests that Amazon is a 'typical' e-business – if such a beast exists. Amazon is predominantly a B2C operation, although nowadays it also has B2B involvements. The 'typical' dotcom would probably be a company that collapsed in about 2001. In that year, *USA Today* described Amazon as 'the company that legitimized e-commerce', and Jeffrey Bezos (its founder and chief executive) was able to boast 'We are the only e-commerce company of scale'.[1] In terms of consumer recognition, Amazon is far out ahead of the e-commerce pack. By 1999, just four years after launch, Amazon.com was reported as being the 57th most valuable brand worldwide, above long-established names like Guinness and Hilton. Amazon is arguably an outstandingly successful company.

My students sometimes boggle at the word 'arguably'. My reply is: 'If you had started a business eight years ago and by now you were counting your cumulative losses in billions, how successful would you say you were?'

Typical or not, Amazon makes a good case study – partly because its high profile means that plenty of data are available. Amazon was first with many technologies that have proved significant in e-business. The shopping-trolley metaphor, for instance, which we take for granted nowadays in the e-tailing context, was an Amazon invention. And most of the business-strategy themes that analysts see as potentially decisive for the success or otherwise of e-businesses can be illustrated in connexion with this company.

1. Quoted by Byron Acohido, 'Amazon: We'll be profitable by year's end', *USA Today* 26 Mar 2001, wernomad.notlong.com

Amazon is founded

Jeffrey Bezos was born in 1964; his adoptive father was a child refugee from Cuba to the USA and worked as an engineer for Exxon. Jeffrey graduated in computing from Princeton, and by 1992 he was the youngest senior vice-president of a high-tech-oriented Wall Street firm. Two years later he threw the job up to create an internet bookshop. To those who queried this seemingly rash move, Bezos's answer was:

> I knew that when I was eighty there was no chance that I would regret having walked away from my 1994 Wall Street bonus ... I wouldn't even have *remembered* that. But I did think there was a chance that I might regret significantly not participating in this thing called the Internet, that I believed passionately in. I also knew that if I had tried and failed, I wouldn't regret that.[2]

Bezos founded Amazon, aged 30, with a few hundred thousand dollars of his own and relatives' money; the website was launched under the slogan 'Earth's Biggest Bookstore' on 16 July 1995. By early 1996 venture capital funds were competing to invest, and Bezos shifted his sights up to a higher plane of ambition. In May 1997 Amazon.com was floated as a public company; the opening share price valued it at $423 million. The prospectus was explicit about the fact that Amazon was losing money fast and expected to lose it faster for the foreseeable future.

Amazon's initial business model

In the year Amazon was founded, 1.5 billion books were bought in the USA, a third of which were children's books. The market was divided into the following sectors:

bookshop chains	25%
independent bookshops	21%
book clubs and discount stores	32%
second-hand, mail order, etc.	22%

The largest and second-largest chains were respectively Barnes & Noble and Borders.

The standard distribution pattern in the USA was that publishers sold books to wholesalers, the largest being the Ingram Book Group, with seven warehouses in different parts of America stocking about 400,000 titles; wholesalers supplied books on a sale-or-return basis to retailers, who sold to consumers (large retailers might also supply small retailers).

Amazon's initial business model involved occupying the retailer slot in this value chain: it bought books from Ingrams and sold them to the public through its website. Because its 'shop' was a website, it could sell nationally or internationally without the expense of bricks-and-mortar branches with salaried staff. Furthermore it did not need to tie up capital in inventory. In theory, the operation

2. This and later Bezos quotations are taken from a speech at Lake Forest College, Illinois, 26 Feb 1998, quoted by Spector (2000).

could have been totally inventory-free: when a customer ordered a book, Amazon might have arranged for the wholesaler to ship it to the customer directly. In fact, books moved via Amazon's premises, but paused there only long enough for packing and forwarding. A conventional bookshop maintains a large stock to enable customers to browse before deciding to buy, and a high proportion of this stock is never bought and eventually returned to the publisher for refunds. Amazon's customers 'browse' via Web pages; they can return books they order, but Amazon expected to have a far lower return rate than a conventional bookshop.

Thus the capital and operating-cost requirements both favoured internet selling over bricks-and-mortar book retailing. The cashflow pattern was favourable too, since Amazon (like any retailer) would pay its supplier in arrears, but customers paid up-front through their credit cards. By contrast, even when a conventional bookshop does sell a particular book, on average the sale occurs two or three months after the shop has paid its supplier.

The online book-buying experience

Not all differences favoured the online model. Bezos never expected to put conventional bookshops out of business: he knew that people enjoy spending time in them. As he said in 1998, 'We will never make Amazon.com fun and engaging in the same way as the great physical bookstores are … You'll never be able to hear the bindings creak and smell the books and have tasty lattes and soft sofas at Amazon.com.'

But there are other things an online bookshop can offer that a conventional bookshop cannot, which might enable the online bookshop to capture a worthwhile share of the market. These things could well even expand the total market for books, so that Amazon's share would not be entirely at the expense of conventional competitors.

One of these is using data on customers' buying histories to predict titles that are likely to interest them. Amazon greets a returning customer by name: 'Hello, Geoffrey, we have recommendations for you'. The recommendations are generated by sophisticated algorithms which compare a customer's buying history with those of other customers whose purchasing patterns overlap. After one has been an Amazon customer for a while, the recommendations become eerily well-targeted; it takes a strong will to avoid letting one's book spending get out of control.

We cannot talk about 'business process re-engineering' here – Amazon is new, so there was no previous process to re-engineer. Nevertheless, it is important to understand that what is significant in the Amazon operation is not just about selling through an electronic interface rather than over a counter. It is also about things happening electronically 'behind the scenes'. One of the things that e-commerce is good at is *cross-selling*, often symbolized by the tag 'Do you want fries with that?' But Amazon goes far beyond merely suggesting an item that complements the item which a customer has just chosen. Using records of many customers' past buying to predict individuals' future choices among 1.5 million titles is a powerful marketing tool that would be quite unfeasible without IT.

Another Amazon technique is to draw customers into membership of a *virtual community* focused on the site. Someone who looks at a book description is invited to contribute a review; reviews are rated by other site visitors, and at some periods Amazon has given cash prizes to the highest-rated reviewers. These reviews serve two purposes. They can help customers decide whether a title is worth buying, in a way that briefly scanning a physical copy cannot. But also, participants are involved in a relationship with the company that might encourage a kind of loyalty that is unlikely with a physical shop. Some commentators see virtual communities of this kind as an important marketing tool (cf. Chapter 8).

The significance of things like these for the Amazon operation is symbolized by the fact that Bezos avoids the term 'e-commerce', preferring to describe his business as 'e-merchandising'. According to Bezos, 'commerce is the simple find-it-buy-it-ship-it action. E-merchandising is much more about customer behavior online', and he sees Amazon as an 'experimental laboratory' for studying this: 'we can use advanced technology to not only understand our products on an individual product-by-product basis but to understand our customers on a customer-by-customer individualized basis.' Bezos even claims that Amazon should be seen 'as sort of a small Artificial Intelligence company.'

Amazon adopted many other, more straightforward techniques to encourage customers to accept this novel method of shopping. It was, for instance, the first e-tailer to respond to orders by e-mailing an immediate confirmation. Robert Spector notes that 'As late as 1999, of the ten most visited shopping sites on the Internet, Amazon.com was the only one that offered on its home page a link to its "shipping policies", where a chart explained shipping and handling fees' (Spector 2000: 152). Bezos focused from the start on doing everything possible to please customers, from obvious points such as large discounts and fast (and sometimes free) delivery, to editorial write-ups and site illustrations which aim to give the visitor 'a sense of the quirky, independent, literate voice, and that behind it all you're interacting with people'.[3] Bezos's 'mantra' is 'to obsess over our customers and not our competitors'. Space does not allow us to survey the many methods which Amazon uses to make online shopping a good experience.

Getting physical

The initial business model did not last long. Beginning in November 1996, Amazon acquired premises to keep its own stock of the 200,000 best-selling titles. It continued to buy titles ranked from 200,000 down to 400,000 through wholesalers; the long tail of slower-selling books were ordered directly from the publishers. To the original customer service centre in Seattle, Amazon added another in Delaware on the opposite coast; in 1999 five more were added, scattered round the USA. More premises entailed many more staff salaries.

There were two reasons for this development. One was that Amazon's leading competitor, Barnes & Noble, tried to buy the wholesaler Ingram in 1998. Anti-trust

---

3. Amazon executive editor Rick Ayre, quoted by Peter de Jonge, 'Riding the wild, perilous waters of Amazon.com', *New York Times* 14 Mar 1999, muezinck.notlong.com

rules prevented the sale from going through, but the attempt drew attention to a vulnerability in Amazon's original business model.

More crucially, though, the inventoryless approach proved inconsistent with Amazon's ambition to dominate the field. When a customer knew he could walk into a bricks-and-mortar bookshop and buy a best-seller then and there, he was not likely to wait too much longer for an online purchase to be delivered; only by holding its own stocks of popular titles at strategic locations could Amazon fulfil orders within a day or two. Once Amazon had attracted serious investment, the outside investors (and Bezos, who originally thought in terms of profitability at a lower level of market share) wanted it not just to make a living but to dominate its market sector. The inventoryless model would not allow that.

Get Big Fast

This large ambition was one way in which Amazon became a typical dotcom. The new world of online commerce was seen as vacant terrain ripe for colonization, like the American West waiting for pioneers to stake their claims; with a one-off opportunity like that, the important thing was to grab as much territory as possible, and worry about profits later. The syndrome was identified by Neil Weintraut (1997): rather than 'build[ing] businesses in a methodical fashion, Internet businesses … adopted a grow-at-any-cost, without-any-revenue, claim-as-much-market-real-estate-before-anyone-moves-in approach to business. This mentality has come to be known as "Get Big Fast."'

Get Big Fast has been such a standard e-commerce principle that it is often reduced to an acronym, GBF. It might seem to contradict the idea in Chapter 2, that lower transaction costs in internet commerce lead to smaller firms: but there is no contradiction. Coase's theory is about the 'vertical' size of companies – how large a segment of the long value chains leading from raw materials at the top down to consumer goods or services at the bottom is typically contained within a single organization. Get Big Fast relates to 'horizontal' company size: how large a share of a given market, and how broad a range of 'sister' business activities, are controlled by one firm.

Globalization of trade, and the global reach of the internet, promote a winner-takes-all business environment. Instead of many comparable firms within a given sector each surviving in its own geographical or specialist niche, it becomes easier for one company to conquer the entire sector and leave few pickings for the rest. Dotcom startups typically raced to try to ensure that they were the ones to win. E-commerce was seen as creating a large *first mover advantage*: being first away from the starting blocks gave a good chance of sweeping the prizes.

Achieving large scale is particularly attractive for a business whose costs relate mainly to developing a website and software for serving customers online. These costs may be heavy, if the site and software are complex, but they do not rise in proportion to the scale of the selling operation. A physical bookshop which doubled the range of titles it carried would probably need to double the size of its premises, and perhaps almost double its staff of shop assistants. When an e-commerce site is up and running, adding numerous Web pages similar to existing ones is only a marginal extra expense.

Considerations like these are why investors were so happy to put large sums into e-businesses which spent money like water and did not expect to see profits for years.

Technology lock-in

Investing to get big fast makes sense only if, having won the race and taken a large market share, one can keep it. Any high-street greengrocer could corner the custom in his town by giving away a five-pound note with every bag of vegetables sold, but that would not help him: once the fivers stopped, customers would drift back to the greengrocers they used before (provided they were still there).

It is often claimed that customers for technical products do not – or rather, cannot – behave like that. They get *locked in* to a technology, so that a company which gets big fast not only corners the market but keeps it.

The example of technical lock-in that almost everyone has heard of is the QWERTY keyboard. When typewriters were invented more than a hundred years ago, the story runs, engineering limitations meant that rapid typists jammed the keys; this was combated by distributing the alphabet around the keyboard in an arrangement which forced typists to work slower. In the 1930s, when the technology had improved and jamming was no longer an issue, a much better arrangement – the Dvorak keyboard – was invented: but it never took off, because the English-speaking world was locked into QWERTY. Manufacturers that might market Dvorak keyboards would find no buyers, because touch-typists were trained on QWERTY; typists that might train on the Dvorak layout could not, because it was not manufactured. Many people would be better off if we all switched from QWERTY to Dvorak, but there is no way to get there from here.

The suggestion is that this is not just a tale from ancient history, but a vivid illustration of a phenomenon which is pervasive in high-tech markets. Technology by its nature produces lock-ins: so the first mover advantage is huge, and getting big fast at any cost makes sound business sense.

This idea has been very influential among investors in e-commerce. But it ain't necessarily so.

Do lock-ins exist?

The flaws in the lock-in idea have been exposed by Stan Liebowitz (2002), who points out in the first place that the QWERTY story is false. Although the QWERTY layout was chosen to prevent jamming, it is also a good arrangement for fast typing. Impartial experiments comparing QWERTY and Dvorak show little difference. The one widely-quoted experiment that seemed to show a significant advantage for Dvorak was conducted by August Dvorak himself and was clearly biased.

What is true of keyboard layouts is true more generally, according to Liebowitz. Alleged cases of technical lock-in dissolve when looked at carefully. Either a technology which dominates its market is about as good as (or better than) alternatives which are failing to make inroads; or, if an alternative technology really is superior, then it does succeed in displacing the market leader.

The most plausible cases of lock-in are cases where the benefit of a technology to one individual depends on how many others use it. If some better word-processing format were invented, I might be reluctant to switch from Microsoft Word while the people who swap WP files with me still use Word. If they all make the same calculation, Word could retain our allegiance. According to Liebowitz, in practice even *network effects* like that are not enough to prop up inferior technology. But in any case, network effects are often irrelevant to e-business. If I decide to stop buying from Amazon, the fact that many people do still use it will not be a reason for me to reconsider.

First versus best

All this suggests that 'first mover advantage' and 'get big fast' may be principles whose significance has been exaggerated. Being first to market may enable an e-merchant to gain from customer inertia – a later competitor will find it hard to gain market share by being only equally good; but a competitor which offers customers more can win in the end. Liebowitz is in no doubt: 'If you are faced with the choice of either rushing a weak product or Web site to market in order to be first or taking the necessary time to be best, go with best.'

Amazon has achieved its success because it was not only first but, arguably, remains best. Amazon soon acquired competitors – Barnes & Noble launched an online operation in February 1997; but we shall see evidence in Chapter 11 that online book buyers do prefer the Amazon experience to that offered by other online bookshops. The consumer rating service BizRate (p. 52) gives Amazon one of the highest scores for any e-tailer.

Elusive profits

The original e-commerce vision was of companies that sink scarcely any capital into inventory or buildings, and simply conjure profits out of the electronic network, by providing virtual links between customers and suppliers.

This vision blurs when Web-based companies expand their physical operations, as Amazon did when it began to hold its own stocks of books. The costs of the virtual side of company activities can soon be dwarfed by the costs of the physical side. Gary Rieschel notes that 'it takes between $15 million and $25 million to build a top-of-the-line Web site. Yet it costs at least $150 million to build a warehouse and distribution system for a consumer Web operation'.[4] Consequently the economies of scale which are such an attractive feature of e-business become irrelevant, because operating costs are dominated by areas where outgoings rise in closer proportion to growth in activity.

4. Reported by Michael J. Mandel and Robert D. Hof, 'Rethinking the Internet', *Business Week* 26 Mar 2001, bouqueca.notlong.com

By early 2001, Amazon's annual revenue was running at $2.8 billion, but it had yet to make a profit in any accounting quarter. In that year, Bezos cut back hard to try to get into the black – 15 per cent of employees were let go, and some customer service centres were closed. Amazon did finally achieve profits in the fourth quarters of both 2001 and 2002. (Any bookshop makes far more sales in the period leading up to Christmas than in the rest of the year.) But it will take many profitable quarters before Amazon earns back the $2.3 billion it had lost by 2001, so that the net economic consequences of its existence are the same as if Bezos had stuck to his day job in 1994. I do not mean to make light of Amazon's remarkable success at satisfying numerous customers. But, so long as Amazon continues to make losses, on average each instance of customer satisfaction is costing more than Amazon charges in return. The greengrocer is still tucking £5 notes in with the carrots.

Diversification

In pursuit of the Get Big Fast principle, Amazon expanded not only internationally but into many other retail sectors. At different times Amazon has moved into selling music, pet products, kitchenware, clothes, consumer electronics, and other categories – even cars at one point. Some of these ventures did not last, but others continue. The slogan has changed from 'Earth's biggest bookstore' to 'The World's Largest Selection'.

One reason for diversifying is that books are *low-margin* goods. Amazon has built up a huge customer base and knows its customers perhaps more closely as individuals (through their tastes in books) than any other large company. It would like to exploit that body of data to sell products for which the difference between price paid to the wholesaler and price charged to the customer is wider.

But, in the first place, it is not clear that internet selling is as suited to other products as it is to books – nor that the data Amazon has accumulated on book buyers will be helpful for selling other things. I have been vaguely puzzled, the last few times I bought from Amazon.co.uk, to find a flyer advertising kitchenware included with the books. It is hard to believe that the type of books I buy make me seem a good prospect for pots and pans. In any case, while physical contact is not very relevant for book-buying decisions, in our house if we need new kitchenware we want to see it and touch it before buying. If that meant waiting a fortnight to visit a distant shop, that would be fine because our saucepan purchases are never urgent. Is the Sampson family unusual in these respects? I doubt it.

So getting big fast by greatly expanding the categories of goods sold is a problematic strategy. But there is another, more general issue about margins.

Many e-tailers began with the idea that the low overheads of running a website should make it easy to undercut conventional merchants who have the expense of maintaining and staffing bricks-and-mortar shops. Amazon offers larger-than-normal discounts on book prices, even though normal discounts yield low profit margins for conventional bookshops. However, beyond the short term it is not conventional retailers that an e-tailer needs to compare its profit margins with – it is other e-tailers.

With categories of product that consumers are happy to buy online, it may well be that conventional retailers will be driven out of business because they cannot match e-tailers' prices. To date that has happened much less than some expected; but, even if it does happen, it will not leave e-tailers free to make profits by charging prices that are just a little less than the prices which made conventional retailing viable. Competition between online merchants in the same market sector is likely to be even fiercer than competition between conventional retailers, because it is so easy for buyers to compare prices online. So, even if some goods are currently associated with larger profit margins than books are, where online selling of those goods turns out to be feasible the margins are likely to narrow considerably.

Alliances

We saw in Chapter 2 that alliances are often seen as key to the success of e-business. Amazon was slower than some to take this road, but it has done so in recent years. For instance, in 2000, Amazon joined forces with Toys'R'Us to create a website selling toys and video games. Toys'R'Us buys and manages the inventory and takes the risk of goods failing to sell; Amazon is responsible for website development, order fulfilment, and customer service.

One special type of alliance-building began much earlier, in 1996, when Amazon started its 'Associates' programme. Businesses or organizations which run sites devoted to a particular topic link their book recommendations to Amazon: a visitor to the associate site can click to buy a book, and Amazon fulfils the order, paying a 15 per cent commission to the associate. By the end of 1999 Amazon had more than 300,000 associate sites. For Amazon this is a valuable source of new customers; the analysts Forrester Research see associate programmes as the best method of driving traffic to an e-commerce site. Also, it gives Amazon access to editorial expertise on books in specialist areas, which is useful for marketing the same books to customers who arrive by other routes.

Furthermore, Spector (2000: 158) points out that Amazon's associate programme, being the first in the field, was set up in a particularly advantageous way: once a customer makes a purchase through the programme, Amazon 'owns' that customer and pays no subsequent commissions. Many other e-businesses have imitated the Amazon Associates programme, but in later versions the associates have typically required continuing benefits from customer relationships which they initiate.

Intermediation and disintermediation

Another aspect of e-business strategy which we need to examine, although Amazon happens not to be a good illustration, is the aspect referred to by the terms *intermediation* and *disintermediation*: see for instance Alina Chircu and Robert Kauffman (2001). People sometimes talk of 'digital intermediation' or 'electronic intermediation' to underline the fact that they are describing business innovations which are made possible by IT.

The idea here is that computer technology can enable value to be created by inserting a new step at some point into a value chain (intermediation); or conversely that the technology can make some existing step redundant (disintermediation). In Chapter 2 we saw that IT may be causing value chains to split up into different-sized segments from before; that does not imply a change in the total number of steps, only in how many steps are executed within the bounds of a single organization. The idea of electronic (dis)intermediation is that the value chains themselves might change length, in terms of the number of steps by which goods or services reach the consumer.

Although these terms are widely used, they involve a confusion. Some may feel that, in a book like this, it would be better to avoid ambiguous terms and to write about e-business only in language that does not lend itself to misunderstanding. Unfortunately, that would leave the reader defenceless when he encounters these words elsewhere – and they are used so frequently that many readers will encounter them. It seems better to be explicit about the confusion and help readers to see what is really going on behind the ambiguities.

It is reasonably easy to quote cases that fit the definition of disintermediation, as I explained it above. One example would be airline websites such as Travelocity, which have made it easy for consumers to buy flight tickets directly from airlines, 'disintermediating' the high-street travel agents who used to represent the only practical way for most individuals to book flights. It seems much harder to identify clear cases of electronic intermediation. One example offered by Chircu and Kauffman is the American website Priceline, which enables tourists to buy hotel rooms, flights, package holidays, etc., by naming their own price which suppliers fitting the tourist's requirements decide whether to accept. If one assumes that the conventional way for a tourist to book a room is to contact a hotel directly, then Priceline does add an intermediate step, which benefits tourists by making it easy for them to arrange discounts, and benefits hotels by helping them to fill their rooms. With most other things sold through Priceline, such as package holidays, tourists typically would have used an intermediary before the internet: the innovation relates to the novel bargaining power which Priceline bestows on the consumer.

We should surely distinguish cases such as airlines selling flights directly to the public, which cuts out a link in a conventional value chain, from cases where the number of links remains constant but an e-business takes over some link from conventional competitors. Chircu and Kauffman fail to make this distinction: they quote Amazon as another case of intermediation, but Amazon's presence does not increase the number of steps along the value chain linking authors and publishers to readers – it just replaces a conventional link with an electronic link (which is why I said, above, that Amazon is not a good illustration of the (dis)intermediation concept).

Chircu and Kauffman's third example of intermediation is eBay, which provides a virtual marketplace where individuals can sell one another more or less anything – including, in particular, fleamarket-type junk whose owners would often have been unable to find buyers at any price before the internet made it easy to advertise, and to search advertisements, nationally or globally. (Because the buyers and sellers it brings together are typically individuals rather than organizations, businesses like eBay are sometimes called *C2C* as opposed to B2B or B2C organizations.)

eBay is an interesting e-commerce example – apart from anything else, it is one of the few e-businesses that has been consistently profitable. However, eBay is not a case of inserting an extra link into an existing value chain. The exchanges that eBay facilitates are often ones that would not have taken place at all without IT.

Both in the case of Priceline and of eBay, the economically significant consequence of the internet is not changes in the length of value chains, but making the market more *liquid*. Mutually beneficial exchanges happen that would not have happened before. Without Priceline, hotel rooms would remain empty because would-be travellers would not discover that the hotel was willing to accept a low price to fill them. Without eBay, items that some collector is glad to pay for would end up on the town dump.

'Reintermediation'

Because of the confusion of terminology, when Chircu and Kauffman write about *reintermediation* they are not mainly concerned with cases where middlemen such as travel agents who are threatened with redundancy by e-commerce find ways to preserve their role. What they are really discussing is strategies by which conventional businesses can resist competition by e-only counterparts. Chircu and Kauffman predict that disintermediation will commonly be followed by reintermediation, but they do not mean that middlemen will succeed in reasserting their roles in cases where the internet is enabling their customers to deal with their suppliers directly. That seems implausible. My guess is that high-street travel agents must wither away as internet penetration of households increases. What Chircu and Kauffman mean, rather, is that conventional businesses will commonly find ways of fending off competition by dotcom startups which try to occupy the same point on a value chain. This is a plausible argument.

As Chircu and Kauffman see it, where a *pure-play* (i.e. e-only) e-business tries to compete with an established conventional business, the e-business may win market share in the short term through technical innovation, but in the longer term the conventional competitor is likely to win, by becoming a *clicks-and-mortar* hybrid. A successful business needs more than innovative technology; it is normally easier for the conventional company to acquire the technology than for the e-business to acquire the other necessary assets, such as an existing customer base, a well-regarded brand, expertise in the goods or services traded, and access to a suitable distribution network. Furthermore, economies of scale will favour the large established company, unless the competing e-business succeeds in Getting Big Fast.

Earlier, we found the idea that technology tends to 'lock in' its customers to be questionable. Chircu and Kauffman point out that even if this idea does hold true for some technologies, for any activity based on the World Wide Web in particular it is the reverse of the truth. A crucial characteristic of the Web is to be neutral between different platforms, browsers, and so forth. So where an e-business's technical innovation relates to the Web, it is likely to be highly *appropriable* by established competitors – the conventional business will be able to fight back by developing Web systems that achieve the same results, even if the e-company's code is proprietary.

The technology provider role

One lesson that Chircu and Kauffman draw is that the best strategy for an e-only company in the long run will often be not to compete with conventional companies, but to adopt the role of technology provider, developing and licensing the systems which conventional companies need in order to convert themselves into clicks-and-mortar businesses.

Amazon has succeeded in overcoming some of the problems facing a pure-play startup. It has got fairly big fast; it has built up a large customer base, and developed a valuable brand. Nevertheless, Amazon has also been moving into the technology-provider niche. In September 2000, Amazon licensed its 1-Click software and trademark for use in Apple's Online Store. In April 2001 Amazon contracted to provide an e-commerce arm for Borders (the second US bookshop chain), which had tried to set up its own online operation without great success. The analyst Scott Reamer sees moves like this as crucial for Amazon's future, now that growth has levelled off in the areas of books, music, and video: 'The idea of Amazon becoming an [e-tail] outsourcer makes its business model much more attractive'.[5]

Conclusion

There are many other aspects of the Amazon operation which this book has no space to explore. The aim in discussing Amazon was not to produce a comprehensive analysis of the business, such as a prospective investor might require, but to use it as a concrete illustration of strategic principles that have been seen as important in e-commerce.

Whether Amazon does eventually turn the corner and become profitable, or disappears through bankruptcy or takeover, at this point probably depends on how willing its backers are to go on funding losses, as much as on details of how it is managed. The extent of remaining financial leeway is the last thing one would expect a loss-making company to be frank about. I have an open mind about whether Amazon will be with us in its present form five years from now. (There will surely be something called Amazon – the brand has become too valuable to jettison.)

Whatever its own future may be, Amazon will surely serve for a long time to come as an instructive case study in the strategies of e-commerce.

---

5. Quoted by Penelope Patsuris, 'Amazon must spill the beans', *Forbes.com* 24 Apr 2001, dotkilum.notlong.com

4
E-business and the institutions of society

Institutional barriers

In 1998, when much of the technology that makes e-commerce possible was in place, a study by the University of Freiburg looked into why businesses were proving slow to exploit it. The study (Schoder et al. 1998) looked at almost a thousand large and small companies in German-speaking Europe; as in the economy generally, most were dedicated to business-to-business trading, a minority to B2C. Senior managers were asked about their attitudes to e-commerce. Even those companies which already used the Web were often using it merely as a publicity medium, rather than as a new means of doing business.

The responses made the reasons clear. Most companies believed that their business could in principle be ported to the internet; few of them saw the complexity of the technology, or the speed at which it is changing, as barriers. Instead, overwhelmingly they cited problems about lack of business conventions in this new domain, and inadequate legal regulation together with unclarity about how existing laws applied.

E-commerce presented companies with opportunities, but also with risks – the investigators classified these as:

- *client risk* – customers making contact via the internet are less likely to be 'known factors' whose reliability can readily be assessed

- *financial risk* – the value of goods or money that might be lost through internet trading

- *legal risk* – problems about assigning responsibility for various elements of electronic business transactions and enforcing contracts

For the managers surveyed, legal risk far outweighed client risk and financial risk combined. Even though financial and client-relationship issues are crucial for financial services and consultancy, these sectors did not lay special stress on client or financial risks – on the contrary, they were more than averagely concerned about legal risk. The sector which was least worried about legal risk was manufacturing. Manufacturers produce physical goods and ship them physically to customers, activities to which a long-established framework of law and business convention applies; so for manufacturers the risks of internet trading looked smaller.

The Freiburg findings make clear how crucial for the evolution of e-business are matters which relate to *social institutions* rather than to the technology itself – matters such as law, accepted ways of doing things, and attitudes. The social institutions of the conventional business world developed over centuries. Five years after the Freiburg survey, we can see that it will be a long time yet before society has adapted its institutions to the new medium sufficiently to create a stable framework for e-business.

Wealth, poverty, and social institutions

The fundamental importance of these issues becomes all the more unmistakable when we consider why some societies are rich and others poor. Differences in prosperity between countries are huge. Burundi has an annual income per head of US $200 and falling – despite a lush agricultural environment. Canada's income per head is more than a hundred times higher, though in the colonial period it seemed such a useless territory that in 1763 the British debated whether it would be more advantageous to take Canada or the small West Indian island of Guadeloupe from the French as reparation for the Seven Years' War.

William Easterly and Ross Levine (2002) have analysed economic and social indices to discover how responsibility for differences in prosperity among 72 rich and poor countries should be allocated between three factors: geography (for example, climate, access to the sea); government policies, which may favour or hinder economic advance; and social institutions, such as political stability, established systems of property rights, and so forth. One might guess that all three factors separately contribute to prosperity or its opposite, but that is not what Easterly and Levine found. It turned out that good institutions are the *only* factor that matters directly. With good institutions, Burundi might be as prosperous as Canada; with bad institutions, Canada – or Britain – could be as wretched as Burundi.

The reason to quote this research is to suggest how much there is to play for in the evolution of e-business. Relative to what may emerge from the new technology, we are in a situation like that of the eighteenth-century Canadian colonists: the future is ours to build. Getting the framework of institutions affecting e-business right is likely not just to affect progress marginally; it may make the difference to whether e-business will end up as a minor innovation, or alternatively will explode into a revolution of wealth-generation whose characteristics cannot be guessed at. We do not know which will happen, but it is clearly worth looking carefully at areas where institutions are already proving problematic.

Practical infrastructure hurdles

Some barriers to e-business development relate to practical issues which are 'social' only in the sense that they require new arrangements to be put in place throughout society – no one company can solve the problem alone.

Public key infrastructure

One of these is the need for a *public key infrastructure*. There are several functions crucial for business which in principle can be achieved in the electronic domain through cryptography. These include *authentication* (enabling the recipient of a business communication to be certain that it comes from who it purports to come from); *confidentiality* (ensuring that communications can be read only by the intended recipient); and *nonrepudiation* (ensuring that someone who places an order or agrees a bargain cannot later call the details into question). In the non-electronic world these functions are achieved by diverse physical means. Letters are written on headed paper, signed manually, and sealed in opaque envelopes; in important cases signatures are formally witnessed; and so forth. The electronic domain seems so transparent, fluid, and anonymous that comparable safeguards might be difficult to achieve.

However, *public key cryptography* (see, for example, Levy 2000), invented in 1978 by Ron Rivest, Adi Shamir, and Leonard Adleman, is technically very suitable to serve these functions. (Although the technique is credited to Rivest, Shamir, and Adleman and called the 'RSA algorithm' after their initials, Levy points out that it was invented earlier by scientists at GCHQ Cheltenham, who were forbidden to publicize it for national security reasons.)

How 'public key' works

Public key cryptography begins by agreeing some way of representing messages as numbers. In a computing context, where character-sequences and everything else are treated as long sequences of binary digits, this is not an issue. Each agent using the system is assigned a set of three very large integers d, e, k, selected in such a way that, for any integer x, if x^d mod $k = y$ then y^e mod $k = x$ and vice versa. (The notation x^d means x to the d'th power, for instance 2^3 is eight. The notation p mod q means the remainder after q is repeatedly subtracted from p, for instance 14 mod 6 is two.) Someone, say Alice, who is assigned the numbers d, e, k keeps d secret but publishes e and k openly as her *public key*.

Then anyone can send Alice a message which only she can read, by encoding the message m as the number m^e mod k (using Alice's public exponent e); Alice deciphers it using her private exponent d. Alice can send anyone a message which only she could have written, by encoding m as the number m^d mod k, using her private exponent (recipients decipher it using her public exponent). And Alice can send Bob a message which only Alice could have written and only Bob can read by enciphering it twice, first with her private exponent and then with Bob's public exponent – Bob deciphers it using Alice's public exponent and his own private exponent.

Any change to a ciphertext means that it deciphers not into a different message but into gibberish. Decipherment of a message without knowledge of the relevant private key is believed to be mathematically impossible.

Thus public key cryptography offers e-commerce a communication system that matches and indeed improves on traditional systems. Physical signatures can be forged, but if someone keeps his private key secret there is no way for anyone else to produce a ciphertext which can be deciphered with the first person's public key. Someone who receives a message legitimately can read it, but could not have written it.

Traditionally, cryptography depends on a single secret key which is agreed between the parties to communication. That only allows communication between agents who are already in a mutual relationship. Public key cryptography allows reliable, secure communication between anyone and anyone, whether or not they have had prior contact.

The need for digital certification

For public-key to fill this role, there needs to be a system of trusted authorities distributing keys to organizations and individuals that need to communicate. Anyone with the necessary mathematical understanding could generate his own three numbers and publish two of them, but if bad guys could generate their own keys and publish them as belonging to Microsoft or the Ministry of Defence, the purpose of the technique would be defeated. Just as people sometimes need to show a birth certificate or passport in order to borrow the reputation of the issuing authority to confirm their identity, so a system of 'digital certificates' needs to be underwritten by trustworthy authorities and generally accepted.

To date such a system has been slow to emerge. In Britain, the Post Office (or Consignia, as it was known at the time) opened a digital certification business called ViaCode, but closed it down in May 2002 because slow uptake made it financially unviable; this forced the British Chambers of Commerce to cease issuing certificates to its members, for lack of a technology partner. The banking clearinghouse BACS announced that it would begin trials of a new system in early 2003. Internationally, in January 2003 the standards body Oasis announced new efforts to promote public key uptake. But there is a Catch-22 problem. Digital certification will be expensive until it is adopted by enough users to bring the cost down, but while costs remain high and the user community is small, companies understandably prefer to make do with less satisfactory solutions.

The problem is not just about expense, but about public understanding and trust. Boaz Gelbord points out:

> Though much easier to forge, the old written signature is a system that everyone understands; we are all more-or-less equally qualified to check if a signature matches the one on the back of a credit card ... people are reluctant to place their trust in a system that requires a high level of mathematical knowledge to understand. (Gelbord 2000)

A well-developed public key infrastructure would not, incidentally, be an uncontroversially good thing. Lawrence Lessig (1999) has argued that it will threaten civil liberties; his case deserves serious consideration. This book, though, is concerned with business, and for e-business a public key infrastructure seems highly desirable – some believe that e-commerce will never properly take off without it.

At the retailing level, the Secure Sockets Layer (SSL) encryption system currently used to ensure the confidentiality and integrity of consumer communications includes no functionality for authentication or non-repudiation. (In consequence, considerable fraud occurs, though the average consumer is unaware of this because the cost falls on sellers rather than buyers.) SSL was originally intended to be replaced by the Secure Electronic Transactions (SET) standard, under which consumers would be issued with digital certificates – but experimental systems proved too complex. Currently a hybrid system is planned, involving use of SET among merchants and banks, while banks will authenticate consumers using separate systems (for example, MasterCard SecureCode and Verified by Visa) which are due to be launched in spring 2003. Since this will require consumers to provide additional data beyond their credit card details when making purchases, it is not yet clear how they will be motivated to co-operate.

Technically, there is little doubt that a universally accepted public key infrastructure would be the ideal solution. It is not clear, however, how we can get there from here. This is one example of a social institution needed for e-business progress which is easier to describe than to create.

Fulfilment

Two further areas involving practical hurdles, particularly for e-tailing, are *fulfilment*, and payment.

Fulfilment is the business term for the process of responding to orders by ensuring that customers get the goods. At Christmas 2000, when internet shopping was hot news, journalists wrote stories about how they had decided to join the IT revolution by doing their gift shopping online, only to garner a sheaf of 'sorry you were out' notes from courier companies. People can make special arrangements to receive the odd one-off delivery, but shifting to online purchasing as a routine is less easy. Tesco's online business currently allows consumers to specify two-hour delivery slots, which can be in evenings or weekends; that may be practical for groceries, where every town or village generates numerous orders every day, but might be uneconomic for other commerce sectors with lower density of ordering. In Nottingham in August 2002 the Royal Mail began testing a drop-box service whereby consumers ordering goods online can have them delivered to lockers at their workplace or in public places. This may partly solve the problem, but it remains to be seen whether lugging goods home from a drop-box offers a sufficient convenience saving over conventional shopping to catch on.

Fulfilment is not problematic exclusively for retailing. In the B2B sector there is no difficulty about receiving deliveries; but online trading can generate novel patterns of order flow, which may be hard for the supplier company to satisfy promptly – yet the online medium creates heightened expectations of prompt fulfilment. That, though, is not a 'social institutions' issue. B2C fulfilment is: it depends not only on what is economically viable for retailers but on what patterns of delivery can be made to fit into consumers' lives.

Payment

Even at the B2B level, shifting the payment process from physical to electronic systems is not unproblematic. If internet trading means that a company's customer base becomes international for the first time, for instance, then electronic payment processing will involve complex functions relating to diverse tax régimes, and perhaps to different credit terms for exotic customers.

Early initiatives to create electronic B2B bill settlement systems mostly did not come from established banks, hence many competing systems arose. By autumn 2002, only about five per cent of companies that could take advantage of B2B invoicing and payment software were doing so. But even if convergence on standard systems in this area is slow, that probably does not pose a significant barrier to e-business development. B2B payments are typically for large sums at long intervals, so little efficiency is lost if they continue to be processed by traditional methods.

In retailing, on the other hand, merchants deal with consumers who are largely unknown to them, so they must secure payment at the same time as they part with the goods; and the advantages of e-commerce would largely be lost if numerous small payments had to be processed manually.

The standard way for consumers to pay retailers is by credit card, and this has worked fairly well. There are three problems, though: fraud; local differences in credit-card acceptability; and micropayments.

When e-tailing began, many people were dismayed at the thought of sending their credit-card details into cyberspace. After some brave souls tried it without being taken to the cleaners by fraudsters, the initial resistance had dissipated considerably by the end of the 1990s; but plenty of people remain unwilling to take the risk, or are far more cautious about who they will buy from online than they are when shopping conventionally. This is not necessarily irrational: SSL technology (see above) protects card details very well en route to the merchant, but there is no saying how the details are handled or stored after the merchant receives them. (Nevertheless, it seems paradoxical that people who will happily allow a waiter to take their card away to the till – and perhaps clone it – are so twitchy about online card use.)

Secondly, not all countries use credit cards as widely as Britain or the USA. Germany and Japan are two countries where the credit-card culture has made few inroads.

The micropayment problem

If credit cards are not used in a B2C context, the logical alternatives are to create electronic analogues of cheques or cash. In particular, 'e-cash' of some kind would *have* to be used for *micropayments* – sums smaller than £5 or so, which are not economic for merchants to process through the credit card system. Since e-commerce began, many people have predicted that there will be a lively market in selling items – a page of useful information, a track of music – online for pence, once society has managed to converge on some generally-accepted micropayments scheme.

Numerous e-cheque and e-cash systems have been floated. One type of system works like a pay-as-you-talk mobile phone account: consumers are given 'e-wallets' which they top up at intervals (perhaps using a credit card) and use to pay out small sums when making online purchases with no need for time-wasting authentication.

To date, no e-cheque or e-cash scheme has been adopted widely enough to attain critical mass. At the time of writing, there are signs that PayPal may – perhaps – take off in the e-cheque role, but since it depends on the credit card infrastructure to process payments it cannot solve the micropayments problem. Again society faces Catch-22: few consumers or retailers are interested in adopting a particular micropayments scheme unless they know that many others accept it, but large numbers can be achieved only if individuals join while numbers are small. Many micropayment schemes – Beenz in Britain, CyberCoin and Millicent in the USA – have come and gone. BT launched a new Internet Payments service in October 2002, under which online micropurchases will be charged via consumers' internet service providers to their phone bills, but some feel that this will suffer by association with unsavoury premium-rate phone business models. Microsoft plans to launch a new e-wallet scheme.

Do we need micropayments?

Some believe that the collapse of one micropayments system after another is not an accident. Clay Shirky (2000) describes micropayments as 'an idea whose time has gone'. Shirky believes micropayments are a non-runner because consumers set a higher value on the time and effort needed to decide whether to accept a particular bargain than they set on the thing to be bought; micropayments 'create in the mind of the user both anxiety and confusion'. He believes that consumers prefer to subscribe to sources of useful information via one-off fees rather than to make separate decisions about paying for specific pages.

Shirky's article has been surprisingly influential, but it seems illogical. People buy low-cost items on a daily basis without anxiety. When I buy lunch in a cafeteria or make local phone calls, I do not conduct internal debates about the cost of each individual item; I know broadly what overall level of consumption I can afford. People often buy individual magazines at newsagents without wanting to commit themselves to subscribing.

The one factor that might make online purchasing different would be if most things that someone might want to sell online for small sums were already made available free by others. It would be difficult to make money selling current share prices or weather forecasts for pence, if they are freely available elsewhere on the Web. But there seems little reason why a recognized financial publication should not sell pages of market analysis, a popular band sell new songs, or a children's writer sell bedtime stories. Consumers do not want just anyone's analysis, songs, or stories, they want material produced by sources they respect. Sites that currently offer pages of useful information free might prefer to charge a few pence to each of thousands of readers, if they easily could.

Thus there are two open questions. Is the market for microsales potentially large enough to make it worthwhile for society to adopt an e-micropayments system? And, if so, will enough merchants and consumers converge on one system to lead to its general acceptance?

Many commentators feel that the answer to the first question is a clear yes (though Shirky disagrees). If that is right, and if the answer to the second question remains no, then many transactions will fail to occur which would benefit both parties if they did occur – including not only the potentially microtradable goods we already know about, but also the unknown categories that will be created in future, if the e-commerce infrastructure makes it possible to market them. Although each individual transaction is by definition small, losing all of them is potentially a large cost to society from failure to evolve a new economic institution.

Plenty of effort continues to be applied to the problem. A novel approach invented by Ron Rivest (the R of the RSA algorithm) was announced in February 2003. In Rivest's Peppercoin scheme, consumers buy items in exchange for electronic tokens whose values to the merchant accepting them do not match the face value of the transactions – instead, most tokens are worthless, but a randomly-selected proportion are worth sums large enough to process through the credit-card system. Averaged over many transactions, a merchant's total revenue is the same as with conventional payment, but it is not dissipated through numerous fees to the card association. It sounds zany, but perhaps it will be the answer.

Gaps in the law

A chief institution distinguishing prosperous from impoverished societies is the rule of law. Businessmen often say that a business can succeed in any environment, provided the environment is settled and predictable. Law is a central part of the framework which offers that predictability.

One large issue is how the laws of many separate countries apply to a global medium. We shall discuss that in Chapter 5. But even within a single jurisdiction, e-business raises novel legal problems.

No statute can hope to anticipate every detailed circumstance in which it has to be applied. English and American law acquires precision from the accumulation of precedents – decisions in earlier cases which settle how some broad principle is to be interpreted in particular contexts. A technology as new and wide-ranging as IT creates wide areas where no precedents exist; so no-one can say for sure how the law applies.

The law of contract

A good example of e-commerce revealing a legal gap was the January 2002 Kodak case, relating to the law of contract (for business, perhaps the most crucial area of law). The online Kodak store offered a 'special deal' on a digital camera, mistakenly quoting the price as £100. The normal price would have been over £300, so this figure was remarkably low but, arguably, not so low that customers were bound to realize it was an error. Thousands of orders were placed in the few days before the offer was taken down.

In face to face shopping, the law is clear. If a too-low pricetag is put on goods by mistake, the customer cannot hold the shop to that; but once he takes the goods to the till and his money is accepted and rung up, it is too late for the shop to say that a mistake has been made (however genuine). In this case, the Kodak site automatically registered customers' credit card details and e-mailed order confirmations, but the error was caught before the cards were debited or the cameras shipped out. Had binding contracts been created? Kodak said not: what happened was like bringing goods to the till but not yet taking money and ringing up the sale. Legal experts said various things. In due course Kodak blinked, and honoured the orders at the low price.

From the company's point of view that was doubtless the right decision: their reputation is worth more than the monetary loss. For e-business generally, it is unfortunate, because an important area of commercial law remains unclarified. Consequently it is that much more difficult than it might be to set up an online trading operation with confidence that the commercial risks have been accurately assessed. In February 2003 Kodak closed down its online store.

Trademarks

Trademarks are another area of business law where e-commerce is creating new uncertainties. Many readers will know about the tussles that have occurred when similarities between company names that are harmless in conventional commerce, because the companies deal in unrelated products, lead to conflict when both companies want to use the same domain name. But litigation in this area has been throwing up problems that are less obvious than that.

One example relates to paid-for listings on search-engine sites such as Google and AltaVista. Some of these companies earn part of their revenue through deals with commercial website owners whereby, if pages from those sites appear in the results of a user search, they will be placed high in the list. The American company Mark Nutritionals produces a weight-loss programme under the registered trade name Body Solutions; in January 2002 it sued several search engine companies for trademark infringement, because searches on the words 'body solutions' did not yield result lists in which URLs for Body Solutions appeared in the first screen. (At least in AltaVista's case, this was not because URLs of non-paying companies were deliberately pushed down the lists, but simply because the algorithm used to identify URLs relevant to two-word queries was not particularly clever.)

One understands the trademark owner's displeasure. At the same time, it is hard to see how search engine companies could possibly meet the obligations which would be entailed by a decision in favour of Mark Nutritionals. For one thing, as Danny Sullivan puts it:

'Orange' is the name of a mobile phone company in the UK, while 'Apple' is the name of a ... computer company ... Can searches for these words not carry ads without the permission of Orange or Apple?[1]

No decision has been announced to my knowledge at the time of writing.

Intellectual property

Clear structures of property rights are crucial to the success of business. The IT revolution has scarcely affected property in the core sense – land and physical goods; but it has large implications for intangible property, such as copyrights and patents. In an information-based society these categories are increasingly important.

Because it is so easy for digital content to be copied perfectly at zero cost, many commentators have suggested that traditional copyright laws will become unenforceable and wither away.

In many respects this might not matter. The original reason for creating laws of copyright was to stimulate production and publication of worthwhile literary and intellectual work, by granting the creators temporary monopolies on exploiting it commercially. In present-day conditions it does not seem likely that the flow of ideas would be much reduced in the absence of copyright law. Nonfiction is largely written by employees, such as academics, whose royalties are small change relative to their salaries. Creative literature is often written for the pure love of writing. It occasionally happens that books like the *Harry Potter* series transport a J. K. Rowling from penury to riches, but this is quite unusual: it would be sad to have no *Harry Potter*, but surely it would not make enough difference to justify maintaining a complex legal framework?

The main significance of copyright today has to do with things rather different from those which motivated its introduction. It allows entertainment companies to make serious money out of mass media, such as music and films.

Early signs have tended to confirm that IT is destined to kill off this sector of business. Peer-to-peer file sharing systems such as Napster have made it easy for anonymous individuals to download copyright music tracks. True, a copyright-infringement action succeeded in closing Napster down in 2002 (to some observers' surprise, since its own activities had not seemed obviously illegal), but other organizations such as KaZaA sprang up to achieve the same functions by techniques that made them safer from legal attack.

Many commentators, though, believe that the *content industries* (such as music companies, and Hollywood) will succeed in fighting back, now that they have rather belatedly understood their danger. Some, such as Lawrence Lessig (currently arguing against extension of copyright before the US Supreme Court), hold that the longer-term danger for society is the reverse (Lessig 2002). The content industries may use their financial muscle to achieve levels of technical and legal protection for

1. Danny Sullivan, 'Lawsuit over paid placements to define search engines', *SearchEngineWatch.com* 19 Feb 2002, dogvanes.notlong.com

their products which end up stifling the creativity that copyright was originally intended to foster.

Copyright has never been absolute. The law includes a doctrine of *fair dealing*: thus, when I write a book I may freely quote brief passages from earlier authors, so as to explain my own case by showing what I am building on or reacting against. Lessig foresees a situation in which technology will be able (through so-called *Digital Rights Management* hardware built into the internet) to prevent even minor recycling of elements from existing intellectual products, and this will be supported by law, not because it benefits society – quite the reverse – but merely because the content industries form a powerful lobby.

Business processes and patent law

A related development is the extension of the patent system to business processes. Traditionally, patents covered things like novel machines or physical processes. The routines which a business uses to get its work done were not thought of as patentable things – they were just part of the culture that recruits learned. Now, business methods are often explicitly coded in software, and can be covered by patents – the patent-monitoring company Derwent Information claimed to have catalogued 200,000 business-method patents internationally by November 2002. In one widely-discussed case, Amazon sued its rival Barnes & Noble for using technology similar to Amazon's '1-Click' system, which minimizes the quantity of data that online customers need to enter – though the case was settled on undisclosed terms, leaving it unclear how much protection the 1-Click patent actually provides.

The overall consequence is that companies can find themselves in legal difficulties for aspects of their operations that they never dreamed the law might be interested in. Even if they were doing things the same way before the method was patented by a competitor (so that in theory they should be covered by what is called *prior art* exemption), because business methods are often inexplicit prior art can be difficult to establish. It is almost as if you were to find me suing you for putting your clothes on in the morning in the same sequence that I use, with a damages claim for all the years you got away with it in the past.

Web link permissions

Related to copyright is the changing attitude to incoming links from others' websites.

The World Wide Web began as an academic enterprise, and site owners in the early days took for granted that the more other sites that linked to theirs, the better. With commercialization of the Web, this has ceased to be axiomatic. There are different ways in which a site can incorporate a link to someone else's web page, from links that cause a graphic on the external site to appear as part of one's own page, down to cross-references like Local restaurants include <u>Chez Nicole</u>, the <u>Peacock Inn</u>, and <u>Riverside</u>. Even in the former case, the website expert Jakob Nielsen (2002: 91) expresses uncertainty about whether copyright law is actually violated – the point may not yet have been tested in court, but when it is the answer will probably be yes. On the other hand many people would still assume that the latter type of link requires no permission. Nowadays, though, businesses are beginning to say things like 'If you want to link to us, show us your website and we'll tell you if that's all right'. Businesses want to locate themselves in salubrious virtual neighbourhoods, just as conventional businesses like to inhabit salubrious physical neighbourhoods – and inward links help to define a virtual neighbourhood.

Whether this desire is enforceable at law, for instance by treating use of someone's URL as a copyright violation, is I believe at present wholly unknown. The fact that businesses are trying to impose such constraints implies that they see this as a possibility; and it is an area where new legislation may come, if the law as it stands does not satisfy business needs.

The problem of trust

We saw in connexion with digital signatures that the problem of achieving social institutions which enable e-business to flourish is not only a problem about creating the technical infrastructure and persuading companies to adopt it. It is also a problem about public knowledge and trust. This problem applies more generally. By now, trust is recognized as a crucial barrier to the development of e-commerce. The UK E-Commerce Minister, Stephen Timms, commented in October 2002 that, in discussions about constraints on e-business progress, 'The issue that comes up time and time again is trust.'[2]

Traditional business functions as well as it does because the average citizen inherits knowledge about how the world works and how to assess risks, who or what to trust and who or what not to trust, through hearing what his elders say and seeing how they behave. If nobody took anything at all on trust, economic life would surely grind to a halt. The social theorist Francis Fukuyama (1995) has argued that the level of trust endemic in a society is an important determinant of its ability to prosper. But e-business is a domain where this cultural inheritance does not help. Often, older people understand the domain less well than younger ones.

After I opened an account with a highly-regarded online British savings bank, for months whenever I logged on to operate the account I would see a message saying that the bank's 'Verisign security certificate' had expired. The first time, I queried this via e-mail and got a gobbledygook reply; after that I ignored the messages. Was this reasonable? Was it foolish? I haven't a clue, and I have no idea who could tell me. That is a very common situation at the present juncture in history.

In the online world, there is a near-total absence of the subtle cues – the way people dress and speak, the quality of stationery, the appearance of company premises or vehicles – which in offline interactions help us to form or revise our judgements about how much confidence to place in people or organizations. The cues that do exist are often ambiguous or misleading.

2. Quoted in Emma Nash, 'Now is the time to start building trust', *Computing* 31 Oct 2002.

> If someone tells us that a serial killer is locked up in a secure prison, we would rightly expect the chance of an escape to be extremely unlikely. But when designers tell us there is a 'secure connection' for the http protocol, we do not know what level of security we can expect. Note too that the padlock-and-key icon in Netscape Communicator conveys a type and level of security that is not comparable to our experience with the icon's physical counterparts ... designers routinely use misleading language and images to convey to users greater reliability and security in the technology than is warranted. (Friedman, Kahn, and Howe 2000)

Batya Friedman et al.'s closing comment suggests that the problem stems from deceitfulness, but that seems harsh. There are deceitful traders out there, but there are also plenty of honest ones. The root problem is lack of shared social assumptions, because of the unfamiliarity of the online world. Even if dishonesty were no commoner online than in conventional business, e-business would be severely hobbled by lower levels of trust.

The problem is made worse by the fact that established patterns of trust are different in separate human societies, which are linked by the internet more immediately than they have ever been linked before. Fukuyama points out that the default level of trust among unrelated individuals is higher in America, Germany, and Japan than it is in France, Italy, or China, for instance. Statistical analysis of data on 28 countries by Claudia Keser et al. (2002) shows that even level of internet penetration correlates closely with societies' trust level. So a user may be comfortable with the technology but yet have good reason to withhold trust online: he may be dealing with systems developed by people whose social expectations and assumptions differ from his own.

Misplaced trust

Apart from people fearing to trust an online interaction, there is a converse phenomenon: people do give trust online in circumstances where, in the offline world, this might seem inappropriate.

Thus, the internet is reducing the perceived value of professional qualifications. Now that people can get medical or legal advice free from Web forums (where the advisers are not necessarily recognized professionals), they are often less inclined than they used to be to respect the expertise of qualified doctors or lawyers.

Michael Lewis (2001) describes an extreme case: a 15-year-old boy, Marcus Arnold, living in a small town in the Californian desert, who in 2000 took up the hobby of answering questions about criminal law on a 'knowledge exchange' site, AskMe.com, based on expertise picked up mainly from watching television courtroom dramas. Initially he pretended to be older than he was; the ratings which the inquirers assigned to his advice soon pushed him close to top in the ranking of AskMe.com criminal-law advisers (who included many professional lawyers), at which point he came clean about his age. This did not stop him reaching the No. 1 rank a month later. Defendants who knew he was fifteen were asking him to accompany them to hearings; he was writing motions for his 'clients' which they would get properly-licensed lawyers to submit to court.

One view of this is to say that the legal profession, and other professions, have been exploiting their monopoly status to pretend that their special expertise is more valuable than it really is. By making it easy to locate enthusiastic amateurs, the internet is showing these pretensions up. Undoubtedly there is some truth in that.

On the other hand, Lewis does not pretend that Marcus Arnold knew enough to give correct advice in tricky cases. Trained lawyers do know a lot of detail that cannot be picked up just by watching television dramas. It may be that in practice most cases require only elementary knowledge. But many of us are willing to pay solicitors' fees because, lacking the training, we cannot be sure that our case will not turn out to need deeper knowledge – and also because, with a professional, we have a comeback if the advice proves bad.

So an alternative view of the situation is that the internet fosters the mind-set which, in another professional domain, prefers an incompetent doctor who exudes confidence and reassurance over a chilly-faced doctor whose knowledge and skill are outstanding. It encourages misplaced trust.

Privacy

The less trusting we feel, the keener we are to safeguard our privacy. Whereas unfamiliarity leads to lack of trust in online interactions, with privacy the current situation seems to be opposite: often, people are happy to engage in online commercial interactions only because they have little grasp of how much privacy they are forfeiting.

To get a feeling for how closely our web-browsing habits are monitored, for instance, David Manasian (2003) suggests the experiment of setting one's browser to warn about 'cookies' rather than silently accept them,

> then browse the web for a few minutes. You will soon be bombarded with messages telling you that almost every website you visit is trying to plant cookies – small text files that collect information about your browsing habits – on your computer. ... Your every move on the internet is being recorded by someone, somewhere.

Many of us who were vaguely aware of receiving cookies imagined, naïvely, that the information they gathered remained between us and the individual cookie-planting website, making them fairly harmless – but that is far from true. Cookies collect valuable marketing information which is sold by the sites that harvest it to companies which share it with other sites. 'The largest of these, DoubleClick, has agreements with over 11,000 websites and maintains cookies on 100m users. These can be linked to hundreds of pieces of information about each user's browsing behaviour.'

Web surfing is only one area of life where Big Brother is watching us, or soon will be watching us, in a way that was hardly conceivable only a few years ago. Barcodes on goods are beginning to be replaced by RFID (radio frequency identification) tags, which in terms of business efficiency have three advantages: they are tiny ('half the size of a grain of sand'); they can be read automatically at a distance rather than needing to be scanned manually; and their 64-bit codespace allows individual items, not just product types, to be given unique identifiers. No privacy worries surfaced in January 2003 when Tesco began experimenting with RFID tags in place of barcodes, which should enable the store to monitor stock levels and sell-by dates more efficiently and detect shoplifters reliably. (For its initial trials Tesco used packets of razor blades.) But it was a different story in March when Benetton announced plans to embed RFID tags into its garments. Commentators woke up to the fact that consumers could be 'bombarded with intrusive advertising[,] since a history of customers' purchases and their identities would be linked with the tag even after they leave the store.'[3] Burglars will be able to check out the contents of houses without needing to get out of their car. 'Future divorce cases could involve one party seeking a subpoena for RFID logs – to prove that a spouse was in a certain location at a certain time.'[4] Faced with a boycott, in April Benetton announced a rethink. But although this particular company may refrain from making its customers go around wearing identity beacons, for the time being at least, it is hard to believe that the technology will not spread. The European Central Bank plans to embed RFID tags in euro banknotes. Before Benetton, Prada had already begun putting the tags into its luxury garments, apparently without attracting adverse comment.

In any case, RFID tags in clothes are not needed to monitor people's whereabouts. CCTV cameras are so widespread in public places that one estimate in 2003 reckoned that the average Briton is recorded 300 times a day; automatic face-recognition technology is advancing rapidly. Credit cards leave data trails, and as mechanisms for issuing bus and train tickets, admission tickets, and the like are computerized these things will add to the detail available on everyone's movements.

All this has come about so quickly that the public is only now beginning to react; but the signs are that many people dislike it strongly. David Manasian believes that 'privacy is likely to become one of the most contentious and troublesome issues in western politics'. Particularly since the 11 September atrocities, some people are willing to concede the need for surveillance by the State, without feeling any happier when private-sector organizations do the same thing.

Privacy may be a lost cause. Scott McNealy, chief executive of Sun Microsystems, says 'You have zero privacy anyway. Get over it.'[5] And David Brin (1998) has argued that if everyone can monitor everyone else, 'mutually assured surveillance' will ensure that personal information is not abused (as the prospect of 'mutually assured destruction' kept nuclear arms unused during the Cold War years). But many people will find it difficult to be as sanguine as Brin. At the B2C level, this could be a very significant factor limiting future participation in e-commerce.

3. Elisa Batista, 'What your clothes say about you', *Wired News* 12 Mar 2003, tagizate.notlong.com
4. Declan McCullagh, quoted in *vigilant.tv* 14 Jan 2003, vigilant.tv/article/2716
5. Quoted in Sterne (2001: 210).

Consumer ratings

Many approaches are being tried in order to create the kind of confidence in e-commerce which people have long taken for granted in conventional commerce.

One straightforward technique is to publish ratings of online merchants by their customers. The best-known service of this kind is the American site BizRate, launched in 1996. E-merchants who agree to participate arrange for BizRate to poll consumers electronically at the time when they make a purchase (and again some days later, to allow for assessment of delivery performance, etc.). Purchasers give the merchant marks out of ten for criteria such as 'ease of finding what you were looking for', 'clarity of product information', 'on-time delivery', and ten or twelve others. Moving 90-day averages are published as a display of smiley and sad faces. Non-participating merchants are reviewed also, at shoppers' initiative – though this mode of assessment is less immediate and perhaps less unbiased than electronic polling at point of purchase. Participating companies display the BizRate 'Customer Certified' logo.

BizRate is a commercial operation: to keep things fair it does not charge e-tailers for listings, but it sells them the detailed customer comments from which its published ratings are distilled. Nevertheless Americans take BizRate seriously as a source of unbiased information about e-tailer quality. BizRate puts effort into ensuring that, for instance, its ratings cannot be manipulated by the merchants themselves posing as customers.

The value of an operation like this depends on how comprehensive its coverage is. In 2003 BizRate claims 'over 2000' participating merchants, which must mean that many have not chosen to participate; only a small number of these seem to be reviewed at customers' initiative, and we have seen that those ratings are likely to be less reliable (though some non-participants receive thousands or tens of thousands of reviews – BizRate claims to have over 1,300,000 active reviewers).

Customer feedback seems to be a rather successful mechanism for creating trust in online commerce. Paul Resnick et al. (2000) argue that this mechanism actually functions much *better* in practice than, logically, ought to be possible. On the C2C auction site eBay, 'the overall rate of successful transactions remains astonishingly high for a market [so] "ripe with the possibility of large-scale fraud and deceit"'; Resnick et al. attribute this to buyers' and sellers' surprising willingness to rate each other fully and honestly on eBay's Feedback Forum.

Site certification services

Apart from services like BizRate which assess e-tailers on features which are apparent to consumers, there are also non-profit certification schemes that focus more specifically on privacy and trustworthiness, which are harder for shoppers to judge for themselves. These certification services are better developed in the USA than in Europe; the best known is TRUSTe. (Another is BBBOnLine, run by the US Council of Better Business Bureaus.)

TRUSTe is a nonprofit organization sponsored jointly by companies such as PricewaterhouseCoopers and Microsoft, which has been working since 1997 under the slogan 'Make privacy your choice' to encourage the growth of e-business by fostering user trust and confidence. It has several methods, for instance its Watchdog system provides a resolution mechanism for disputes about customer privacy; but its chief activity is certifying the practices of online companies with respect to customer privacy, via a badge (the 'trustmark') which a site displays to demonstrate that it has been audited and found to meet the TRUSTe norms. By 2001 more than two thousand companies were participating.

Initially, the plan was to define a range of symbols, since not all customers necessarily require the same privacy approaches. For instance, some people may object to receiving third-party mailings unless they have actively opted in for them, while others may be satisfied if they are given the opportunity of opting out. Different privacy policies may be suitable for different business sectors. Because the details of commercial privacy policies are subtle and complex, it is unrealistic to think that many consumers will actually read them even if they are posted on the Web. So TRUSTe planned to develop a system of icons to encode the significant variables visually. Lori Fena, chairman of TRUSTe, said in June 2001:

> Just as the traffic light was created for drivers to understand easily and quickly the rules of the road, this initiative will create common language and symbols for consumers to make informed, yet quick, decisions about who gets their personal information and, more important, who doesn't.[6]

Two years on, however, these ideas appear to have stalled. And there has been serious criticism of TRUSTe, with sceptics suggesting that the requirements for its trustmark are so minimal as to make it worthless or even misleading. In 1999, when it emerged that the RealJukebox site was distributing software that surreptitiously gathered personal data from users' hard discs, TRUSTe decided that since the privacy violation was linked only indirectly to site visits it lay outside the scope of a TRUSTe audit. Batya Friedman et al. (2000) compare this to 'a hotel garnering a five-star rating simply by promising not to guarantee its customers good service and then faithfully keeping its promise'.

In Britain the Consumers' Association ran a certification scheme, *Which?* Web Trader, with aims comparable to TRUSTe's, but the scheme closed in January 2003 because it was unable to cover running costs. A comparable scheme run by IMRG (Interactive Media in Retail Group) continues, but it is on a small scale and has not achieved wide recognition. Currently, the most likely way forward may be through the government-sponsored TrustUK organization, which announced a new accreditation scheme in February 2003 to replace the Consumers' Association scheme. No such scheme will achieve much, though, unless it becomes near-universally accepted. The TrustUK secretary has reported reluctance by online traders to pay the fairly modest fees needed to make the new scheme work.

6. www.truste.org/about/lori_speech.htm

Platform for Privacy Preferences

The World Wide Web Consortium (W3C) is pursuing another approach, under the title *Platform for Privacy Preferences Project* (P3P). This has grown out of what was originally, in 1997, described as an 'Open Profiling Standard', and version 1.0 of P3P became a W3C Recommendation in April 2002. (Two years were lost after a company claimed in 1998 that P3P infringed one of its patents – the complaint was eventually withdrawn.)

P3P is concerned not with ensuring that companies stick to their stated policies on how they use customer data, but with making it easy for people to avoid visiting websites whose policies do not suit them. P3P provides a standard format that companies use to post an encoding of their policies on their site; individuals encode their privacy requirements via controls on their browser. Then, as the user surfs the Web, his browser can check automatically that visited sites are acceptable, without the user needing to consider the issue case by case.

By November 2002, many e-commerce sites had adopted P3P, including about a quarter of the top hundred sites; the rate of adoption was slowing, though, probably because the economic downturn meant that companies had fewer resources to spare for technical innovation in their websites.

Single sign-on

Initially, P3P was intended not only to automate checking of privacy policies, but also to allow users to encode their personal-profile data (address, age, etc.), so that tedious retyping of the material for site after site would be eliminated, but the user could impose general constraints on the circumstances in which different subsets of the data would be given out. Various principles were elaborated, for instance 'Under no circumstances is the reader notified whether the sender simply did not have requested information available or whether the sender actively chose not to share their information'. But, for various reasons, this data-exchange aspect of P3P was dropped.

Single sign-on technology has clear advantages, though. It is not merely that people do not like endlessly typing in the same details, but also the need to keep track of passwords for different sites forces people to write their passwords down, negating much of the security benefit. Currently, the single sign-on goal is being pursued by others. Liberty Alliance, a consortium initiated by Sun but deriving its impetus largely from industrial users of technology rather than suppliers, announced a specification for user authentication in July 2002, covering just transmission of information required for identity verification. Microsoft has its own system, Passport, which aims to do more; but Passport has been running into difficulties. At one stage users' personal data were to be held on Microsoft's own servers, but this concept was abandoned in 2002 not just because consumers disliked the idea but because merchants objected to losing direct links with their customers. Then in January 2003 the EU determined that Passport's treatment of personal information violated European privacy law, and Microsoft was forced to agree to modifications that may take some time to implement.

Another system for users to control what categories of data are released to various sites, Nightingale, was announced by RSA Security in early 2003. And in July of the same year, IBM announced a new and different approach: a programming language, Epal (Enterprise Privacy Authorization Language), which allows privacy control to be embedded in the detailed texture of application software.

Winning hearts and minds

There is no shortage of technical initiatives to address the problems about trust and privacy. But technical fixes will achieve little, unless they succeed in winning general public acceptance.

From what we have seen, it seems that on the whole acceptance is occurring less rapidly than some had hoped. It may be unrealistic to expect attitudes and assumptions which have evolved naturally over centuries to be matched by online analogues within a few short years.

5

Jurisdiction, regulation, taxation

E-commerce across frontiers

In the heady early days of the Web, idealists envisaged it creating a new world in which national borders and governments would lose their significance. Many remember the 'Declaration of the Independence of Cyberspace',[1] published in 1996 by John Perry Barlow (lyricist for the Grateful Dead), beginning:

> Governments of the Industrial World, you weary giants of flesh and steel, I come from Cyberspace, the new home of Mind. On behalf of the future, I ask you of the past to leave us alone. You are not welcome among us. You have no sovereignty where we gather.

People really thought it might be so – but of course it never could be. Sovereignty must always be exercised somehow, by good governments or by bad governments. And for the foreseeable future, the domains within which sovereignty applies will be divided up geographically. Perhaps the most salient of all legal problem areas for e-commerce is the question of jurisdiction: whose laws apply, when the parties to a transaction are based in different countries?

This is not a new problem. Any international trading requires agreement about what law applies to disputes. But before the internet, when some physical effort was involved in communicating across national boundaries, it was not a pressing problem. To B2B traders the issue was obvious and was provided for in contracts: either the jurisdiction applicable to disputes was specified explicitly, or by default the laws of the seller's location applied. Consumer goods were rarely bought by mail order from abroad.

Now that the Web makes it easy for consumers sitting in their own homes to buy things from across the world, many governments feel that it is not acceptable for their legal protection to depend on the seller's home law. A consumer is unlikely

---

1. www.eff.org/~barlow/Declaration-Final.html

to know about relevant ways in which another country's law differs from his own; more important, it is impractical for most private individuals to invoke the protection of a foreign legal system. Repeatedly, governments have responded to e-commerce by trying to impose their own legal requirements on sellers anywhere selling to their citizens.

In 1997, for instance, the State of California introduced a law which imposed, on anyone (not only retailers) selling online to buyers in California, detailed requirements about matters such as disclosure of seller's street address and refund policy – the rules specified not just what should be stated but in what size of lettering and where on the website (Mougayar 1998: 66–7). The rules may have been reasonable and sensible; but if each of the hundred-odd nations of the world (and indeed the fifty separate State jurisdictions of the USA) were to impose independent requirements at this level of detail, it is not clear how merchants could realistically comply – or how compliance could be enforced.

The E-Commerce Directive

Some observers saw this Californian legal initiative as a naïvely over-ambitious early response to a novel technology. But the European Union is currently trying to move in a similar direction. The European E-Commerce Directive was due to be embodied into the law of member states by January 2002 (though the legal complications involved meant that most missed this deadline). Under this law, in theory a retailer in one European country, say Britain, selling to consumers in another, say France (or even, possibly, in a non-European country), can be required to defend disputes under the legal principles of his home country but in a court in the consumer's country. Many doubt that this will work. One lawyer asks 'Is a French court going to ignore French law? It is just not going to happen.'[2] The Alliance for Electronic Business (a group representing relevant British organizations such as the CBI) warned that the Directive is likely to damage e-commerce take-up.

Furthermore, the Directive imposes detailed requirements that might be technically impossible to meet. If mobile computing takes off so that people use personal digital assistants or mobile phones for shopping, there is no way that small screens could display the masses of detailed information which the Directive requires merchants to disclose.

Another EU law, the Brussels Regulation (which came into effect in March 2002), gives consumers the right to sue in their home courts a trader who 'by any means, directs [commercial or professional] activities' to their country, so that legal remedies depend crucially on whether a website has features which suggest that it is adapted to audiences in a particular country. If prices are shown in pounds, it might be easy to decide that British buyers are targeted; does the same follow if, say, the site uses British rather than American spellings?

Clearly these are laws which could only provide a clear structure of rules once their various ambiguities and impracticalities have been clarified through expensive test cases. In an international context, the legal structure that emerges

---

2. Quoted by Jean Eaglesham, 'A troubled deal on the internet', *Financial Times* 10 Feb 2002.

will have as much to do with what can be enforced in practice as with legislators' original intentions. (In December 2002 the European Commission launched consultations with a view to bringing forward revised proposals.)

A Framework for Global Electronic Commerce

One way in which a successful legal basis for global e-commerce might be created would be through agreement by the main commercial nations on common principles. President Clinton's administration in the USA attempted to give a lead: in July 1997 it published *A Framework for Global Electronic Commerce*,[3] which urged the governments of the world to join America in implementing policies that would minimize the risk of interfering with the benefits expected to flow from internet commerce. Thus, principle 1 of the Framework was 'The private sector should lead'; principle 2 was 'Governments should avoid undue restrictions on electronic commerce' – so, among other things, 'governments should refrain from imposing new ... taxes and tariffs on commercial activities that take place via the Internet'. One might see the *Framework* as proposing an e-commerce régime that comes as close as one could get in real life to the idealistic vision of independent cyberspace.

In the months following publication, the *Framework* principles were influential – as Walid Mougayar (1998: 68) put it, 'the world seems to be listening'.

One reason why the world was willing to fall in with the *Framework* principles in the late 1990s was the widespread conviction that the internet would soon generate immense wealth, though no-one was quite sure how. The priority was to avoid injuring the goose that was going to lay golden eggs, and there was no telling what seemingly harmless regulation might prove injurious.

Another reason for agreement was that the hands-off attitude promoted by the *Framework* document chimed with ideas about the role of government which had become popular independently of IT. The decades following the Second World War had been a period when people throughout the Western world believed in achieving universal welfare through active government intervention and regulation of the economy. In about 1980 there was a turning point. Many people came to feel that welfare states were incapable of fulfilling their promises, so it was better to limit the State to the minimal roles of maintaining security and the rule of law, and to leave it to individuals to pursue their own welfare. In Britain this change was symbolized by the premiership of Margaret Thatcher – but Lady Thatcher was only the most prominent representative of an international shift. Britain is currently governed by the party which opposed Thatcher's Conservatives, but Tony Blair's Labour party has adopted many of her principles.

The fact that the internet crosses national boundaries freely, and gives individuals and small enterprises access to domains which previously were limited to a few big players, means that government regulation is often harder to impose than it was. For believers in small government that is an excellent thing, and the internet is a useful ally in the task of reducing government interference.

3. www.ecommerce.gov/framewrk.htm

Darwinian versus sports competition

Consider a specific area: stock exchange regulation. Before IT, physical practicalities meant that share trading was carried out by a limited number of brokers in known locations who accordingly were easy to regulate, and they were tightly regulated. In America, the Securities and Exchange Commission has historically enforced an onerous system of rules designed to achieve perfect fairness, for instance there are heavy penalties against 'insider dealing' – which became illegal in most Western jurisdictions in the 1970s and 1980s, having previously been seen as all part of the game.

The internet makes it easy for small-scale stock exchanges to be set up and for individuals to trade in stock from houses in the suburbs. Detailed regulation becomes impossible in that environment, so the question arises how far the rules should be relaxed to permit the technical possibilities to be exploited. In September 1997 Steven Wunsch, who was running a small specialized electronic stock exchange in the USA, wrote a now-famous open letter[4] to the Securities and Exchange Commission, arguing that the Commission's aim of creating a perfectly fair level playing field was misguided. It is generally agreed that economic competition benefits society, because it keeps prices down and stimulates creation of new products and services; but, Wunsch pointed out, there are two kinds of competition – *sports competition*, and *Darwinian competition*. In sports competition, everything is done to make competitors' chances as equal as possible. It 'requires highly defined, specific forms of competitors, common fields of engagement, and alert referees to make sure the rules are followed.' In Darwinian competition, on the other hand, 'there is no fair, there are no rules, there is no referee; the name of the game is survival.' What bodies like the Securities and Exchange Commission are trying to impose is fair competition in the 'sports' sense. But, Wunsch argued, the kind of economic competition that society needs is Darwinian competition. It is Darwinian competition that 'discovers which new forms of competitors are better at surviving than old forms'. Darwinian competition

> is inherently unfair by the terms of sports competition. But, far from hindering the effectiveness of evolution, this unfairness is essential to producing ever more capable competitors and ever more complex forms of biological, social and economic organization. In a very real sense, Darwinian competition must be unfair to work properly.

The case of Jonathan Lebed

The contrast between old and new philosophies is well illustrated by the case of Jonathan Lebed. Jonathan Lebed was a youngster from a blue-collar family in Cedar Grove, New Jersey, who in 2000 became the first minor in the USA to be prosecuted for stock market fraud. Beginning at age 13 he had traded in shares from a computer in his bedroom, creating a website and using existing online forums in order to talk up the shares he owned. He did this in a professional

---

4. Reproduced as Chapter 23 of Steve Wunsch, *Auction Countdown*, 2001, outkilsh.notlong.com

fashion, and apparently without factual misstatements; over a couple of years his profits approached a million dollars. (With a small part of the profit he bought a bright-green Mercedes sports utility vehicle, which his parents drove him round in.) The Securities and Exchange Commission came down like a ton of bricks: if a child makes money by tipping shares, this must be illegal 'manipulation' of the market – share tipping is the province of adult professionals.

The trouble is, professionals are not specially good at it. A 1999 study showed that share-price predictions from amateur websites (so-called 'whisper numbers') were wrong by, on average, 21 per cent. Predictions by Wall Street professionals were wrong by 44 per cent on average – more than twice as much. Jonathan Lebed seems in fact to have been an unusually astute stockmarket analyst and investor, and in the end the SEC settled out of court for confiscation of a fraction of his profits; it was not at all clear what he had done that was illegal. His real 'crime' was to expose the pretensions of those claiming to regulate the market in the public interest. As Michael Lewis (2001) puts it in his entertaining account of the Lebed case:

> That's the trouble with fourteen-year-old boys – from the point of view of the social order. They haven't yet learned the more sophisticated forms of dishonesty. It can take years of slogging to learn how to feign respect for hollow authority.

Some may feel that it is morally wrong to talk up publicly things in which one has an economic interest. In a gentlemanly world, such things would perhaps not happen. But when anyone, anywhere is free to place postings on websites, a convention like that is quite impossible to maintain.

If the internet is making it hard to enforce regulatory régimes, and at the same time is revealing that traditional regulations are often irrational, then one may well conclude that the Darwinian free-for-all encouraged by the *Framework* document is the right and only practical way forward.

Increased e-business regulation

It is easy to see how the *Framework for Global Electronic Commerce* attracted support when it was published. But there are converse points of view. Six years later, after the goose has laid fewer and less-golden eggs than expected, some of these counterarguments may seem weightier.

Although the international trend has been to remove purely commercial constraints on economic competition, there has been another tendency since the 1990s to increase regulation in the name of goals such as 'health and safety' and 'equal opportunities'. This tendency affects e-business along with other domains.

Security standards

The idea of regulating e-business on security grounds is emerging in response to government perceptions that the sector is irresponsible about security (even though surveys regularly show that security is IT managers' top priority). In

January 2003 the Slammer worm caused damage estimated at $1 billion worldwide, although a patch had been available for eight months previously. Doubtless some of the damage affected customers or trading partners who were not responsible for failure to deploy the patch. Various standards, such as British Standard 7799, are available to define requirements for secure information management, but companies are slow to adopt them – David Hendon of the Department for Trade and Industry announced in February 2003 that only eighty BS7799 certificates had been issued to UK firms to date.

Hendon commented 'There comes a point at which society can't allow the corporate equivalent of train crashes to keep happening'.[5] He suggested that standards such as BS7799 may be made legally mandatory. If compulsion arrives, no doubt it will turn out to entail significant consequences for e-business beyond the purposes that motivate its introduction.

Disability discrimination

Disability discrimination is a good example of regulation in the name of equal opportunities. The UK Disability Discrimination Act, 1995, comes into full force in 2004, but it already requires services offered by websites to be accessible to disabled (for example, blind) users. Until test cases have been fought out it is not clear exactly how this will translate into specific requirements on websites. The World Wide Web Consortium has been attempting to flesh out the general principles through its Web Accessibility Initiative, and courts may well treat conformance with the W3C guidelines as meeting the legal requirements – though this is not guaranteed, since the W3C has no statutory authority. Whether or not they are legally recognized, the W3C guidelines are clearly not simple. The latest set to be released (in January 2003), namely version 1.0 of the 'User Agent Accessibility Guidelines', were four years in development and cover only one of three aspects of accessibility for which W3C guidelines have been issued to date. Conforming will presumably be a serious challenge to small businesses running websites on a shoestring; a UK government investigation in April 2003 found that even in the public sector, 78 per cent of sites are currently in breach of this law. Furthermore, there is no guarantee that well-intentioned rules designed to make life easier for the disabled might not make it impossible to develop new e-commerce services which would be highly beneficial for society as a whole.

Bodies representing the disabled, such as the Royal National Institute for the Blind, are naturally interested in bringing test cases to show reluctant businesses that they must take legislation like this seriously. On the other hand, even in the domain of conventional commerce, there is anecdotal evidence that smaller companies nowadays are beginning to find regulatory legislation too complex and onerous to attempt to comply with. So at present it is a very open question how far this type of regulation will take hold in the e-commerce sphere, where there is the additional complication of global reach.

---

5. Quoted by Gareth Morgan, 'Whitehall security standard warning', *Computing* 20 Feb 2003.

Conflicting ideals

Making life easier for the disabled is at least an ideal on which there is broad international public agreement. Some societies see it as a higher priority than others, but so far as I know no society actively rejects the principle. The situation for e-business is even more difficult when different societies have conflicting principles.

Libel

One instance is libel, which for publishers is a very important area of law (and much of e-commerce depends on Web publication). Even closely related societies can have very different libel laws. British libel laws are often seen as draconian, with cases easy for plaintiffs to win and damage awards large; in the USA the law of libel is so weak as barely to exist. One might suppose that whether a website contains a libel depended on the law of the place where the Web server is located; but in December 2002 an Australian court ruled otherwise. Joseph Gutnick, an Australian businessman, sued the online version of *Barron's* magazine for defamation, and although Dow Jones (who own *Barron's*) argued that the article was published from its server in New Jersey, the Australian High Court decided that the alleged defamation occurred wherever the article was read. This is now a precedent which is likely to influence cases in other countries whose legal systems are based on English law, and it seems to create an almost impossible burden on website owners to comply with an open-ended range of national laws on defamation.

The Nazi memorabilia case

A different kind of legal issue was brought into focus by the Yahoo! Nazi memorabilia case. France, like some other Continental countries, has fierce laws against activities which condone Nazism. US law upholds freedom of expression for all political points of view. These approaches came into conflict when in 2000 French anti-Nazi groups sued Yahoo! for allowing items such as SS daggers to be advertised on its online auction site. The French court ordered Yahoo! to prevent surfers in France from viewing these adverts, with a penalty of about $13,000 a day for non-compliance. Then in November 2001 an American court cleared Yahoo! by ruling that the First Amendment to the US constitution (on freedom of speech) trumps more restrictive overseas laws, with respect to content generated by Americans within the USA. The direct contradiction between these decisions happened to go away because Yahoo! meanwhile voluntarily removed the offending adverts from its site. That enabled all concerned on this occasion to ignore the fact that (as it was put by Vint Cerf, an expert witness for the French court) 'if every jurisdiction in the world insisted on some form of filtering for its particular geographical territory, the world wide web would stop functioning'.[6]

6. Quoted in Mark Ward, 'Experts question Yahoo auction ruling', *BBC News Online* 29 Nov 2000, golgetop.notlong.com

The *Framework* approach to conflicts of principle like this is that the principle of freedom should win. To the American compilers of the *Framework* document, that was equivalent to saying 'the principle which makes it easiest for e-commerce to flourish should win'. Seen from elsewhere, though, the same approach can seem to amount to 'the principle which suits the USA best should win'.

Preserving national cultures

That same contrast of perceptions arises in an area that is less acutely inflammatory than Nazi souvenirs, but more significant: namely the extent to which national cultures should be protected against the levelling effect of globalization.

Many countries have in the past taken steps to preserve their distinctive cultures through, for instance, legally restricting the proportion of foreign programming and films that can be shown on television and in cinemas. France, with its remarkable history and civilization, has been a leading example. The *Framework* urges that on the internet that approach should be outlawed. Countries which want to promote home-grown content should subsidize it from general taxation, rather than limiting the flow of content from elsewhere.

To a Frenchman that might sound like 'French taxpayers must pay to keep France French'. He might wonder why they should have to. The *Framework* principle maximizes freedom; but the media happen to be a more important revenue-earning sector of the economy in the USA than in most countries, so the principle is again one that favours American national interests.

This may be a less important issue than it looks to politicians, though. As entertainment media mature, there is plenty of evidence that consumer preferences lead to more localization of content than governments would dare to impose. 'The days when "Dallas" or "Kojak" filled British prime-time are long gone';[7] broadcasters in every EU country are now far over the legal minimum quota for EU-made programmes.

The Hague Convention

At present, the trend seems to be to move away from the free-for-all approach towards the opposite extreme, that anything on the internet which would be objectionable in one jurisdiction should be eliminated everywhere. This poses obvious practical difficulties for e-business because of the need to get to grips with large ranges of exotic regulations. To many, the trend will also be objectionable morally or politically. Plenty of people might be happy with global bans on, say, Nazi souvenirs, or paedophile sites – but those are the easiest cases. The same people might find it unacceptable if, for instance, internet advertising of alcohol, or discussion of interest rates, were outlawed because some Islamic nations object to these things.

---

7. 'The one where Pooh goes to Sweden', *The Economist* 3 Apr 2003; cf. 'Cultural imperialism doesn't sell', *The Economist* 11 Apr 2002.

Contradictions between national legal principles such as arose in the Nazi memorabilia case may be eliminated in future through international acceptance of a convention under development since June 2001 by the Hague Conference on Private International Law, which would require courts of each signatory country (the UK and the USA are two of them) to enforce one another's decisions in the areas of commercial and civil law. This is perhaps more practical than the approach taken by the European E-Commerce Directive, which requires courts to make decisions using other countries' laws. But, as one commentator put it in August 2001:

> imagine this: you live in England and create a website based in England that breaks no English law. Then, because of a court ruling in Turkey, the English courts close you down simply because the website can be viewed abroad and the Turks don't like it.[8]

Richard Stallman, founder of the GNU project, has produced a trenchant analysis (Stallman 2001) of the various uncongenial implications of the Hague Convention.

If this is the way forward which the world chooses, e-commerce will come to be limited to what is totally bland and inoffensive – very different from the anything-goes, let 'er rip attitude of the 1997 *Framework*.

When such contrasting principles can be influential at times only five or six years apart, it is clearly far too early to predict what kind of stable legal régime for e-business is destined in due course to emerge.

Taxation

An obvious way in which government intervenes in business is by taxing it. The activities of government have to be paid for, and two significant sources of revenue are tariffs (customs duties) on goods entering a country, and taxes such as corporation tax and value-added tax on internal business activities. (Tariffs often serve a second purpose, in protecting domestic industries against foreign competition.)

The *Framework* document advocated international agreement to levy no tariffs at all on goods which are delivered over the internet, such as films or music (so-called *online delivered content*, see Chapter 6); and not to impose any novel taxes on e-commerce. Domain names, or ISP subscriptions, for instance, are the kinds of thing which a government looking for ways to maintain its revenues might be tempted to tax – they are easily identifiable, and (unlike cases of little old ladies living in large houses faced with massive property-tax demands) obligation to pay is likely to be broadly matched by ability to pay. The *Framework* urges that this temptation should be resisted.

As online delivered content becomes a more significant proportion of the total flow of trade, and as e-commerce develops new forms to which, probably, existing taxes will sometimes fail to apply, the overall effect must be to put downward pressure on total government revenues.

8. 'Superbyw@ys' by 'Webster', *The Oldie* Aug 2001.

Many economists would see this as thoroughly healthy. Few dispute that spending by governments is inherently inefficient. Other things being equal, a lower-tax economy will be a more vibrant economy. But, of course, countries with high-tax régimes have them not because they think taxation helps the economy to flourish, but because they want their State to do various expensive things for the populace, such as providing health services. That is a political choice. Someone sceptical about the *Framework* principles might ask whether we want to allow the new technology to pre-empt political decisions.

There has been a trend, in line with the *Framework* recommendations, to reduce or abolish tariffs on IT-related goods. But then, recent decades have in any case been a period of repeated international rounds of tariff reductions. Economists argue that tariffs are a bad thing: people everywhere prosper more, if each country concentrates on producing whatever it is naturally fitted to produce, rather than diverting effort towards inefficient production of goods that can be made cheaper elsewhere. Again, while this argument has been influential in recent decades, some prefer on political rather than economic grounds to defend industries that could not survive, if they were fully exposed to overseas competition – as small farmers in France and Germany are defended through the EU Common Agricultural Policy. Conceivably, in future the world in general might choose to turn back towards protectionism, as in the years before the Second World War. If so, it is not obvious that the world would see good reason to exempt goods traded via the internet.

The *Framework* principles on taxation may well be the best way to help e-commerce to flourish. They are not politically neutral principles.

Tax neutrality

Many states of the USA derive their income largely from what Americans call 'sales tax'. When Britain had an equivalent tax, it was called 'purchase tax', and this is a more accurate name: in mail-order sales across American state boundaries, the tax is determined by the location of buyer rather than seller. It has to be that way: if the seller's state determined tax levels, businesses would migrate to low-tax states and a decision to increase sales tax would guarantee economic decline. (Consumers are unlikely to move just because of minor differences in sales-tax levels, on the other hand.)

This illustrates the point that tax systems should be neutral. So far as possible, they ought not to alter the patterns of economic activity that evolve naturally. The *Framework* document advocates tax neutrality with respect to the internet; but the very fact that taxing e-commerce is discouraged means that the overall tax system is not neutral as between electronic and conventional trading – it favours the former.

The US states have since 1998 accepted a moratorium on sales taxes on internet transactions. This seems unfair to conventional merchants: e-commerce may often be a good thing, but people should shift to using it because they find that it does in fact serve them better, not because governments have made it artificially cheaper. It is problematic also because it erodes the total tax base. Either other taxes have to be made heavier to compensate, or total government revenue declines.

For the American states, the latter effect is creating large problems (not just because of the e-commerce tax moratorium but because in general consumption is increasingly switching to services, while state sales taxes apply mainly to goods). In consequence, by 2002 a high priority for American state governors was to overturn the internet moratorium. From July 2003 the EU has decided to levy value-added tax (VAT) on people who sell things through sites such as eBay.

A tax-free zone?

If tax régimes were easily reshaped to suit changing economic patterns, an optimist might argue that governments will not lose by reducing taxes on e-commerce, because that will help the companies which engage in it to flourish and become more profitable, and hence they will pay more in corporation tax (the equivalent for companies of income tax on individuals). In reality, though, tax régimes have a momentum of their own and cannot be radically recast from year to year – in practice a government which depends mainly on sales tax probably could not suddenly switch to dependence on corporation tax instead. But, in any case, it is a large assumption that eliminating one kind of tax will stimulate enough extra economic activity to produce fully-compensating increases in other tax yields.

So the idea of allowing e-commerce to become something like a tax-free zone involves major difficulties. Yet so too does the idea of treating e-commerce for taxation purposes as just another form of trade.

American mail-order retailers are used to dealing with the different sales-tax regulations of the various states; it must be a fairly complex aspect of their work, but at least there are likely to be family resemblances between state tax régimes within one country, and all the tax laws are written in English. Furthermore, with mail order there is no question about which state the purchaser lives in. How would an American, or British, e-tailer be able to cope, if he had to take account of tax laws in, say, Moldova or Laos, which might not be written in English or even in our alphabet? What if he were selling online delivered content to an e-mail address ending in .com or .net rather than a national suffix?

If e-commerce becomes a major fraction of world trade, it will pose large questions about the financing of governments. It is not clear that anyone yet has come up with thoroughly persuasive answers.

6
Shifting to an intangible economy

Intangible products and inputs

E-business is about the *processes* of business becoming intangible. Streams of bits are replacing paper invoices transported in post-office vans and trains, wooden advertising hoardings, and other heavy, slow-moving paraphernalia of business life. But hand in hand with this there is another economic evolution under way, by which much of the *substance* created and distributed by economic activity is becoming intangible.

The idea that the balance of the economy is shifting towards intangible goods is a modern cliché, and people who discuss it are often thinking about intangible consumer goods – radio and television programmes, computer games, education, and many others. Not all of these things come under the IT heading (in the list just given, only computer games do), but all of them are intangible rather than physical goods; and between them they are certainly accounting for an increasing proportion of consumption. One statistic, for instance, is that in the year 2000 the average American spent about seven hours a day watching television or listening to radio. It may seem staggering that so many people have so much free time, but the figures come on good authority. Surely, a generation or two earlier, this category of intangible consumption would have been sharply lower.

Intangibles are growing in importance also as input factors of production. Some further statistics are that the relative share of raw materials and energy input in manufacturing output has been falling by about one per cent a year for the past half-century, while the relative share of information/knowledge inputs has been rising at a similar rate since the 1880s. By now, to take two sample physical manufactures, intangible inputs account for 70 per cent of the cost of producing butter, and over 70 per cent of value added in car manufacture.

The statistics just quoted are taken from Charles Goldfinger (1997), the most insightful analysis known to me of the shift to an intangible economy: much of the following discussion will be based on Goldfinger's work. That shift does not relate exclusively to IT, and it began long before the computer was invented; but IT is giving the shift a large fillip, by creating new categories of economic good, and by making it easier to decouple intangible goods from the physical objects in which they used to be embodied. Although intangibles always were somewhat exceptional with respect to the standard assumptions of economics, before the computer revolution this was a marginal problem. Most economists ignored it most of the time. Now, it is no longer marginal and cannot be ignored.

Incidentally, the categories under discussion are often slippery. I listed education as an intangible consumer good earlier, but insofar as education represents training to enable a worker to do a job or do it better, it is an input factor of production rather than a consumer good – some kinds of education have more of the former quality and some more the latter. For that matter, aspects of education which involve direct one-to-one contact with a teacher would be better classified as services than as intangible goods. Nobody claims that these distinctions, between goods and services, and between tangible and intangible, are clearcut. They are not – there is much debate in the literature about precisely how best to define them. In this book we shall content ourselves with using the terms in a rough-and-ready way.

Injuring the invisible hand

For the IT specialist, the shift towards an intangible economy is important because it relates to new applications of his expertise. For owners of intangible property, IT is opening up new ways of making that property yield revenues, as well as undermining established business models. (Claudia Loebbecke (2001) offers some enlightening case studies in this area.)

But, for people interested in economic aspects of the functioning of society, the shift towards an intangible economy matters because it is changing many of the assumptions on which rational economic calculation is based. Adam Smith's 'invisible hand', which uses the price mechanism to bring about the optimal deployment of society's productive resources, may be becoming rather arthritic under the impact of IT.

Intangibles are economically odd

Sticking for the moment to the case of consumer goods, Goldfinger identifies a number of different respects in which intangible goods are 'special' or contradict common economic assumptions. Intangible goods can be:

- *non-destructive*: the same product, for instance a film or a piece of music, can be consumed repeatedly by the same person or by different people.

- *joint*: an intangible good is frequently inseparable from a tangible good – reading a novel involves handling a physical book, watching a video involves getting hold of a cassette or DVD.

- they are often *volatile*, in the sense that their value can be highly time-dependent. To someone working in the City, a particular piece of financial information may be worth millions in the morning but may be valueless that same afternoon. That extreme case falls outside the area of consumer goods; but, for instance, on a pay-per-view television system the average viewer would be far more willing to pay to see today's news programme than yesterday's.

- there is a problem about *infinite regress*: if the good to be consumed is information, often the only way to discover whether it is worth consuming is to consume it.

Features like these may be a thorough nuisance to academic economists. Do they matter to the rest of us?

Yes, they do. We saw in Chapter 2 that a successful economy depends on a complex web of price-signals, by which for instance orange-growers, and the people involved in the various stages by which television sets are manufactured, are led to serve (among many others) a Brighton student unknown to them. If the signals are blurred, because of the peculiarities of intangible goods, this matters to individual companies because it will be hard for them to work out how to act in order to be profitable; and it matters to all of us as consumers, because less value for us will be produced from the resources available than could be produced if the signalling system was functioning well.

Pricing intangibles

The special properties of intangible goods create many problems for price-setting. Traditionally, prices of goods were determined by reference to the cost of production and/or to what buyers were willing to pay. Both factors are problematic in the case of intangible goods.

Production costs do not yield a straightforward method of setting prices, because with intangibles there is typically no proportionality between inputs and outputs. For oranges, producing two tons requires about twice as much input of various categories as producing one ton. But a popular piece of music may be consumed – listened to – by tens of millions of fans, and yet it may have required no more input to produce than is required by a flop that few hear.

Willingness to pay for intangibles is problematic for two reasons. One is the infinite regress problem. How is a consumer to decide what he is prepared to pay for something, if he has no way of assessing its worth without paying for it? The second reason is that intangible goods are typically so easy to copy or share; consumers will not be willing to pay out a sum corresponding to the true value to them of an intangible good, if they can get it without paying. This does not relate just to 'piracy'. Many cases of sharing intangible goods are perfectly legal and usual. A student union lounge may subscribe to one copy of a newspaper that is read by dozens of students. But we all know, too, that the ease of copying electronic files often makes it near-impossible to enforce laws that attempt to control this, even when such laws exist. We discussed Napster and KaZaA in Chapter 4.

Traditionally, the difficulty of price-setting for intangibles was often masked by the fact that intangible goods were inseparable from their physical embodiment, which could be priced in a normal way. So, for instance, books would commonly have prices set in terms of physical size and quality of paper and printing – rather than in terms of the value of the information they contain, or the literary quality of the writing. As a way of pricing the content, this is not economically rational (price signals set this way will have no particular tendency to match production of different kinds of content with the varying levels of demand for them), but at least it works after a fashion. Once intangible goods are digitized, on the other hand, it is very easy to decouple ('unbundle') them from their physical embodiment. It is then impossible to overlook the problem of pricing the intangible element.

Goldfinger points to the many alternative models for selling software, as one illustration of this kind of problem. A software package may be sold as an independent product, nowadays usually on a CD-ROM (though, in that case, unlike the case of a printed book, the price will bear no relationship to the tiny cost of manufacturing the CD-ROM). It may instead by sold bundled with hardware: Microsoft has commonly sold the Windows operating system as part of a hardware package. Some serious software is more or less given away as shareware, or absolutely given away as freeware; and while some software producers who do this are essentially hobbyists who are not aiming to develop a profitable business, there is also a respectable point of view (which we shall look at in more detail in Chapter 12) according to which the best business model for a commercial software house involves giving away the software products and charging to support them. Brad Cox (1996) argued that it would be better to sell time spent accessing software, through usage metering, rather than selling copies of the software itself; recently Marc Benioff of Salesforce.com has implemented this approach.

With tangible goods, one does not often seem to meet this level of disagreement about the basic question of how to sell them.

Intangible assets

So far we have been discussing intangible aspects of the goods made and sold by companies. Another area where intangibles are increasingly important, and quantification is very difficult, is that of company assets. In business life one of the central things one wants to know about a company is what it is worth. Nowadays, everyone agrees that intangible assets are a large and growing proportion of companies' total assets, and that they can often be more important for a company's success and indeed survival than its physical assets; yet there is little agreement even about what kinds of thing should be listed as intangible assets – let alone how they should be valued. This, then, is another way in which the transparency of a traditional market economy, based mainly on physical things, is now being made murkier by the growth of intangibles, posing a threat to its self-optimizing operation. IT is a chief factor in that growth.

Companies produce balance sheets, which means that accountants have to take a position on how to count intangible assets: but they take different positions. Goldfinger quotes a 1992 analysis by the (at that period, highly-regarded) accountancy firm Arthur Andersen which recognized four categories of intangible company assets: *brands* (for many leading consumer-goods companies such as Coca-Cola or Danone, managing their brand is the central priority); *intellectual property* (for example, patents); *publishing rights* (copyrights); and *licences* (for example, rights to use a technology granted by the patent owner). This is broadly a consensus classification, but Goldfinger points out that it excludes other things that might be seen as important assets, for instance 'human capital' – the knowledge, working habits, and so forth possessed by a firm's workforce – and 'company culture'. Firms often like to boast that their employees are their most important asset; a problem about including human capital as an asset on balance sheets, though, is that employees are not slaves – an employer does not own them.

Even if one makes a decision about what categories of thing to recognize as intangible assets, it is commonly very hard to put specific values on them, for many different reasons.

- For one thing, a particular category is normally much more *heterogeneous* than in the case of physical assets. One kilogramme of fresh unsalted Danish butter should be fully equivalent to another, but with software development, for instance, it is notorious that the value of one programmer/day may be wildly different from the value of another programmer/day, even if the programmers have the same formal qualifications – classically, Frederick Brooks (1975: 30) quoted a productivity ratio of 10:1. In the physical economy some workers perform better than others; but with manual work the differences are usually smaller, and in the case of factory production lines, the work situation enforces equivalence between one man-hour and another.

- Then, with intangibles it is harder than with physical goods to distinguish *capital purchases* from *current spending*. If advertising functions to strengthen public perceptions of a company brand, it is building capital, but if it functions to jog consumers into making a purchase this week then it is a cost to be set against current income – yet the same advert may serve both purposes. Similar remarks could be made about spending on employee training.

- The ways in which intangibles *interact* in business activities are so complex that it is hard to factor out the contributions of different assets.

- Physical assets tend to *depreciate* in recognized ways; for practical purposes, it may be reasonable to say that a given type of machine has a useful life of, say, ten years and loses one-tenth of its value each year. The time/value graphs for intangible assets are far more diverse and often irregular. In some areas, brands become more valuable with time (think for instance of the inscriptions 'Established 19xx' – or, even better, '18xx' – over the doors of luxury-goods retailers). Other intangibles may gain and lose value with the vagaries of fashion, or may retain value for years and then lose it unexpectedly overnight, in the case, for example, of a patent which is overtaken by the invention of a better technique.

- One approach to accountancy determines current value of assets as a function of the *historical cost* of acquiring or creating them. But this tends to be as irrelevant to the true current value of capital assets as manufacturing cost is to pricing intangible traded goods.

- The obvious criterion of *market value* rarely applies. Intangible assets are not often bought and sold separately from the company that owns them. Even when a brand is detached from its parent company, what moves to new ownership will commonly be not the intangible marque alone, but the portion of physical plant devoted to manufacturing that marque.

Some accountants simply exclude many classes of intangible asset from balance sheets. But the consequence of that is that the 'book value' of a company (what it is worth according to its accounts) can be wildly different from its market value as revealed by share price or in a takeover. In 1995 the market value of Reuters was about six times its book value, which explicitly excluded (among other intangibles) the global databases of financial information that are one of its core operating resources. The 1992 accounts of Coca-Cola included $300 million for intangible assets; *Financial World* estimated the value of the Coca-Cola brand at that time as $35 *billion*. In principle there have always been problems about quantifying intangible assets, but until recently they scarcely mattered because this asset category was less important. Forty or fifty years ago, a child at a shop counter might ask simply for 'a bar of chocolate', which implies that confectionery brands were far less significant then than now, when no child would dream of being so unspecific. And although IT has nothing to do with that particular case, the increasing importance of intangible assets is to a very large extent related to the new role of IT in the economy. If intangibles are hard to count, it seems inevitable that the economy must in consequence have become more of a casino than it used to be.

Economy of abundance

Economics has traditionally been about how to manage scarce resources. Thanks to the ease of reproducing intangible goods, though, an economy based on them tends to be an economy of abundance, which again interferes with many longstanding assumptions. One of the words frequently associated with 'information' nowadays is 'overload' (whereas we do not hear about 'clothes overloads' or 'car overloads'). In the physical economy, many consumers could consume, without being specially greedy, more than they can get; in much of the intangible economy, consumers can easily get far more than they could possibly consume.

True, the Western economy of the last half-century has been much more productive than before of physical goods. Even if individuals do not describe themselves as suffering from a clothes overload or food overload, people are sometimes called fashion victims, and the European Union has had its food mountains and lakes. This is one of several ways in which intangibles are taking to a greater extreme tendencies that are visible to a lesser extent in the physical economy. Food, clothes, and cars are relatively cheaper than in former times, but still there is no parallel in these physical sectors to the bombardment of our senses by media products, from television programmes to academic articles, all competing for a share of our finite attention.

Stan Liebowitz, a leading critic of the idea that IT changes the basic rules of economics, is sceptical about the 'economy of abundance' concept (for example, Liebowitz 2002: 208). But (it seems to me) one can recognize that the ease of reproducing some classes of goods introduces a novel quality to some areas of economic life, without agreeing with the crazy ideas about abolition of economic principles that were flying about at the time of the dotcom bubble.

One consequence is that the intangible area of the economy is becoming a casino economy in a second sense, apart from the sense discussed in the previous section. Bringing an intangible product to market can be more like entering a lottery than earning a predictable return from a day's labour. Goldfinger quotes the case of Hollywood film-making, where out of every hundred 'scenarios' under development only one is turned into a completed film, and out of every six films released only one returns a profit – but, with luck, that one returns enough profit to cover the other five films and all the work that led nowhere. Or consider the pharmaceutical industry – where the products themselves are tangible, but the share of scientific research and similar intangibles among the inputs to production is so large that this might best be seen as part of the intangible economy. Only one in 4000 synthesized pharmaceutical compounds becomes a marketed product; and only about a third of those earn back the costs of their development, so the industry as a whole can keep going only if some of those rare successes are very profitable indeed.

Goldfinger argues that in these circumstances the goal for management is not to increase the chances of success for individual products – if companies do that, they are like spectators all standing on tiptoe to see over one another's heads – but to capitalize on the rare successes they achieve: 'to transform hits into megahits'. Thus, Disney makes two or three times as much revenue from spinoff products associated with a successful film (videotapes, computer games, toys, etc.) as is generated directly by people buying tickets to see the film.

It is an interesting explanation for the phenomenon of media-related merchandising, though the logic of Goldfinger's argument is not totally clear. However low the probability of a hit, mathematically it seems that working to raise that probability by N per cent should be as effective a way of maximizing profits as working to increase the revenue from hits achieved by N per cent. Perhaps the tacit assumption is that doing the second is easier than doing the first – though that does not follow merely from the fact that the former figure is low.

Reweighting the value chain

Another consequence of the shift from scarcity to abundance, according to Goldfinger, is that the weight of influence over value chains is shifting towards the consumer's end. Goldfinger quotes the management expert Peter Drucker as saying in 1992 'Power in the economy of developed countries is rapidly shifting from manufacturers to distributors and retailers'.

This is clearly true for industries supplying basic needs such as food and clothing. In recent years farmers and garment manufacturers have had to dance to the tune of retailers such as Tesco and Marks and Spencer in an unprecedented manner. Goldfinger gives other examples from higher-tech domains. In the early 20th century, he says, the lion's share of power in the market lay with the company which assembled components into a complete product: Renault and Citroën were in a stronger position than, say, Michelin – that last company did more than the car-makers to foster the early development of motoring in France, through installing road signs and publishing maps and guides, but no-one makes car purchase decisions by reference to choice of tyres. With personal computers, on the other hand, Intel and Microsoft are in a stronger position than companies who assemble and market the finished machines.

Again, though, it is not clear whether Goldfinger's analysis is as logical as it might be. He presents these various developments as instances of the same trend defined by Drucker – but are they? Marks and Spencer is nearer on the value chain than its garment suppliers to consumers; but a chip manufacturer like Intel is surely further away from consumers on the PC value chain than the company which assembles and markets machines incorporating that chip. In terms of position on value chains, Intel and Dell (say) correspond to Michelin and Renault, respectively, not the other way round. The powerful position of chip and software producers surely relates less to position on the value chain than to performance and branding. For the user, it makes much more difference what software his machine is running and what chip it is running on than who put the box together, whereas a motorist's overall experience of his car commonly depends more on the marque than on any one component-supplier's contribution.

So, while Goldfinger has raised a range of important issues relating to the intangible economy, there remains room for debate about some of his conclusions.

7

Enterprise resource planning

The vision

Among business applications of IT, the largest single area is *enterprise resource planning* or ERP. In 2001, ERP accounted for slightly over half of all enterprise application spending in Europe. This proportion is expected to decline in future relative to other application areas (which we shall examine in later chapters); but that is not because ERP is an obsolete technology – it is because the ERP market is now mature, so fewer companies are coming forward to adopt it for the first time than in the case of some younger applications. Also, ERP is expensive; a company which has not adopted it yet might not care to take the plunge in the current economic climate.

A vision of what we now call enterprise resource planning was expressed in the 1980s by Sir John Harvey-Jones, the legendary chairman of ICI who after retiring in 1987 made a second career as hero of BBC Television's 'Troubleshooter' series. In his book about industrial leadership, *Making It Happen*, Sir John wrote:

> It saddens me that when people look at the impact of information technology they think so frequently in terms of organizing business in the ways that we have in the past. The enormous powers that are now within our grasp are used merely, so to speak, to mechanize what we have done rather imperfectly before. I see the advent of information technology in a rather different way. ... We have already got all the knowledge and information available to operate a system where an industrial purchaser will order automatically, through his computer system, from an industrial supplier. The computers at the supplier's end will order up the raw materials, program the production, make out the invoices and the records, almost certainly ensure automatic

payment of the raw materials supplier, while collecting from the customer. ... what is needed is a totally different relationship between the customer and the supplier. They will have to work together to achieve the enormous savings and the greater efficiencies that will come from such systems, and this means increasingly that the customer/supplier relationship will become more and more like a partnership ... (Harvey-Jones 1988: 328–9)

This is a fair description of enterprise resource planning, before the thing itself existed in its modern form. Fifteen years later it is surprising to read that Sir John's chief reason for looking forward to such developments was the prospect of 'more choice, more freedom, and more self-determination': he seems to have envisaged e-business as liberating the employee almost in the way that 20th-century technology liberated women from heavy housework. To date things have not worked out like that. In other respects, though, Sir John was accurate in anticipating that computers were destined to do much for business processes than merely mechanize what was currently done by hand.

A question of terminology

Although 'enterprise resource planning' is by now universally accepted terminology, the phrase 'resource planning' is not particularly helpful as a description of the main functions of ERP systems. The terminology is historical. As far back as the 1960s, software was developed for managing inventory, and in the 1970s this was extended to automate related functions such as production scheduling (which entails forecasting materials requirements) and planning inventory holdings to match them with future distribution needs. 'Resource planning' is a suitable term for these functions, and the systems developed to handle them are ancestral to the ERP systems marketed today. But, from the late 1980s, these systems evolved to cover further business processes. Some people use the term ERP in a very broad sense; Ravi Kalakota and Marcia Robinson write 'e-commerce is the front office, and enterprise resource planning (ERP) is the back office' (Kalakota and Robinson 2001: 239), which implies that ERP covers everything except the marketing and selling interface to a company's customers.

Others (and Kalakota and Robinson, elsewhere in their writing) use 'ERP' in a narrower sense than that, and I shall use it in a narrower sense. Part of the terminology problem comes about because suppliers of the technology are themselves extending the functions of their various systems in different directions, in the attempt to capture larger shares of the total business-IT market. Oracle, for instance, was originally a relational-database company which now supplies ERP software also – databases are central to the operation of ERP, but ERP is much more than a database. Conversely, the leading ERP vendor, SAP, offers systems which nowadays handle customer relationship management as well as more standard ERP functions – traditionally CRM was quite distinct from ERP.

The suppliers have no motive to encourage us to think of business processes as rigidly partitioned into separate domains. This book's categorization of the total range of business software into discrete enterprise applications may seem a little old-fashioned, as companies spread the coverage of their offerings into increasingly overlapping subsets of the complete range. But, for the reader new to e-business who is trying to make sense of all the complexity out there, a treatment which focuses separately on distinct core areas may be the most helpful approach.

The core ERP functions

From this point of view, then, ERP denotes centralized, company-wide software systems which handle in a unified way a large proportion of what one might call the mechanical aspects of keeping a business running, including at least the 'upstream' functions connected with ordering from suppliers and managing the inventory of supplies received, as well as managing the inventory of products awaiting distribution. For several years now, 'downstream' functions such as processing orders received from customers and sending out invoices have standardly been integrated into the same systems. Currently, the 'upstream' ERP functions are beginning to spread beyond the boundaries of individual companies: a large company that has adopted ERP may seek even greater efficiency by giving its key suppliers access to its network, so that routine aspects of the ongoing supply process can be handled with minimal human intervention. David Linthicum (2001: xvii) quotes a finding that 'almost half of the Fortune 500 executives surveyed had already opened up three or more corporate data systems to their business partners'.

All of these functions might be called 'mechanical' because they involve little or no human judgement. If a customer has ordered a thousand widgets at a quoted price and the widgets have been shipped, there is no need to debate whether the customer should be invoiced. Customer relationship management, on the other hand, is connected to the winning of orders, so it is an area of business where human judgements are central.

Since its introduction in 1992, the market-leading ERP system in this sense has been SAP's R/3 – for a third-party technical description, see Linthicum (2001: 349–62). SAP AG, based at Walldorf near Heidelberg, is Europe's largest software company. The name stands for *Systemanalyse und Programmentwicklung*, German for 'system analysis and program development'. SAP was founded in 1972 by five German former IBM employees: their first client was the German subsidiary of ICI – the story goes that IBM declined to take on a contract to develop production-planning software for that company, so the systems analysts resigned from IBM to take the job on themselves. Other leading ERP vendors include PeopleSoft, Oracle, and Baan (which was acquired by SSA Global Technologies in 2003).

Thomas Davenport (1998) offers a survey of the various elements commonly included in ERP systems, as well as the problems that implementing these systems can entail. I shall not attempt to state a hard-and-fast boundary between 'what counts as ERP' and what does not. The field is changing so fast that it would be pointless to try imposing rigid definitions.

Linking information islands

The chief motive for a company to adopt ERP is not merely that it automates functions which were previously executed manually. By the beginning of the 21st century, a firm will probably have been carrying out most of the individual functions automatically for years already. It has more to do with integrating different functions across separate departments.

In the first place, this gives managers more detailed and up-to-date knowledge of what is happening in their company and hence more ability to control it. Kalakota and Robinson (2001: 245) quote a manager in a large company:

> You can't manage what you don't know. Before our ERP implementation,
> it was four to six weeks after the close of the month before we had
> information reconciled, and we still weren't sure of the accuracy.

This issue is vital even for a firm that is not expanding its sphere of activities. But also, globalization means that the information and control problem for managers in many companies is taking on new levels of difficulty. Keeping tabs on what is happening at a separate site or indeed in a separate building is always much harder in practice than keeping abreast of what is going on under a single roof. The chatting in corridors or coffee lounges, which superficially looks trivial or time-wasting, in reality serves vital communicative purposes. Monitoring activities on the other side of the world introduces a higher dimension of difficulty, and not just because of physical distance and timezone differences: language, currency, and tax-régime differences add to the manager's problems. ERP is seen as a large part of the answer to these.

Then, the very fact that many individual business processes were automated years or decades ago means that the systems will often be creaky, perhaps full of patches installed as business needs and processes evolved. It might not seem worthwhile to replace an individual application that still just about does its job with a newer package serving just that function, but ERP represents an opportunity to make a clean sweep and replace many separate legacy systems. (Kalakota and Robinson suggest that ERP systems not only embody modern business practices but are 'capable of adapting to changes in the business environment of the future' – though one must be wary of hype here. Vendors of any software commonly claim that it has the flexibility to adapt to future change, but the future is often surprising.)

One particular area which Kalakota and Robinson identify as a driver for replacement of legacy systems is changes stemming from government policies and regulations. Replacement of Continental currencies by the euro, for instance, had major business-software implications for firms within and outside the Eurozone. The year-2000 issue triggered a massive shake-up in areas using software inherited from a period when programmers saw that date as too distant to worry about. (Now we have come through to the 21st century with no signs of civilization breaking down, even in countries that spent far less than Britain on the Y2K problem, we may wonder what all the fuss was. Beforehand, the issue was seen as very serious, and in many cases law required systems to be changed.) 'Government regulation', here, includes the wave of *deregulation* that has affected Western economies over the last decade or two. With deregulation of industries that were formerly served by national monopolies, we see companies such as BT being required to sell services to competitors, and therefore having to deal with 'non-native' formats with respect to pricing structures, customer contracts, and the like; one can easily imagine that this enforces changes which go beyond what could be handled by adapting software inherited from the monopoly period.

The largest single selling point for ERP, though, is the prospect of linking 'information islands' into an integrated continent of information spanning a company from side to side. As Kalakota and Robinson put it (2001: 246), 'most large enterprises find themselves contending with a hodgepodge of disparate, disjointed applications, creating an environment of confusion, misunderstanding, errors, and limited use of corporate information assets'. That last point is crucial. One of the most valuable assets of a modern company is often the information it possesses, distributed across the minds of its individual staff and in filing cabinets and desktop hard drives. Frustratingly, the asset is often wasted, because not all the relevant pieces of knowledge can readily be retrieved and brought to bear when and where they are needed. ERP holds out the prospect of a solution to this problem.

BMW Hams Hall

As a case study, consider the introduction of SAP R/3 at the BMW Group's Hams Hall car-engine plant outside Birmingham, to date regarded as 'the most modern engine factory in the world'.

Hams Hall opened in February 2001 to manufacture four-cylinder petrol engines, currently used in BMW 3 Series cars. The plant represents a £400m investment; when running at full capacity it is expected that a 1500-strong workforce will be turning out 400,000 engines a year.

Hams Hall came into being shortly after a complicated passage of company history. In 1994 BMW had bought Rover (previously the state-owned British Leyland Motor Company, which earlier still resulted from a merger between Austin, Morris, the lorry-manufacturer Leyland, and other companies); then in 2000 it sold Land Rover to Ford and sold the Rover and MG marques to a management buyout which is again trading under the Rover name. In consequence, the workforce at the new Hams Hall site had diverse backgrounds, with a high proportion having been BMW employees for only a few years. Furthermore, the difficulties besetting British car manufacture in the late 20th century meant that BMW's inheritance from Rover included a history of IT underinvestment; and the various Rover divisions, and BMW, used different systems – causing isolation of one part of the current company from another, unnecessary waste of human time and computing resources, and, perhaps most seriously, the danger of unintended variation in data as it migrated between systems.

The fact of Hams Hall being a new facility on a new site made it a favourable opportunity to draw a line under the past and adopt a new IT infrastructure. The features of SAP which appealed most to BMW were that it is modular, yet network-based so that any particular datum is entered or updated once and then available wherever needed; a clear upgrade path was foreseeable, with the possibility for instance of extending coverage out beyond Hams Hall or BMW to embrace some of its suppliers; and that as the years went by, data entries would cumulate into an efficient 'corporate memory', instead of records of diverse kinds being distributed across many different locations in the company, making efficient information retrieval very difficult.

See for instance Figure 7.1, a screenshot of an engineering change report relating to a modification to the specs of a particular screw at one particular location in the engine, with knock-on implications both for the screw supplier's tooling and production process, and for other areas of the BMW Group that use the same screw in other engines or vehicles. (Parts of Figure 7.1 are blanked out for reasons of commercial confidentiality.) Via the 'traffic lights' at the foot of the screen, the sign-off status with respect to various responsible parties can be checked at any time, by anyone in the company with appropriate access privileges; after the issue is resolved, the history of this event (together with countless others like it) becomes part of a comprehensive electronic archive, which can be consulted efficiently whenever someone involved in BMW's global activities needs to do so.

Changing company culture

It is easy to see why BMW saw large benefits to be gained by adopting electronic ERP. But it was a large undertaking. As a BMW engineer put it to me, it represented a 'massive culture change'. An extensive and costly programme of training was required. Each worker was given two and a half days training in 'SAP culture', in addition to training in the specific SAP module(s) relevant to his or her work, and 'key SAP users' were designated to provide one-to-one follow-up tuition as individuals required it. Apart from this, sensitive industrial-relations issues were created. Workers who previously used pen and paper methods often perceived computer data entry not as a new and better way of doing their existing job, but as an additional responsibility, of a kind that might be expected to attract extra pay.

Discovering how to achieve the culture shift was itself a learning process. Often it became clear that workers did not appreciate the power of the system they were interacting with, and hence did not get from it the value that was in principle available. And, like any complex IT system, SAP's software was itself evolving, making learning all the more challenging. So long as the old systems were available alongside, it was too tempting for staff to revert to them to complete immediate tasks, which was all right in the short term but meant that the intended corporate memory was not getting off the ground. So BMW pulled the plug on the old systems, while making SAP more palatable by creating user-interface screens that

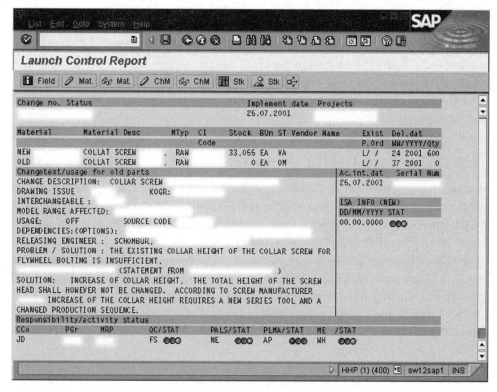

Figure 7.1

emulated the previous systems, and incorporating temporary fixes within SAP to cater to work habits formed under the old systems.

Two years after the start of operations, Hams Hall see SAP as a success. The company envisages beginning to integrate its suppliers into the network, with a long-term vision in which the value chain from BMW's component manufacturers through to the consumers who drive its cars are all connected into a skein of electronic communication that allows instant feedback on quality issues.

Owens-Corning

One problem car-engine manufacture is not faced with is supplying large numbers of small-scale customers. Kalakota and Robinson quote a case where the need for the integration that ERP permits was more extreme: Owens-Corning, an American-based building materials supplier. This company trades worldwide from factories in some twelve countries apart from the USA, and before ERP the company

> operated as a collection of autonomous fiefdoms with an estimated 211 legacy systems. Each plant had its own product lines and pricing schedules, built up over years of cutting deals with various customers. Trucking had been parceled out to about 325 carriers, selected by individual factories. (Kalakota and Robinson 2001: 258)

This was problematic for the company, but it was problematic also for the builders who buy from it: they had to order the various materials needed for a single job separately from separate Owens-Corning plants. Owens-Corning implemented SAP R/3 to enable its customers to order from a single site and monitor the progress of their orders on a 24/7 basis. Apart from the improvement in customer service, the resulting integration of company operations delivered large cost savings.

The other side of the picture

Not all companies who have chosen to go the ERP route have fared so well as BMW or Owens-Corning. BMW Hams Hall, a new site with a handpicked workforce, was particularly well placed to make the leap to ERP; Owens-Corning had particularly acute needs. But there are downsides to ERP.

Precisely because ERP is so comprehensive, the decision to adopt it carries large risks. It is possible to implement just an individual module of a modular ERP system, but the benefits which the technology potentially offers will not accrue if one just dips a toe in the water: one must go the whole hog. Jim Prevo, chief information officer of the Vermont company Green Mountain Coffee, commented in 1998:

> An ERP implementation is like the corporate equivalent of a brain transplant. We pulled the plug on every company application and moved to PeopleSoft software. The risk was certainly disruption of business, because if you do not do ERP properly, you can kill your company, guaranteed.[1]

Kalakota and Robinson quote a case of another American company, FoxMeyer Drugs (a pharmaceutical wholesaler), which claimed that it was indeed killed by trying to implement ERP. After beginning a SAP implementation in 1993, FoxMeyer filed for protection against its creditors under US bankruptcy law in 1996 (and was eventually taken over by a competitor). Rightly or wrongly, FoxMeyer blamed its collapse on the ERP software; it sued SAP's American subsidiary, and its implementation partner Andersen Consulting, for giving false assurances about it.

Leaving aside the risk of triggering company collapse (which is no doubt remote in most cases), two more general downside issues with ERP are that it has a reputation for being difficult to use, and that it is very expensive.

The usability issue was examined by the analysts Forrester Research in January 2003; they tested software from eleven leading ERP vendors for ease of completing three routine tasks. The conclusion was that the poor reputation is merited. According to Forrester's reseach director Laurie Orlov, 'Overall, the usability of these products is not acceptable for the amount they cost'.[2]

1. Quoted by April Jacobs, 'Business process software pays off', *Computerworld* 31 Aug 1998.
2. Quoted by Gareth Morgan, 'Poor usability forces up ERP training cost', *IT Week* 20 Jan 2003.

This may be a relatively curable problem. SAP believe (and others agree) that user difficulties with their own software relate not to the logic of the functionality it provides, but to the way in which that functionality is delivered. Their new product MySAP, which is gradually taking over from R/3 as their flagship ERP package, has a Web-based user interface which SAP hope will greatly reduce usability complaints.

The expense issue is harder to challenge. These systems are some of the most complex software in use nowadays for any purpose; the costs of developing them were large, and the charges to users are correspondingly high. The analysts Ovum found in March 2003 that the cost of implementing SAP or PeopleSoft systems ranges up to £60,000 per seat.

For a long time, only large companies used ERP since only they could afford it. Recently, the software has been marketed to medium-sized or even small companies – there are few prospective new customers left in the large-firm sector. The vendors have developed cheaper, cut-down versions of their systems, and lowered their licence fees; but licence fees represent only a small fraction of total implementation costs. Rather than making a large capital investment, companies can rent the use of ERP (and other enterprise application) software from so-called *application service providers* (ASPs), but this approach tends to be too inflexible in many circumstances.

Ian Wesley, senior manager at Ovum, argued that, for many companies, the leading ERP systems are simply not cost-effective solutions – they are too expensive, and their complexity means that firms which operate internationally cannot rely on finding support available at all their locations. A more reasonable strategy, Wesley believes, is to install fullscale 'tier one' software such as SAP R/3 only at a company's home base, and to make do at overseas locations with lesser, 'tier two' packages from other vendors – despite the obvious loss of seamless intercommunication this implies.

Reforming business practices

The implementation issue is not just about money, but about the impact on a company's business practices.

An ERP implementation embodies a set of business processes and rules. Companies such as SAP sell versions of their systems tailored to particular market sectors, for example, Insurance or Apparel & Footwear; but a particular firm will typically have its own procedures which will not be exactly the same as those of other firms in the same sector. The firm will be attached to its own ways of doing things, and often with good reason – its distinctive procedures may provide part of its competitive edge.

With ERP, either the firm pays to have the software customized to fit its procedures, or it must change the procedures to fit the off-the-shelf package. But significant customization of a large ERP system is a hugely expensive undertaking, and it is the kind of software project which can easily fail – the Ovum report already quoted recommends that companies should not attempt it. So adopting ERP may mean operating more efficiently, but it also means agreeing to operate in ways that a firm has not chosen for itself.

One can see this in a positive light. Inherited business processes may be out-of-date processes; ERP vendors aim to make their software embody best current practice from the relevant industrial or commercial sector. The clean sweep of old processes required when ERP is installed may be a blessing in disguise, enabling senior managers to push through, as a technological necessity, working reforms which they lacked the political clout to push through as desirable in their own right. (Compare the way that companies often pay management consultants to recommend unpopular actions, such as laying off staff, which they recognize the need for themselves but find it difficult to carry out without outsiders to shoulder the blame.) From this point of view, customizing ERP to fit the company may be not just too expensive but actually undesirable, because it preserves bad old ways and makes it harder to replace them with good new ways.

Kalakota and Robinson point out that a successful ERP implementation begins by analysing a firm's business processes (which may have been understood tacitly without ever being systematically written down), and then rationalizes them, making them simpler overall and cutting out anything that does not add value. Only after a firm's business processes are rationalized should they be crystallized into ERP software: 'Automation without simplification only immortalizes ineffective processes' (Kalakota and Robinson 2001: 262). Kalakota and Robinson are bullish about the positive impact on firms' operations implied by adopting ERP. But Kalakota and Robinson are cheerleaders for the new technology. If one accepts their axioms uncritically, they seem to imply that no firm has worked effectively before ERP. Doubtless any organization has room for improvements, but a generalization as blunt as that seems self-evidently exaggerated.

Kalakota and Robinson ought to appreciate this, since they give a graphic example of the opposite situation, where a poor ERP implementation had serious negative effects on business processes. In 1996, the US subsidiary of the Japanese company Brother Industries entrusted SAP implementation to its IT staff, with inadequate input from staff who understood the business realities. In consequence, the implementation prevented managers from monitoring and controlling manufacturing costs in detail, because the techies assumed that it was enough for the system to report overall labour and materials cost totals, without appreciating that management needed refined information about the cost of separate input factors. This is an extreme case, and the problem was not inherent in the software; after a bad beginning, Brother eventually sorted things out. But it shows that one cannot presuppose that the impact of ERP software on business processes will always be beneficial or even neutral.

Political problems

Another negative issue is the political resistance which is unavoidable with a culture-changing phenomenon like ERP.

Kalakota and Robinson, in their cheerleading role, present this as little more than instinctive hostility to any change: 'Never underestimate the reluctance to change processes'. That conservative instinct is indeed a powerful force in any human organization, but if that were the only human problem there would be ways to address it – Kalakota and Robinson suggest sensible approaches, such as finding ways of sharing the vision motivating the change with the staff who will be asked to operate the new system, and giving them small pieces of the system to play with at an early date so as to dissolve their fear of the unknown.

There are weightier reasons than that for staff to resist ERP, though. Thomas Davenport (1998) explains that, because ERP links together what were previously islands of information, managers use it

> as a lever for exerting more management control and imposing more-uniform processes on freewheeling, highly entrepreneurial cultures. An executive at a semiconductor company, for example, says, 'We plan to use SAP as a battering ram to make our culture less autonomous.'

People do not enjoy finding themselves on the wrong end of a battering ram.

Ben Worthen, in the course of an enlightening case-study of a difficult and long-drawn-out implementation of SAP by Nestlé, quotes Nestlé USA's chief information officer Jeri Dunn as saying 'When you move to SAP, you are … challenging [people's] principles, their beliefs and the way they have done things for many, many years.'[3]

Those at the top of an organization may be enthusiastic about seeing internal boundaries within the organization melted away by an integrated software system, but it would be naïve to expect the heads of those units to share the enthusiasm. If they do not share it, they have plenty of ways to resist. Speakers at a Cranfield University IT Directors' Forum in February 2003 listed some of them. A department head may allocate his worst staff to a project, for instance, or he may try to ensure that his department is last in line to implement it (by which time, perhaps, the project will have been abandoned). One speaker claimed that most organizations realize after the event that they should have put more resources and expertise into the human aspects of business re-engineering, as opposed to the purely technical aspects.

The danger of over-centralization

It is far from clear that this resistance to centralization will in fact be against the interests of the company. Kalakota and Robinson assume that it is 'unhealthy' for local managers to strive to maintain their autonomy. But a great deal of thinking from outside the IT sphere suggests that it may be very healthy.

The point is made concisely in the same book by Sir John Harvey-Jones with which we began the chapter:

3. Ben Worthen, 'Nestlé's ERP odyssey', *CIO Magazine* 15 May 2002, domdasaw.notlong.com

> Vast amounts of human effort have been made in large organizations to coordinate and optimize, so to speak, at the centre of the wheel. ... it is perfectly possible for all those at the rim of the wheel to self-optimize ... The reality of life is that they are the only people who can optimize, and so much of past management theory has been to try to find ways in which they can be encouraged to do so. (Harvey-Jones 1988: 329-30)

Again it seems ironic that Sir John in 1988 saw IT as helping the people 'at the rim of the wheel' to optimize their local activities in the light of their detailed local knowledge, whereas ERP unquestionably has the reverse tendency. But there is a weight of opinion about business and social issues which would side with Sir John in saying that over-centralization of the affairs of any organization cannot lead to good outcomes. From this point of view, what should be seen as 'unhealthy' is perhaps not the local autonomy that ERP batters into submission, but the natural inclination of people at the top to micro-manage their subordinates, which ERP tends to encourage.

Integrated systems versus middleware

Whether it is desirable or not, some people see integrated ERP systems as the direction in which businesses are sure to move: the advantages are obvious, the possible disadvantages (cost apart) are nebulous and hypothetical. However, there are commentators who disagree from a technical perspective.

David Linthicum points out that before the days of integrated ERP we already had separate applications linked together by *middleware*, and he is sceptical about whether the integrated approach is as different as it is cracked up to be. 'Middleware' (some prefer the newer term 'enterprise integration applications') refers to various diverse systems for allowing separate applications to communicate with one another, whether 'point-to-point' (i.e. one particular application linked to one other application – examples are IBM's MQSeries, DCE from the Open Group) or 'many-to-many' (for example, BEA's Tuxedo). If the reader feels ignorant about middleware, he is in good company; as Linthicum says:

> Middleware remains a great mystery to most people. It is difficult to use and even more difficult to explain. Most users typically never see middleware plumbing, as they do application development and database products. (Linthicum 2001: 149)

It became fashionable to run down middleware as 'stovepipes'. 'Stovepipe' here is an American figure of speech referring to devices which transport a specialized type of content from one location to one other location, like a mesh of rusting tubes criss-crossing space in some old-fashioned factory. What is needed is for everything to be available everywhere. But Linthicum argues:

> Packaged applications such as SAP, Oracle Financials, and PeopleSoft ... are natural stovepipes themselves ... [and] have only compounded the problem. Sharing information among these systems is particularly

difficult because many of them were designed not to access anything outside their proprietary technology. (Linthicum 2001: 11)

An ERP system may integrate the flow of data within a single large company, and a company may even link a limited number of key business partners into its ERP network; but no sigificant company has dealings only with a small fixed list of partners. If we are moving into a world where not just company-internal activities but interactions between company and company are frequently automated, then integrated data handling within companies and their close partners will not be enough, if the data cannot easily flow from one integrated network to another. Planning an integrated ERP system encourages the designers to assume, inappropriately, that it will be a closed universe.

Susan Osterfelt of the Bank of America commented in September 2000 that the tide was turning once again: from stovepipes to integrated systems and now back to stovepipes. One reason why the integrated approach was coming unstuck was that the need to respond rapidly to a changing business environment forces companies to outsource some of their systems by turning to application service providers, who in some cases will house the client companies' data in the process (but will not be within the integrated networks owned by those companies); so then, 'All of a sudden, we not only have disparate legacy systems whose data we need to integrate, but brand new outsourced systems whose data is not even within the confines of the organization!'[4]

Susan Osterfelt believes that the logic of this situation is pushing business not towards integrated ERP systems but towards the use of middleware and XML – the latter being a technology (discussed in Chapter 10) which facilitates exchange of data between computers that 'have not been introduced to one another', so to say. She quotes analysts Forrester Research as predicting that general adoption of integrated business software just 'ain't gonna happen'.

Conclusion

Clearly, the level of investment that companies have made and continue to make in ERP systems means that this is a technology which any student of e-business needs to know about. Many important companies are satisfied that they have achieved remarkable benefits by using SAP R/3 or comparable packages. At present, sceptical voices like Linthicum's and Susan Osterfelt's are in a minority.

How things will develop in the future remains to be seen.

---

4. Susan Osterfelt, 'Business intelligence: a stovepipe by any other name ...', *DM Review* Sep 2000, wexforrs.notlong.com

8

Marketing and customer relationships

What marketing is

Marketing is the activity of promoting and planning how to sell a company's products to customers. The distinction between marketing and the actual selling activity is colourfully expressed by Robert Cringeley:

> Marketing is the creation of long-term demand, while sales is execution of marketing strategies. Marketing is buying the land, choosing what crop to grow, planting the crop, fertilizing it, and then deciding when to harvest. Sales is harvesting the crop. (Cringeley 1996: 204)

Unless a company has customers, all its other activities are an expensive waste of effort. Accordingly, some would argue that marketing is not really a separate aspect of overall company operations. Peter Drucker, perhaps the single most influential management guru of recent decades, wrote:

> Marketing is not a specialized activity at all. It encompasses the whole business. It is the whole business seen from the point of view of its final result, that is from the customer's point of view. Concern and responsibility for marketing must therefore permeate all areas of the enterprise. (Drucker 1968: 54)

But it is one thing to say that every area of a company's activities ought to be conducted with an awareness of its contribution to fulfilling customers' needs or wishes. A sensible company does not design and make products, and only then begin to think about who it can sell them to and how. It would be another thing, though, to suggest that we cannot identify particular areas of activity and decision-making which are most directly involved in the marketing goal: we can.

Marketing and e-commerce

In the context of this book, an important feature of those areas is that much of what there is to say about them is not greatly affected by whether a company is involved in new or old technology. It is always important, but it is specially important in connexion with marketing, to stress that *an e-business is a business*. The principles laid down in standard business primers, such as David Needle's *Business in Context* (Needle 2000), are as relevant to e-companies as they are to any other kind. The following pages will draw heavily on Needle's excellent treatment, which goes far deeper into the subject than is possible here.

At the same time, IT has introduced new considerations into the picture. In particular, *customer relationship management* (CRM) systems are, after ERP, by most reckonings the second most important enterprise application category.

In the early part of this chapter, we shall look at the general principles of marketing. Later, we shall move on to examine the various special contributions made by IT.

Like it or not

The first thing that needs to be said about marketing is that, to many people, it seems the least admirable side of business. Particularly at the B2C level advertising is often seen as persuading people to buy things they don't need, and it is blamed for creating an excessively materialist tone in turn-of-the-millennium societies.

On the other hand, defenders point out that marketing fulfils essential functions, giving consumers (and business purchasers) product information that they need in order to exercise choice intelligently, and obtaining information about their wishes and preferences which business needs in order to serve them better. There have been societies in the recent past, for instance Eastern Europe during the Cold War decades, where individuals were not subjected to the endless bombardment of selling messages that are such an irritating feature of our time. That made for a certain dignity in everyday life which arguably we have lost; but the reason for it was that producers had no motive to attract custom. The goods and services available were few and often of poor quality; purchasers had to take what they could get.

We cannot have it both ways. Many feel that the selling messages are a price worth paying in exchange for the styles of life which are made possible by a modern market economy. In any case, within our society as it actually exists marketing is a very necessary function for any business, so we need to learn something of its principles.

Changing orientations

Needle (p. 361) draws attention to historical shifts in the attitude of business in the Western world towards the relationship between production, marketing, and sales. A century ago, populations were growing rapidly, and the assumption was that consumers would buy anything that industry could make available – the problems for industry were producing sufficient goods and distributing them, not finding buyers. Then as those problems began to be solved, it was supposed that provided goods or services were of sufficient quality they would sell themselves. Between the World Wars, particularly in the USA, economic depression and mass production techniques between them put the relationship into reverse: industry had to focus on actively selling its output, using methods such as advertising, promotions, and incentives to the sales force. In the decades after the Second World War, the *selling orientation* began to make way for the *marketing orientation*, advocated in a classic article by Theodore Levitt (1960): instead of focusing on what a company was offering and looking for any way of persuading people to buy it, companies shifted their focus to discovering what consumers wanted and findings ways to satisfy their wishes. This was a consequence of increased competition, but also of developments such as rational management (whereby business managers select strategies in the light of systematic market research and analysis rather than 'flying by the seat of their pants'), and of various moves to deregulate markets that occurred from the 1980s onward.

Needle distinguishes a further, recent *societal marketing* orientation, in which business no longer focuses simply on satisfying individual consumers but aims to do so in ways that take into account how its activities impinge on society or the environment. One may wonder, though, whether this ranks as a shift on a par with the others identified. Marketing must always take into account what is fashionable and what the customers care about. Fifty years ago, British consumer goods gained a cachet through associations with royalty, so names like 'Tudor', 'Windsor', 'Imperial' were frequent. Nowadays, many consumers like to feel that their buying behaviour links them to the survival of tropical rain forests or the welfare of poor Africans, so goods are marketed accordingly. When the fashion changes again, marketing details will change with it, but the principle of giving customers what they want will not thereby change.

Market research

Any marketing strategy will involve elements of guesswork and instinct, but modern companies aim also to use objective research. They monitor their own current performance, in terms of total sales and market share, and look at figures broken down by region, by salesman, and by any other available variable. Either directly or via reports commissioned from outside researchers they monitor developments in the marketplace, for instance relating to changing patterns of buyer preferences, or to new products or price changes from their competitors. They explore the feasibility of launching new products of their own, by studying the nature of the market and working with focus groups to discover how a proposed new offering is likely to be received.

Business intelligence

A software category relevant to market research is so-called *business intelligence* systems – Cognos is a leading supplier. As with many other terms in the enterprise applications field, business intelligence is a broad label with shifting boundaries, but at their core business intelligence systems are a packaging of data-mining techniques for business use.

Any business which has been computerized for several years will have generated a massive archive of data on the various aspects of its operations. Just extracting answers to known questions from that data mountain is difficult in itself, and one function of business intelligence systems is to make it easy to answer specific queries and to generate reports on current business performance. But data mining goes further, to discover answers to questions that no-one had thought of.

In that mountain of data there will be trends and generalizations unsuspected by those running the business. Perhaps sales of one of the product lines are more dependent on weather conditions in the North of England than in the South. No-one would have guessed that; but if it is so, the company certainly wants to know it and bear it in mind in planning its marketing and distribution operations. Data mining uses sophisticated statistical techniques to uncover unknown relationships.

Market segmentation

One aspect of market research involves looking at differences in buying behaviour between separate market segments, breaking the universe of potential customers down in terms of region, social class, sex, age, lifestyle, and (according to Needle 2000: 387) increasingly by race. The findings may be relevant in terms of developing variant products to appeal to separate market segments, or promoting the same products to separate segments in different ways.

Needle offers striking examples of the success of segment-based marketing. In the 1970s and 1980s, the advertising of Coca-Cola emphasized the concept of 'one world' – some readers will remember commercials based round a pop song, 'I'd like to teach the world to sing in perfect harmony'. In 1993 Coca-Cola changed tack. It began to distinguish many different market segments and promoted its product differently to separate segments. Over the following four years, sales rose by 21 per cent (Needle, p. 388).

Needle also discusses, as another case of the same thing, the way that Thomson Holidays sells holidays to separate market segments under many different brand names: Thomson Summer Sun for the mass market, A La Carte for tourists with high disposable income, Young At Heart for those old in years, Superfamily for parents with young children, and so forth. But these are really different cases. Coca-Cola is the same drink, whatever the social class or age of the person buying it. On the other hand, what older holidaymakers commonly hope to buy is, in part, absence of noisy children: Thomson Holidays are using their separate brands to sell importantly different products.

Segmentation can be an expensive marketing strategy, and it does not always achieve the benefits hoped for. Some commentators have regarded it as overdone; by 1975 Theodore Levitt saw the 'marketing myopia' he had deprecated in 1960 as beginning to give way to 'marketing mania'. Michael Lewis (2001: 167) sees demographics as 'falter[ing] as a tool for explaining and predicting consumer behavior', because generalizing about people in this way is becoming as taboo in connexion with selling as it already is in other areas of life.

In conventional business, the evidence is that segmentation does often work: while it remains legal for companies to divide their markets into segments, for many of them it will be important to do so.

In e-commerce, though, commentators such as Cutler and Sterne (2000) see market *segmentation* as irrelevant, because websites can be organized to tailor their marketing and selling messages to *individual* visitors, based on data elicited from the visitors about their detailed personal profiles and preferences, and on the pattern of individual visitors' clicks within the site. They quote a Forrester Research report: 'Firms struggle to identify profitable individual activity, hobbled by antiquated segment-based approaches.' (On the other hand, Cutler and Sterne quote little concrete evidence that click-tracking techniques actually deliver higher sales volumes.)

Categories of marketing

Consumer goods are what everyone thinks of first as the subject of marketing. But there are many other categories of marketing, with important differences of method.

In the first place, what Needle calls *organizational marketing* – B2B or B2G marketing – is very different from retailing. Buying decisions are made professionally. Retail purchases may be made on impulse, and may be motivated partly by 'soft' considerations such as status or lifestyle aspirations, but purchasing by companies is hard-headed and decided by objective issues of utility and small cost differences. Purchasing by national or local government may be influenced by political considerations, and may be less cost-sensitive than B2B or B2C buying.

Then, marketing of services is different from marketing of goods: there are no tangible products to show off. In the past, marketing of services was a small-scale affair – partly because many services are themselves provided by small organizations, and partly because advertising of professional services such as those of lawyers and doctors was strictly limited or banned by the professional bodies in the recent past, and to some extent still is. But many services, for instance banking, are now heavily marketed.

Marketing of high-tech products has many special problems of its own. To readers wanting to learn about these I cannot do better than recommend Geoffrey Moore's *Crossing the Chasm* (1999). In this book we are concerned with use of high-tech methods in producing and selling goods and services of all kinds – not specifically high-tech goods.

Often, marketing aims to create a favourable attitude not towards specific products or services but towards the organizations that supply them. Current television commercials for Boots the chemists, for instance, focus more on creating an impression that the company cares about your safety and welfare than on any particular product line, which in the case of prescription medicines would be inappropriate.

The public sector is often involved in marketing ideas or attitudes rather than goods or services. Campaigns against drinking and driving, and encouraging smokers to give up, have been some of the more powerful 'commercials' on recent British television.

There is a fine line between using public money to disseminate public-interest announcements, and using it to promote the policies of the government of the day – the latter raises ethical problems in a democracy, but in Britain some feel the line has become unduly blurred.

Needle points out that business has traditionally seen marketing for export as a separate area from marketing for home sales: products may be adapted to suit foreign preferences, cultural assumptions, or legal constraints, pricing policy may be different in different countries. On the World Wide Web it becomes hard to maintain this distinction. The global reach of the Web looks like an advantage from the seller's point of view, making it as cheap and easy to communicate with customers on other continents as at home. But if essentially the same product line has been priced differently in separate national markets, perhaps because it is marketed as a luxury in one country but as a good-value purchase in another, the Web may give customers a new ability to compare prices internationally, leading to resentment in countries where people see themselves as overcharged.

Marketing in different countries

The problems of marketing to a multinational audience go much deeper than issues about price structure. Cultural differences between nations mean that, standardly, one cannot sell things the same way in different countries. Needle (pp. 401–2) describes some of the differences. Germans stress 'product development and careful targeting'. Americans stress active promotion and selling. In Japan, competition focuses on product differentiation and service rather than on price. Such cultural differences can require large differences in the way the same product is marketed to different national audiences. The resort chain Club Med succeeded in Europe by promoting an image of laid-back hedonism; a similar campaign in Japan fell flat, and the emphasis had to switch to self-improvement, for instance by drawing attention to facilities for organized sports.

One might imagine that these cultural differences are a hangover from a past age, and that globalization of the media and trade – and the internet itself – will soon make them entirely irrelevant. As a statement about the world as a whole, this view looks naïve since the 11th September atrocities. Even as between the richer Western nations, there is plenty of evidence that cultural differences still matter and need to be reckoned with in business.

The famous case of a company which bet the other way and lost was Euro Disney (now called Disneyland Paris), which opened in 1992 (the case is analysed at length by Needle, pp. 371–4). The French government of the day had been enthusiastic about getting a Disney theme park; the Disney Corporation assumed that the recipe which worked in the USA would work essentially unchanged in France. The outcome was a public relations disaster, widely discussed throughout Europe at the time. Negative responses ranged from arts commentator Anane Mnouchkine's characterization of Euro Disney as a 'cultural Chernobyl' down to baffled outrage by adult visitors who found they could not buy a glass of wine with their lunch. Many changes were made to adapt to French culture, and losses were eventually turned into profits.

The Four Ps

Standardly, a marketing strategy is broken down under headings called the *Four Ps*:

- *product* (its nature and design)

- *price*

- *promotion*

- *place* (i.e. channels of distribution)

The fourth P refers to the channels by which a supplier's goods physically reach the buyer, and to decisions about whether and how to use intermediaries. We have considered the issue of intermediaries in e-commerce in Chapter 3, and we shall not revisit that topic here. The other three Ps are considered in turn below.

Product

It might seem that a product is what it is, and the marketing function must simply accept that. But a manufactured product or commercial service is designed with a market or markets in mind. Deciding to introduce a new product is an investment decision, made after studying whether the investment is likely to pay off.

Furthermore, in many business sectors, what a company brings to the market is typically not a single product but a product line. When a car manufacturer creates a new model, say Ford's Focus or the Vauxhall Agila, it will be sold in a base version and various higher-level or specialized variants, and similar differentiation occurs with other goods. Differentiating between separate variants of a product is expensive, and deciding how far the potential market calls for such differentiation is itself a marketing function.

Also, even physical goods are in many cases not simply sold as such in isolation. Often, they are bundled with associated services: free delivery, routine after-sales servicing, guarantees lasting beyond the legally-required period, etc. Again it is a marketing decision what elements of this sort to include and which to omit, or to offer as options for additional payment.

Price

In economics textbooks, prices are determined as the crossing-points of smooth supply and demand curves such as those of Figure 2.4 (p. 14). Real life is more complicated. Supply and demand may be accurately represented by smooth curves in the case of agricultural products, say; but with manufactures, these are only an idealized approximation.

For one thing, to consumers price is not a featureless linear scale. Arithmetically, the difference between £93 and £98 is identical to the difference between £98 and

£103, but – for consumers who pay in pounds – the latter jump breaches the two-figure barrier.

This can influence economic behaviour in two directions. Often, market research will show that people shopping for Xs will typically be unwilling to pay more than £Y: instead of being a smooth curve, the demand schedule has a kink at the £Y mark. This may then feed back into the product design process, via *target costing*: the price of a future product is set first, and then the product is designed so as to be sellable at that price.

Robin Cooper and Bruce Chew (1996) have argued that globalization and the electronic-speed economy make target costing more important than it used to be. In the past, a company that marketed a novel product had a de facto monopoly for a while. It took competitors some time to catch up, even though no legal monopoly barred them from supplying similar products. In present circumstances, innovators get so short a free run before imitators begin to compete that products have to be sold on price rather than on unique qualities from day one.

The other side of the picture, though, is that where high quality or luxury status are part of a product's attraction, setting a higher price (within reason) can actually reinforce this image. Rather than steadily falling from N.W. to S.E., the demand schedule may level out or even turn upwards a little way.

When a company decides a product price, manufacturing cost and the competition set a floor and a ceiling respectively. A company that sells its output for less than cost cannot keep going indefinitely (though, if investors are sufficiently optimistic about the company's future, it may survive for quite a while – as in the case of Amazon and many other internet retailers). Likewise, a company that sells things identical to what a competitor sells but at a higher price will lose its customers – though this is a less clear-cut barrier: except for agricultural produce, the products supplied by different companies are rarely quite identical. If customers see the differences as important, a company's pricing may be less constrained by that of its competitors.

Even if the floor and ceiling are fixed, a great deal of thought goes into where to set prices between those limits. For maximum profit, points near the ceiling are indicated. But a company may be more interested in building market share than in immediate profit, in which case it will choose to set its prices lower. And, in the B2B domain, whatever a company's overall strategy may be it will sell at lower prices to favoured (usually large) customers – a supermarket chain will get better prices than a corner shop from the same supplier, because 20 per cent profit on £100 is far less worth having than 5 per cent on £100,000.

Promotion

'Promotion' covers the obvious cases of advertising and direct marketing (for example, mailshots, leaflets delivered house-to-house, telephone selling), but also sales promotion techniques such as point-of-sale displays in supermarkets, free samples given away by company representatives seconded to stores, cheap off-peak fare offers, and many similar techniques – Needle (p. 376) tells us that more than 70 per cent of all spending under the 'promotion' heading relates to sales promotion rather than advertising or direct marketing.

Another promotional activity is seeking to place stories about a company or its products in the media: independent news stories or features carry much more weight with readers than paid advertising. One advantage for e-commerce startups in the early years was that journalists were so keen to produce stories about this new phenomenon, and at the same time knew so little about it, that they would often print dotcom press releases more or less word for word – any marketing manager's dream.

Products are promoted also via the individual relationships which suppliers' representatives are often able to cultivate with buyers, particularly in the B2B world. The importance of these is demonstrated by the way companies structure their marketing efforts. Any company selling a wide range of product lines to a diverse spectrum of buyers has a choice between structuring its selling round its product lines, or round the different industry sectors to which customers belong. The more complex the products, the more appropriate it might seem to opt for the former choice, so that supplier representatives can develop fuller expertise about what they are selling. But in practice IT companies nowadays usually structure marketing the second way, so that their representatives have a better chance to forge close relationships with buyers.

Advertising in the doldrums

The period since 2000 has been a difficult time for the advertising industry. By the end of 2002 *The Economist* was describing the mood in the industry as one of 'panic',[1] and it seemed likely that direct marketing and sales promotion were increasingly destined to achieve more for companies than advertising.

If advertising is a declining force, this has both favourable and unfavourable implications for e-commerce.

On the one hand, when people began to try making money via the World Wide Web, many business models depended heavily on selling advertising on websites. If advertising in general is in the doldrums, that is one more reason why this kind of business model is unlikely to work. But in any case there are deeper reasons why Web advertising seems to be a loser. The Web guru Jakob Nielsen was arguing as early as 1997 that 'advertising doesn't work on the Web':

> TV [is] much more suited for the traditional type of advertising which is flashy and promotes superficial qualities of products. While watching TV, people approach a vegetable state ... [On the Web] the user is *actively engaged in determining where to go* next. The user is usually on the Web for a purpose and is not likely to be distracted from the goal by an advertisement ...[2]

1. 'High hopes in adland', *The Economist* 7 Dec 2002.
2. Jakob Nielsen, 'Why advertising doesn't work on the Web', 1 Sep 1997, www.useit.com/alertbox/9709a.html

In 1997 Nielsen noted that *clickthrough rate* (the proportion of those seeing a Web advert who click on it) was only about one per cent; a year later it had fallen to half that. In February 2002 Nielsen added a PS to say that the sole type of Web advertising that is worthwhile is paid-for listings on search engines: since people visit those sites in order to find others to go to, and the visitor's search terms provide a basis for deciding which listings may interest him, a well-targeted advert may attract custom.

(Nielsen also noted that classified advertising works *better* on the Web than in newspapers – but small-ads are not the kind of 'advertising' we are concerned with here.)

On the other hand, the growing importance of direct marketing could be favourable for e-commerce, because the nature of the internet medium makes it much easier than in traditional commerce for suppliers to tailor their communications to individual customers. We discussed in Chapter 3 the way that a past customer logging on to the Amazon site is greeted by name and shown a page which includes displays of specific books likely to interest that individual. The nature of books makes this perhaps a special case, but many other e-commerce sites will display home pages that differ subtly, depending on the identity of the visitor.

Customer satisfaction versus customer loyalty

Marketing managers who devote effort to choosing suitable marketing strategies would like to have theories to predict people's response: what actually leads people to decide to buy or not to buy? Perhaps fortunately, from the point of view of human freedom, such theories as have been advanced seem rather unsuccessful. Most human behaviour is too subtle to be reduced to formulae.

One idea that has been influential in recent years – and which has special relevance for e-commerce – is Nigel Piercy's argument (Piercy 2002: 26–35) that customer satisfaction and customer loyalty are independent variables.

It is a marketing cliché that the costs of making further sales to an existing customer are many times less than those of acquiring a new customer – Jim Sterne (2001: 15) suggests a ratio of five or ten times less. If for no other reason than keeping costs down, then, a company needs to look after its existing customers well enough to encourage them to keep coming back for more. Before Piercy, people tended to assume that a satisfied customer was a repeat customer, and vice versa. But Piercy argues that what we have is really a two by two matrix, in which all four cells are populated:

		customer loyalty	
		high	*low*
customer satisfaction	*high*	satisfied stayers	happy wanderers
	low	hostages	dealers

In conventional commerce, this leads one to query the value of marketing devices intended to foster loyalty, such as supermarket 'clubcards' or airline frequent-flyer incentive schemes. They may merely create 'hostages' rather than 'satisfied stayers' – and, in the long run, can hostages be valuable customers? (Of course, loyalty-creation is not the only and perhaps not the most important function of supermarket clubcards: by generating streams of data about individuals' buying habits over time they create banks of information with many potential uses in marketing, irrespective of whether shoppers with cards are more loyal than those without.)

The relevance of Piercy's analysis to e-commerce is that, in the online world, discovering alternative suppliers and switching is far easier than before. Does e-commerce push more of us from the 'satisfied stayer' into the 'happy wanderer' or even the 'dealer' cell? Or does it merely reduce the number of 'hostages'? – and which of the low-loyalty cells do they typically migrate to? Even if these questions have clearcut answers, it is probably too early yet to know for sure what they are.

Branding

Branding means using distinctive names and logos to create artificial differences between similar products or product lines, over and above the 'real' differences that may exist in terms of intrinsic product features or quality.

With goods whose quality is hard to check by looking at them, for instance pharmaceuticals or engineering parts, branding has always been an important quality-assurance mechanism. But in the consumer-goods domain, branding has become far more important since the 1980s than it was before. With clothing, for instance, thirty years ago suppliers' logos were discreet, either small or placed where they were not seen when the garment was worn; less clothes-conscious men might be barely aware of the names of any clothing companies. Now, people often wear suppliers' logos blazoned across their chest, and light fiction is filled with designer-label names.

There can be little argument about the fact that this change has taken place. It is not so easy to explain why. Needle (p. 384) offers several reasons, all of which seem problematic.

We have seen that globalization and the speed of modern technology transfer give producers less time than before to profit from 'de facto monopolies' when they introduce new products. Needle suggests that branding is taking over from technology as the basis for product differentiation: monopolies of technical innovation quickly melt away, but the right to use a registered trademark is a legal monopoly and hence relatively secure.

The trouble with this is that it seems to imply that customers are stupid. Believing that a product is better because of a technical difference may be rational; believing it is better just because of a name defies reason. It is not contradictory to suggest that consumers are growing less rational, but it flies in the face of much other economic analysis which claims that consumers have grown more sophisticated (because better-informed) in recent decades.

Alternatively, Needle suggests that the market for most consumer goods in the Western world has grown stagnant through over-supply, so producers have to clutch at any possible way of expanding market share. This view of branding as a kind of counsel of desperation seems to contradict the previous idea: if technical innovation is rife, markets should not be stagnant.

Thirdly, Needle suggests that in market segments such as clothing, where fashion is significant, image-conscious young people are attracted to designer labels which are currently in the swing. That is clearly true, but it merely restates the question. *Why* are youngsters so much more interested in brands than their parents were at a similar age?

Branding has become so important for business that it would be good to have some more satisfying explanation for the development. Failing that, we must simply accept the phenomenon as a brute fact which marketing strategies have to deal with.

Global brands

The new significance of branding, together with the phenomenon of globalization, has led to the rise of *global brands*, such as Coca-Cola or Intel, which are recognized everywhere. Even when a car company sold into different national markets, it would often in the past give the same model different names, with their own local resonances, in different countries; nowadays it is more likely to use 'international', culturally-vague names.

On the face of it, global brands ought to suit Web commerce very well. But, as Needle shows, even when brands are international, what they stand for is often less globally uniform than it might seem. McDonald's sells fast food worldwide and is often seen as an icon of globalization. In reality its food range is increasingly differentiated from country to country. Audi cars are marketed as technically advanced in Britain, as sporty in the USA, and in South Africa they are mainly sold as taxis. So, again, the global reach of the Web may work against rather than reinforce the existing marketing strategies even of companies which operate globally.

Customer Relationship Management

We have seen that there are solid financial reasons to encourage customers once found to remain loyal. Customer Relationship Management (CRM) software provides automated support for that goal.

Automating relationships with customers might sound like the worst kind of dehumanizing computer application. A more realistic understanding, though, is that in modern circumstances, where much commercial interaction inevitably has to be electronic rather than face-to-face, CRM software helps companies to treat their customers *more* as individuals than would otherwise be possible.

In May 2003 the large British law firm DLA placed full-page advertisements in the national press, boasting of how well they were regarded by independent observers. *The Lawyer* voted DLA 'Law Firm of the Year' for 2002. DLA knew what clients cared about: 'In the past, law firms have sometimes given the impression that they are doing their clients a favour. Nowadays, clients tell us they ... want lawyers they can get to know and who can be bothered to get to know them.' *The*

Lawyer's view was that DLA's 'approach to client relationships borders on the fanatical'. And DLA were explicit about how this was achieved: it had invested the resources needed 'to introduce effective Client Relationship Management ..., a process that is now at the heart of our business.'

> Our CRM sets up a system of control and feedback that means we can service our clients according to their particular needs. It means the client always knows what is happening, and we can provide solutions more quickly and control costs – for our clients as well as ourselves.

Law is a very distinctive type of business – hence the use of 'client' rather than 'customer' to gloss the C of CRM. If the highly sensitive services provided by legal advisers can be made more individual through CRM systems, then it would be strange if CRM in more workaday business sectors had the converse effect.

The essence of CRM is to integrate the various contacts which a company has with a customer or sales lead, so that a coherent history of the company's dealings with that person is available whenever a new interaction occurs.

A particular customer may be in contact at different times via a company rep visiting the customer's site, via a phone call to a call centre or to a specific member of company staff, via e-mail, or via the Web. The company may have separate product ranges produced and marketed by different divisions, and the same customer may buy from separate divisions at different times. A CRM system assembles information that enables whoever deals with the customer on a given occasion, wherever he works in the company and whatever the channel of contact, to interact with that customer intelligently and knowledgeably. It cuts out the need for the customer to rehearse much of the background repeatedly in successive calls. It may enable the call centre to route the customer's call efficiently, cutting out the requirement to respond to numerous rounds of 'If you need XYZ, press button 3'. When a past purchaser of the company's equipment phones for advice or support, CRM should arm the service operative with information about that customer's installation, so he can move directly to asking about the problem rather than wasting time establishing the background. The proportion of support queries resolved by a single call increases. CRM is crucial for individualizing the material shown to a customer who visits the company website – we have seen that this sort of individualization is one of the chief marketing advantages of the Web.

The leading CRM supplier, Siebel Systems (founded in 1993), puts it this way in a Web page explaining the CRM concept:

> The challenge is to make it easy for customers to do business with the organization any way they want – at any time, through any channel, in any language or currency – and to make customers feel that they are dealing with a single, unified organization that recognizes them at every touchpoint.[3]

CRM is not relevant only to sales and customer-support functions. It is used in marketing also, for instance to select customers to whom a new product is likely to

3. www.siebel.com/whatiscrm

be of interest and avoid annoying the entire customer base by repeatedly bombarding them with publicity releases about irrelevant products. And it provides data for 'analytics' – discovering generalizations about the preferences and needs of different categories of customer, which may help guide decisions about new product development, for instance. To use the unattractive jargon, CRM makes firms more 'customer-centric'.

CRM under a cloud

The potential value of what CRM promises is obvious, and the technology has been spreading through the business environment. By now it is used widely in the high-tech and general financial-services sectors, and it is spreading into areas like healthcare and insurance. (The law firm DLA is probably ahead of the field in exploiting CRM in a professional-services context.)

Nevertheless, it is fair to say at present that CRM is to some extent under a cloud. It is perceived as an unduly expensive technology, difficult to implement and maintain and difficult to use, and often disappointing in the extent to which it meets its apparent promises. When software purchasers rate suppliers, Siebel tends to rank at or near the bottom. For years Siebel was one of the leading enterprise-application success stories, with revenues doubling year on year and holding up well even for the first year after the high-tech bubble burst; but things started going wrong for the company in 2002.

Some problems stem from the fact that the technical challenges CRM has to solve are quite large. From the user's viewpoint, what CRM aims to deliver sounds simple, but to achieve that the system has to integrate data captured through many different channels, some of which may involve outdated legacy formats; and it has to put all that material together in real time, for instance while a customer introduces himself to a support agent on the phone. The reputation of CRM probably suffers from unrealistic expectations. Furthermore, even when it works well, this technology – like ERP – forces the business which adopts it to change its working practices in ways that it might not have chosen.

Also, though, the technology is still relatively new and not as well worked out as it might be. We do not need to infer this from software purchasers' rankings: Tom Siebel, chairman of Siebel Systems, has been outspoken about the shortcomings of his product. At the company's annual Worldwide User Week in October 2002, he said 'I'm surprised that there's not more outrage on the part of customers ... I'm surprised that they have not taken their enterprise application providers – including Siebel – and just thrown them out.'[4] A few weeks earlier, Siebel was quoted as saying 'There's no market for CRM', suggesting that demand did exist for packages tailored to specific industry sectors, but not for the generic tools which his company has been selling to date.[5] And he predicts that software for managing companies' relationships with their own staff will become a bigger market than CRM. After all this from the chairman of the leading supplier in the

---

4. Quoted in Douglas Hayward, 'Strategy paper', *Computing* 31 Oct 2002.
5. 'Firms must tailor CRM', *IT Week* 2 Sep 2002.

field, it is perhaps surprising that analysts do continue to see the future of CRM as healthy.

Best-of-breed versus integrated suite

One problem for Siebel, and for suppliers of other categories of enterprise application software – ERP, CRM, and genres to be discussed in Chapter 9 – relates to an issue that became a hot topic from late 2002 onwards: *best-of-breed* versus *integrated suite*.

Robert Reid noted years ago that (apart from head-on competition, which is usual in any market) the software market is full of *side-on competition*, which

> occurs when a (generally) larger company, fighting its own battles, expands its products' features in a way that encroaches on the functional space of an apparent noncompetitor. (Reid 1997: 97)

We saw in Chapter 7 that SAP, which made its name as an ERP supplier, has more recently expanded its offerings to include CRM functionality. Likewise PeopleSoft began as an ERP company but has now integrated CRM and e-procurement tools (for the latter, see pp. 114–115 below) into its overall software suite. Microsoft is extending its office-productivity system to include enterprise-application elements. Oracle, a database company, now has an 'e-business suite' comprising ERP, CRM, business intelligence (pp.93–94), and other facilities. For a large player in any one enterprise-application niche, the strategy of broadening to cover the full range of applications in a single suite of software is obvious.

The term 'best of breed' implies that specialized software, such as Siebel in the case of CRM, is better at executing its particular function than the relevant component of an integrated business system is likely to be. This was particularly obvious when Oracle released the first version of its integrated e-business suite in May 2000 and thereby placed the integrated approach on everyone's radar screen. That initial version turned out to be riddled with bugs; so people gave up on the integrated-suite idea for some time.

But Oracle's suite has been improved, and in principle the integrated approach has many advantages for purchasers. It is expensive to buy separate best-of-breed systems for different application areas and pay to create and maintain links enabling them to interact automatically. It can be reassuring to source one's essential business software from a single very large supplier which is unlikely to go out of business, and which cannot disclaim responsibility for glitches wherever in the overall system they crop up.

In most application areas it probably is still true that the best-of-breed specialist system outperforms the corresponding subsystem of an integrated suite, but the question is whether the differential remains large enough to make best-of-breed a wise choice. The CRM components of Oracle's, SAP's, and PeopleSoft's suites are all now contenders, at least, vis-à-vis Siebel. According to Sergio Giacoletto, Oracle executive vice president for Europe (hence obviously not a neutral observer), 'people can buy 80 per cent of the functionality [of a best-of-breed product] for 10 per cent of the price of pre-integrated applications. That's why Ariba, i2 and even

Siebel are suffering. They used to command a premium price because they were the only people with the functionality'.[6] (Ariba and i2 are respectively e-procurement and supply chain management systems – see Chapter 9.)

For its part, Siebel entered partnerships with Microsoft and with IBM in 2002–3 in an attempt to avoid becoming marginalized as too narrowly specialist.

At the time of writing, then, it is an open question whether the specialist suppliers will survive. The downturn has worked against them by making it difficult, financially, for small companies to keep afloat, while the biggest players have enough resources to be able to ride out recession. On the other hand, if the spectrum of companies which purchase software include more large and fewer small firms in future, this may favour the best-of-breed suppliers, because large companies are better able to afford the overhead of integrating separate systems in-house, and may care more about best possible performance. And the cost comparisons are arguable. As best-of-breed suppliers reduce their prices in self-defence, some commentators believe it may actually be cheaper for companies to do deals with separate suppliers which they can play off against one another than to depend wholly on a single large deal with a dominant supplier.

The concept of virtual communities

Contrary to the commonsense viewpoint that sees the function of a commercial website as being to publicize and sell a company's wares, for David Siegel (1997: 18) 'The ultimate goal of many web sites is to create a community.' Many *virtual communities*, of course, have no connexion with business (and note that the concept is quite separate from 'virtual company' or 'virtual organization', discussed in Chapter 2). The virtual community concept was formulated by Howard Rheingold before the internet was commercialized, as a way of describing a sizeable group of people who form a network of human relationships based on some common interest but mediated by the internet rather than face-to-face interactions (Rheingold 1993).

Ever since the business consultants John Hagel and Arthur Armstrong published their influential book *Net Gain* (Hagel and Armstrong 1997), many commentators have believed that these electronically-mediated communities of interest have an essential role to play as links between companies and their potential customer base – at the B2C level, and perhaps also at the B2B level.

Virtual communities as a marketing tool

As P. K. Kannan, Ai-Mei Chang, and A. B. Whinston (2001) see it, virtual communities related to particular business sectors offer a solution to a marketing problem that stems from the anonymity of internet interactions. To market their products successfully, companies need information about customers and potential customers: their demographic categories such as sex, age, and income level, their tastes, and so forth. When sellers and buyers deal with one another physically it is

6. Quoted in Douglas Hayward, 'Questions and answers', *Computing* 24 Oct 2002. In context, Giacoletto appears to be using 'pre-integrated' to mean unintegrated.

often much easier for sellers to gather this kind of information than it is in the online world. Customers cannot be expected to give away useful personal information to commercial organizations for nothing – but if a company fosters a virtual community of interest which buyers of its products see themselves as 'owning' and which gives them, not just the company, value in terms of information, contacts with like-minded people, and so forth, then (Kannan et al. suggest) company and customers can find themselves in a win-win situation.

The key is 'ownership', in the psychological more than the legal sense. A company may set up the infrastructure which allows a virtual community, oriented towards its market sector, to develop; but, to get full value from the existence of the virtual community, Kannan et al. argue that the company must let go. The community must become something that exists to serve all its participants; the company needs to be merely one contributor, not the controller. When consumers seek product information or advice by posting queries on virtual-community bulletin boards, often the most helpful answers will be from other consumers rather than from company representatives. By raising the shared level of understanding and confidence in the product line, C2C interchanges like this may do more to support sales than any amount of company advertising.

The literature on business benefits from virtual communities continues to be predominantly hypothetical in tone, though. One of the few concrete examples, referred to by writer after writer, is Parentsplace.com. This was a California-based site that began as an e-tailing initiative: it was intended to be a business selling child-related products to parents, with social features such as chat rooms included in order to support that goal. Parents who joined the community proved to be much more interested in using it for things like exchanging childrearing advice than in ordering goods from the site; so the site owners changed their business model, abandoning the retail operation and generating a revenue stream instead by selling advertising space to companies marketing the kinds of goods which the site had initially sold.

However, this does not seem to be a good illustration of Hagel and Armstrong's concept, because in this case there was no ongoing business for the community to support. Indeed, there are alternative points of view on the desirability of virtual-community independence. See for instance Sterne (2001: 152–3), who discusses Corel's acquisition of a previously independent virtual community.

A clearer example of a successful virtual community in Kannan et al.'s discussion is taken from the B2B domain: the General Electric Information Systems Trading Process Network.[7] This began as a website set up by the lighting division of the US company General Electric to allow suppliers to tender for GE contracts via standardized Web forms. One motive was to create a level playing field for potential suppliers, and in particular to make it easier for small firms to compete for contracts. Once the facility was in place, though, GE's suppliers found it a useful means of soliciting tenders from *their* suppliers, a step further up the value chain. By now, the site is home to a critical mass of some six thousand companies interacting as buyers and sellers, and it is no longer seen as 'owned' by GE –

---

7. For fuller information on GEIS-TPN see huzvarth.notlong.com

formally, it is run jointly by GE Information Systems, the publishers of the Register of American Manufacturers, and Oracle. This nicely illustrates the idea of a company gaining by giving away control of a forum, though it is a far cry from the original idea of a virtual community as a set of people linked by emotional bonds expressed electronically – business is more businesslike than that.

The concept of virtual communities as catalysts for e-commerce is an interesting one. It was influential in the early years, and it seems worth consideration by companies thinking about their e-commerce strategy today; but it is not such a sure-fire winner as was once predicted.

E-marketing is marketing

To sum up, the point made at the beginning of this chapter bears repeating: an e-business is a business. Marketing in the online world is not radically different from marketing in conventional business. IT gives us new tools; some are more useful than others. Some may be double-edged.

9
More enterprise applications

Automatable and non-automatable functions

In earlier chapters we have looked at the two leading enterprise application areas, enterprise resource planning and customer relationship management. This chapter offers a round-up of some other genres of business software.

It cannot claim exhaustive coverage. Some applications are too specialized to discuss in a book like this; other applications, to do with issues such as security, are not closely enough related to the specific content of business to cover here. But if an application deals with actual business processes, and is general enough to register on the average IT manager's radar, I aim to include it.

It should be said that some application areas are better developed than others. As always in the IT industry, effort is needed to cut through thickets of hype and assess what is actually being achieved. Some areas we shall look at below appear to be reasonably well served by existing systems, but in other cases hopes have not yet been fully translated into realities. From our point of view, it is as interesting to consider business functions that seem resistant to successful automation as functions which have yielded.

It is not just that some functions are hard to automate. People are beginning to suggest that some enterprise application genres may be solutions looking for a problem. Joseph Langhauser of General Motors told a San Diego conference on the future of computing in February 2003 that IT tools had proliferated faster than companies can exploit them: 'We don't need any more IT ... We need to figure out the business processes we have.'[1]

On this negative note, it is worth recalling research by Tom Landauer (1995), who examined industrial statistics to quantify how much impact computerization had had over preceding decades on industrial productivity – what the *return on*

---

1. Quoted by Tony Kontzer, 'A harsh assessment of IT from Peter Drucker', *Information Week* 12 Feb 2003, vizcenal.notlong.com

investment (ROI) had been. His depressing conclusion was that, for the economy as a whole, ROI from computerization since the mid-1970s had been low or zero. (See also Goldfinger 1997: 195.) Computerizing business implies not just spending on equipment and software but paying for people to maintain it, dealing with the business consequences of the many glitches that arise, and so forth. Often, it seemed, these cost factors outbalance the benefits from automating previously-manual functions.

Landauer was researching this question just before commercial use of the internet took off, and before computers were widely used to re-engineer business processes rather than merely to mechanize them. It is probably too soon to quantify the overall return on investment in deploying the enterprise applications discussed in this book. But we must always bear in mind that just because, logically speaking, some function looks ripe for automation, and commercial systems claiming to implement that function are available, it will not always be true that the software systems genuinely yield a business benefit.

Workflow management

Workflow management is a good example of a business function which seems very suitable for computerization, and where various systems have been marketed for some time now, but where 'the great breakthrough has not yet happened' (Gloor 2000: 112). A few years on, Peter Gloor's comment remains valid.

The concept of workflow management is easy to explain. Many businesses involve paperwork in standard formats passing from office to office along standard routes. Gloor's example is a health insurance company. When a client asks to take out a policy, the company collects data from him. On the basis of those data, it decides whether a medical examination is required. If so, the client's details are passed to a health centre allied with the insurance company, and an invitation to attend for examination is printed out and posted. When the client arrives, his attendance is registered by a receptionist, and during the examination the doctor adds medical data to his file. On the basis of the accumulated data, an insurance risk factor is worked out, and the file is passed back to the insurance company, where a decision is made on whether an individual premium must be calculated by an expert, or whether the case is routine enough for automatic computation to suffice – as it will for those clients not asked to undergo an examination. Either via the expert or directly, the file then arrives at a point where a policy and invoice are printed out and posted to the client.

Traditionally, what will have moved from client to office to office, perhaps crossing from insurance company to health centre and back again, will have been paper documents – forms in which data is progressively entered into the spaces. Nowadays, some of the data exchanges might happen via e-mail; but it is not yet usual for the flow of documentation in moderately complex scenarios like the one just sketched to be entirely electronic.

Often, a complex document is transmitted from one point to another as a massive PDF file which has to be downloaded and printed out before being filled in and sent on by post. Bruce Chizen, chief executive of Adobe (owner of the PDF technology), agreed in October 2002 that this way of working is absurdly inefficient, but he pointed out that with documentation such as insurance papers 'presentation is critical, not least because of the laws and regulations concerning the information within the documents.'[2] Chizen believed it would be at least five years before electronic stylesheets like those available in connexion with HTML and XML formats – which in principle can control document presentation without increasing file size much beyond what is needed for the simple ASCII text – become reliable enough for presentation-critical document exchange. Adobe's Workflow Server software, announced in the month that Chizen was speaking, is one attempt to get beyond the need to print paperwork out; it does not address the filesize problem.

Other companies are developing their own solutions. For instance, IBM has its MQ Workflow system (in a previous incarnation known as FlowMark); a specialist company, FileNet, markets Form Manager and related software. The next version of Microsoft's Office office-productivity suite is planned to contain some workflow capabilities – but when the beta version was released in October 2002 the company remained in two minds about how far it would go down that road.

Like many other enterprise applications, workflow depends on agreed standards – particularly when data must cross boundaries between separate organizations, as in the case of medical insurance documents passing between insurance company and health centre. There are organizations working on standards-setting, but forces seem somewhat divided. The Workflow and Reengineering Internet Association (WARIA) has been active since 1992, the Workflow Management Coalition (WfMC) since 1993, and the inadequacy of progress is suggested by the fact that in 1998 the Internet Engineering Task Force set up a third group to work on a Simple Workflow Access Protocol (SWAP) – though this last initiative was short-lived. In 2000, Peter Gloor felt that de facto convergence on agreed systems was not yet visible, and the packages then existing all lacked robustness.

The problem is not just that people have not been trying, or that rivals refuse to agree. The real difficulty is that the task is more challenging than it looks. Those of us who are not administrators often think of that type of work as tediously static, but the truth is that organizational routines frequently change. More awkward still, business processes often contain unstructured components mixed in with the structured aspects. Gloor's example is that approval of a new product will involve a well-defined sign-off process up a company hierarchy, but it may well also involve 'informal soundings' among colleagues. The unstructured elements can scarcely be integrated into an automated workflow system; but, if that means they get squeezed out, the company would surely lose more than it gains through efficient exchange of 'paperwork'.

Group memory

A software genre that has proved more clearly disappointing than workflow is *group memory* systems. I include it here, because in the recent past it was a major

2. Reported in Rod Newing, 'Time to break our paper chains', *IT Week* 21 Oct 2002.

e-business buzzword. When a phrase attains buzzword status, the student needs to know about it if only in order to learn that there is little behind it.

The essence of a business firm, in the eyes of some economists, is that it forms 'a repository of productive knowledge' (Winter 1993: 185) – an institution whose function is collectively to store and apply knowledge of how to execute some complex range of useful economic processes. No one individual in a firm, including its managing director, possesses more than a fraction of this knowledge, which resides rather in the firm as a whole – 'it is the firms, not the people who work for the firms, that know how to make gasoline, automobiles, and computers'. Some of this knowledge is formal and explicit, but much is transmitted through fleeting interactions between staff.

The 'group memory' vision was that electronic systems might enable what was of lasting value in these interactions to be systematically recorded and preserved, reducing the inefficiencies that stem from facts and ideas getting lost from sight as work moves forward.

The original inspiration for group memory software lay in the successful *groupware* program Lotus Notes, which supports collaborative work by colleagues who interact via e-mail, making it easy for them to keep systematic records of how their thinking and discussion on particular topics, and the documents they jointly put together, develop over time. Many companies (for example, eRoom, Webex, Visto) aimed to build on this general concept to create systems which would maintain corporate memory in some grander sense.

But little came of the idea, partly because it seemed too vague. Attempts that were made to implement it often yielded few bankable benefits in practice; the initial enthusiasm for purpose-built groupware diminished after Web technology made it easy to achieve some of the same goals via company intranets. In December 2002, eRoom was taken over by Documentum, a leading content management company. Webex and Visto remain active in 2003, but in the relatively specialized domains of online meeting support and mobile messaging respectively.

Lotus Notes (now owned by IBM) is still a respected name in its original messaging and collaboration niche, and rival groupware products are supplied by other companies – Oracle released its Collaboration Suite in October 2002, the Titanium version of Microsoft Exchange is due in mid-2003. But groupware has not grown into the more grandiose application once envisaged. By 2001, Ravi Kalakota was describing group memory as 'a fad spawned by consultants and vendors' (Kalakota and Robinson 2001: 353). Kalakota suggests that the 'business intelligence' systems discussed on pp. 93–94 are what the group memory concept has morphed into, and he links these and some other e-business technologies as successive approaches to *knowledge management*. But a concept which is so broad that Lotus Notes and business intelligence systems can both count as special cases is perhaps too all-embracing to be useful. More than one speaker at the San Diego future-of-computing conference in February 2003 argued that 'knowledge management' is a mirage, because knowledge simply is not something that can be managed.

Supply chain planning

It is time we turned to more successful enterprise application areas. Supply chain planning is one.

Managing a company's supply chain, monitoring the flow of goods from suppliers and through the successive processes executed within one's own company, re-ordering as necessary, is one of the functions of ERP software such as SAP, which (as we have seen) will often be linked via an extranet to supplier companies. The phrase *supply chain planning* is used for a higher-level activity, which aims to *optimize* rather than merely manage a company's supply chain. 'Supply chain management' systems – the leading name is i2 – cover both things, managing and optimizing, but the optimizing function is the distinctive area that merits examination here.

Thus, some functions included in i2's system comprise (among others):

- *Strategic planning*, which analyses the trade-offs in terms of cost, profit, and service of alternative scenarios for sourcing, manufacturing, and transport. 'Key performance indicators' are identified, and the system flags deviations from these. Worst-case scenarios are simulated to validate a strategy before it is implemented.

- *Collaborative supply planning*, including *factory planning* which generates an optimized production plan for a plant or work unit, taking into account material and capacity; *replenishment planning*, to decide optimal order quantities for restocking, taking into account lead times and supplier and transport constraints; *scheduling*, which sets an optimum sequence for moving orders into production while respecting the various manufacturing constraints; and many other subfunctions.

- *Supply chain execution*, including *transport management*, which distributes loads across various transport modes involving different carriers and tariffs, including complex load consolidation and de-consolidation possibilities; *fulfilment centre management*, which plans pick, pack, and ship processes; etc.

These are merely a sample of supply chain planning functions, distilled from a much longer list in i2's product literature, but the sample is perhaps enough to give a flavour of this application genre.

The i2 company, once very profitable, has had a rough ride lately: in 2002 it had to halve its workforce. But this does not represent a failure of supply chain planning technology – it was merely a consequence of the general economic downturn, compounded by the competition now posed by integrated-suite companies to many best-of-breed software suppliers. (i2 is trying to address the latter problem via new strategic partnerships.)

Currently, there is a notable trend for manufacturers to outsource their *logistics* operations (that is, the organization of physical movement of goods inward from suppliers, through different processing stages, and outward as finished products), in order to take advantage of the more refined logistics alternatives that specialists in that field can offer. This must increase the demand for sophisticated supply chain planning systems. At the same time, new technology such as the RFID tags discussed on p. 51 are creating new scope for supply-chain software to control logistic activities at a level of detail that was not previously possible. There seems little doubt that this application area will be even more significant in the future than it has been to date.

Product lifecycle management

New products are brought to the market, they are sold for a period, and in due course they are replaced by newer products. In a business environment characterized by frequent technical innovation, the expected lifecycle of a product is often not long, and a wise company needs to plan not only for the birth but also for the death of its products. For one thing, customers want to know that there is a thought-out plan for transition to the next product generation – they do not want any risk of finding themselves stuck with an orphaned product which is obsolete but not readily upgradable.

Recently, software companies have begun marketing *product lifecycle management* systems which claim to support this type of planning. MatrixOne is a company which specializes in PLM; many leading enterprise application suppliers now include PLM alongside their main offerings – i2 includes it with supply chain management, SAP includes it with ERP.

Some functions within PLM systems are not clearly separate from functions that might more naturally be discussed under other headings. For instance, we saw in Chapter 2 that car manufacturers are beginning to involve suppliers closely in the development of new models by exchanging CAD (computer-aided design) data electronically: PLM suppliers commonly identify this as a PLM function, since design is an important part of an engineering product's lifecycle, but the activity is clearly valid independently of the concept 'lifecycle management'. However, there are other PLM functions that are more or less unique to this software genre: for instance, asset lifecycle management, which monitors the commissioning and maintenance of manufacturing equipment, and the associated costs, to ensure that the equipment is available to play its part as production is ramped up, that its useful lifetime lasts as long as the product lasts (or else that it is replaced when necessary), and that the impact on company cashflow is anticipated.

It is perhaps debatable whether 'product lifecycle management' will prove necessary in the long run as a discrete software category – though its functions will surely be executed, whether or not the term continues to be used. If integrated suites expand their market at the expense of best-of-breed systems, we can expect that terminology for software genres will be fluid.

e-Procurement

A firm does not need to buy in only the raw materials or parts which it processes into the finished products that it sells. To do its job, it also needs to buy many other kinds of thing, ranging from capital equipment such as heavy machinery to maintenance and repair supplies, office furniture and supplies, travel, advertising, and so on. Buying these things is called *procurement*, and it is normally treated as a separate business issue from buying the materials which go into the products. Procurement activity will typically be more dispersed across a company, and less regular, than purchasing of production supplies.

An important enterprise application niche is so-called *e-procurement*. (The term *operating resource management systems*, 'ORMS', has also been used, because these applications may extend beyond purchasing to include aspects of managing the resources once purchased.) Leading companies in this field are Ariba, and Commerce One.

The essence of an e-procurement system is an application running on the terminal of any employee authorized to make purchases, giving access to the catalogues of approved suppliers, and offering a simple mechanism for placing orders.

Nobody suggests that this is a specially subtle use of IT. But, for companies which use e-procurement, it can be a valuable one. Traditionally, procurement has been an inefficient aspect of business operations, based on complex paper systems that use up large quantities of salaried staff time for transactions which, individually, can sometimes be for tiny amounts: just the kind of scenario for which IT is made. Ariba's list of corporate customers is both long and of star quality.

This is not to say that shifting from manual to electronic procurement is necessarily simple to achieve. Some companies which aimed to use e-procurement on a large scale have been surprised at the difficulties. According to David Metcalfe of Forrester Research, 'It's taken IBM three years to get 90 percent of its procurement online … Unilever was hoping for payback [from] its e-procurement in two years, and it took four.'[3] Commerce One warns that this technology, like other enterprise applications, imposes an element of culture change.

Furthermore it is not always clear that the savings achieved through e-procurement would not have been possible with manual systems. For instance, implementing e-procurement normally implies consolidating a company's range of suppliers into a shorter list, each of which will offer larger discounts in return for the larger volume of business – but nothing stops a firm requiring its staff to use a few approved suppliers while purchasing remains a manual process. However, it is often the case that IT catalyses a development that in theory could have happened without computers, but never did. A survey by Benchmark Research in July 2002 of large firms in the US, Britain, and Germany suggested that the gains from e-procurement were real.

Online B2B auctions

In about 2000–01, Ariba began to move beyond straightforward fixed-price purchasing support into the field of B2B auctions, offering a 'Dynamic Trading' system which aimed to increase liquidity in the market by making it easy for companies to bargain with one another, not only on the price of goods but on non-price features such as exact specifications, delivery dates, and so forth.

3. Quoted by Rachel Fielding, 'E-purchasing goes slow', *IT Week* 29 Jul 2002.

At that time, many people expected auctions to become an important aspect of e-commerce. Many variants are possible: auctions can be *public* (a company advertises its intention to purchase goods or services on a public website appropriate to its industry sector) or *private* (a large company invites bids only from its preferred group of suppliers); and they can be *forward* auctions in which suppliers invite bids from buyers, or *reverse* auctions in which buyers invite tenders from suppliers. In the early days of online B2B auctions, they were used mainly for low-value goods such as stationery; but, in principle, anything traded between organizations may be traded via auction, and online techniques can make the process much simpler.

After the dotcom bubble burst, online auctions seemed to lose their impetus for a while (at the B2B level – C2C auction sites remained successful, but they are a separate story). At the time of writing, the Ariba website suggests that it is no longer actively engaged in this area.

However, there is nothing wrong with the economic logic of trading by online auction. Some analysts are confident that the technique is due to revive and become more significant than ever. One indicator of this came in October 2002, when Consignia (as the Post Office was then called) decided in future to use electronic auctions for half of its £1.5bn annual spend, forecasting that savings would run conservatively at ten per cent. Another came in February 2003, when the very successful C2C auction site eBay launched a B2B equivalent, eBay Business.

Standards for supply chain communication

If companies are to negotiate with one another up and down the supply chain electronically, they need formatting standards for expressing information about the goods and services traded. Ariba saw its position as sufficiently dominant in the e-procurement domain that it initially held aloof from industry-wide standards-setting initiatives, and produced its own Catalogue Interchange Format (CIF). Supplier companies were willing to put in the effort needed to deliver their catalogues in CIF form, for the sake of being able to sell to Ariba's impressive list of clients.

But, as in other areas of e-business, it seems likely that progress overall will be greater if an infrastructure of shared public standards can be created, so that competitors and potential trading partners can all communicate in a common electronic language. Several initiatives are under way.

RosettaNet

The most significant single initiative may be RosettaNet, formed in 1998 as a consortium of technology companies – the forty founding members have since grown to over 400 – which produced a prototype proof-of-concept system in the year 2000. Part of the initial impetus came from a perception that the EDI (electronic data interchange) systems currently used to exchange business data between trading partners were not offering a long-term solution. They are proprietary, and inflexible in face of changing B2B business processes. RosettaNet aims to define a standard, non-proprietary framework for processing business transactions between companies electronically.

For a given business sector, RosettaNet defines a master 'dictionary' specifying properties that characterize products, trading partners, and transaction types, cutting through the confusion that can arise from companies using idiosyncratic terminology. It also defines a standard range of *PIPs* – Partner Interface Processes – so that the kinds of interaction which occur between companies can be specified and understood the same way at both ends. In an early version, for instance, PIP2A2 was 'Query Product Information'; this, and any other PIP, specifies a business document with the vocabulary of the message dialogue, and a business process with its 'choreography'. Using the standard battery of PIPs, interactions that previously had to be executed manually can be automated: the 'choreography' lays down which moves are expected from the respective partners at which stage, so the dance can proceed with neither partner stepping electronically on the other's toes. RosettaNet aims to make these systems sufficiently generic to handle future changes in the nature of B2B communication – though, as always, one must expect the future to be surprising.

BizTalk

As it often does, Microsoft has developed a proprietary system which it hopes to turn into a de facto standard. BizTalk is in part a middleware system intended to allow separate enterprise applications to talk to one another by converting their respective input and output formats into the formats expected by other applications. But BizTalk also has features that make it somewhat akin to 'RosettaNet without PIPs'. It is oriented to exchanging data across organization boundaries, not just between applications within one company; and it offers a graphic interface which gives managers an intuitive means to define their own business processes, rather than providing them with a dictionary of standard business processes.

e-Speak and e-Services

A particularly interesting initiative came from Hewlett-Packard at the end of the 1990s. HP had had little impact in the e-business domain, relative to its general status as a company; it hoped that its e-Services idea might allow it to leapfrog over current activities to move e-commerce to a higher level of sophistication.

Computer scientists have been excited in recent years by a technique called *evolutionary computing*. Software to achieve tasks that may be too complex for human beings to program successfully is instead *evolved* through a Darwinian process in which populations of simple programs mutate randomly and are weeded out, or multiply, depending on how far they develop features approximating to the desired target. Hewlett-Packard's e-Services might be described as 'evolutionary computing meets e-business'.

The e-Speak half of the initiative is an offering comparable to Microsoft's BizTalk: a standard format allowing companies to exchange information on their products and services. As such it might be used independently of e-Services. But e-Services are a very novel vision. A useful commercial service is a complex structure which can be logically decomposed into several or many simple, generic services and electronic resources marshalled together in a specific way. An e-service is an electronic agent which represents one of those modular elements, and which can describe itself over the internet, using e-Speak, to other such agents in other ownership. It can advertise itself, discover complementary services or resources supplied by others, and agree bargains on behalf of its owner.

A human might assemble a group of e-services together manually into a structure capable of delivering a human-level, complex service. But, excitingly, the e-services can band together of their own accord to offer complex services, perhaps services different from anything a human has yet thought of. Peter Gloor (2000: 129) noted that

> HP hopes that entire ecosystems of e-services will grow and change
> dynamically as new e-services advertise their capabilities over the Net.

The internet could become not merely an arena where people can implement their business ideas, but an active participant generating new business ideas of its own.

Both sides of this Hewlett-Packard initiative have since become part of a larger, industry-wide development: what has come to be called *Web services*. This movement is in many eyes the Next Big Thing in e-business, and we shall examine it at some length in Chapter 10.

Conclusion

Many other more or less specialized enterprise applications could be discussed; but we should heed Joseph Langhauser's warning against undue proliferation. The foregoing is perhaps enough to give the reader a sense of the possibilities that are available to an e-business, at the beginning of the 21st century.

10
XML and Web services

A revolutionary formalism

The structured data representation language XML – *Extensible Markup Language* – is suddenly everywhere. What kind of system is it exactly, and why is it so important?

This book has aimed to avoid technical detail in favour of explaining the business logic of various IT innovations. With XML, we need to go just a little further than normal into technicalities, to show the reader how a particular formal electronic 'language' is different enough from everything that came before it that it may have the potential to revolutionize e-business.

Electronic data interchange and its shortcomings

XML is a new kind of solution to an existing function, *electronic data interchange* (EDI). For many decades, computers were seen by the business world as tools to execute various business-internal processes efficiently, but not as communication devices. What moved from company to company up and down value chains, apart from goods themselves, was paperwork – documentation that may have been generated with the help of computers, but was exchanged physically or by fax, and was handled by recipients largely manually. In due course, though, physical paperwork began to give way to EDI. A company would order goods from a supplier, say, via an electronic purchase order in a standardized coded format, rather than via a sheet of paper designed to be read by a human.

In most business sectors the shift to EDI is itself surprisingly recent, and by no means complete. Robert Johnston, Horace Mak, and Sherah Kurnia (2001: 236) still present as a currently ongoing 'paradigm shift' the change in perception 'from the earlier vision of computers as intelligent logic engines (to be applied to problem solving and planning), to a view of computers as a medium for communication and co-ordination between parties and business transactions'. For many small companies, moving from manual to EDI systems would involve costs that are difficult for them to afford, even if they would like to make the transition. In intensely creative sectors such as the fashion industry, where there is naturally a degree of general resistance to computerization, communication between firms seems to be the area where the new technology is least welcome.

EDI developed as a service provided to client businesses by so-called 'value-added network' companies over privately-owned wide area networks (WANs). Electronic files of different types (for instance purchase order, or shipment notice) that are generated by a company's own established systems are translated into an EDI format which is standard within a given industry, before being transmitted over the wide area network. EDI in this sense is very much a going concern. In November 2002 one firm of business analysts was predicting annual growth of over 15 per cent in expenditure by European companies on EDI over the next few years.

However, EDI technology is starting to look like an evolutionary dead end. There are two problems about it. One is that using proprietary networks is expensive, when the internet is available as a cheap alternative communication channel. The deeper problem is that the system of holding data in individual company file formats and translating between these and various industry standard formats is inherently inflexible and unrobust.

It is with respect to that problem that XML is increasingly being adopted as a preferable solution. XML was not originally created to be a general solution to the commercial data interchange problem, but it is rapidly being turned into that.

The limitations of EDI were mentioned in Chapter 9, in connexion with RosettaNet. Although XML and RosettaNet might both be seen in the e-business context as 'alternatives to EDI', they are very different kinds of thing. RosettaNet does something akin to giving a community of experts an agreed technical terminology, as the 18th-century botanist Linnaeus provided scientific names for plants so that botanists everywhere could exchange data unambiguously. XML does something more like giving humanity the English language as a general structure, so that anyone can talk to anyone about anything, slotting in whatever technical terminology is needed for a specific topic.

Problems about file-format details are surely familiar to anyone who has worked with computer files. Take the case of personnel files which record, say, an employee's name, age, annual salary, and date of recruitment. In one computing environment, these data might be encoded in fixed-field records in one sequence, perhaps as (using b to represent the blank-space character):

```
bbbbbbJOHNbBROWNb25bbbb24975.50b19980903
```

while another environment might represent the identical information in variable-length fields demarcated by separator characters and arranged in a different sequence, say as:

```
JOHNbBROWN#24975.50#3bSEPb1998#25##
```

When data such as these have to be moved from one environment to another, there have to be routines for translating between formats. (The example uses personnel data because they are easy to think about; data exchanged between companies along value chains will be about goods rather than about employees, but the same problems arise.) The translation systems require expensive effort to devise and maintain, and there is plenty of room for files to become corrupted. Even in contexts where no translation between alternative formats is involved, we all know how easy it is for data like these to lose, say, the first or the last byte from each record in the course of being copied into a program input stream, leading to errors whose cause can be difficult to track down. And where data are translated between formats, quite minor oversights can easily lead to, say, part of the salary field being mistakenly treated as the age field, again requiring expensive debugging.

The XML alternative

XML offers a way round these difficulties.

By defining a common format usable for any categories of data, it cuts out the need for translation between formats. Because a worldwide community of workers in different fields are all using essentially the same data-encoding format, it is possible to develop an apparatus of support, such as user-interface software, having a level of sophistication and convenience that would not be economically practical for the various individual formats involved in the earlier approach to EDI.

But also, XML files *define their own meaning*, so that it becomes much harder for one field to be confused with another. And perhaps most important of all, XML files *define their own structure*: they are in a sense self-validating. If a byte accidentally gets lost, it will normally make the file not merely incorrect, but actually inconsistent with itself, so that the error is immediately detectable by a machine using the file.

XML is not yet a fully stable system – at the time of writing it is still evolving. And it is probably fair to say that XML does not offer a perfect solution to all the problems that arise in practice. (Systems which are invented for one purpose and end up adapted for various other purposes usually are not ideal.) In the present context, though, the relevant point is that XML is rapidly being accepted as a de facto standard. Even if it were possible to devise some alternative system which in principle might constitute a superior solution to the problems of electronically interchanging business data, in practice XML has already won.

It would be well beyond the scope of this book to give a comprehensive introduction to XML. But the reader will want to know in general terms what *kind* of system XML is, and in the broadest outline how it achieves what it does. On the face of it, the idea of one global standard format that is usable for representing any genre of data sounds contradictory. Surely the chief reason why different sectors of business have evolved separate EDI formats is because they need to encode different categories of information? Precisely so; yet, by moving to a higher level of generality, XML covers the data-encoding needs of diverse industries, and of all kinds of organizations that are not businesses at all, within a single framework.

XML, HTML, SGML

Unfortunately, there is a large practical problem in explaining how XML works: namely, virtually all IT students are familiar with HTML (*Hypertext Markup Language*), the format in which Web pages are encoded. When one begins to look at XML, it seems so similar to HTML that it is hard to avoid the trap of taking XML to be a sister language to HTML. XML looks like 'HTML made difficult', because the parallels with HTML are obvious but one soon encounters non-HTML features whose point is not so apparent at first sight.

For present purposes, it is a nuisance that HTML is so well known, because in the world of markup languages HTML is the strange odd-man-out. Thinking about HTML is likely to be a hindrance, not a help, in grasping how XML works. But most readers will be thinking about HTML anyway, so at various points I shall spell out the contrasts explicitly.

In fact, the easiest way to approach XML is not directly but via yet another acronym, SGML – *Standard Generalized Markup Language*. Historically, SGML was created in the 1980s as a very general model within which one could define data-description languages for different types of data, each appropriately adapted to its own domain, but all sharing sufficient family resemblance to permit various software utilities to be developed once for all to apply to the whole family, rather than having to be developed separately for the separate family members. XML is a revised version of SGML which tightens up the family resemblance, disallowing large swaths of hypothetical data-description systems that count formally as valid SGML systems, while still keeping enough flexibility to include anything that someone might realistically want to use. HTML, on the other hand, is something like a particular one of the huge family of data-description languages allowed by SGML: one designed to describe World Wide Web pages rather than, say, orders for engine parts. But most versions of HTML are not really even that; their conformance to the rules of SGML is more cosmetic than real. In order to appreciate the essence of XML, in computing terms it is vital to think of it as 'SGML– –', not as 'HTML++'.

That is the route we shall take: first outlining the basics of SGML, then saying a little about how XML differs from SGML.

The need for consistent structure

SGML (Goldfarb 1990) has been an ISO standard since 1986. It was created by the publishing industry, which needed a technique for representing complex documents in electronic form in ways that allowed *consistent structuring* to be enforced mechanically throughout long documents, and which made a clear distinction between the *functional* or logical aspects of document structure, and the *formal*, graphical properties with which different structural elements were rendered on paper.

As an illustration, think of a dictionary. A printed dictionary consists largely of a sequence of *entries* for successive headwords. So for instance the entry for the word 'train' in a small hypothetical dictionary might look something like the following (I am sure a good dictionary compiler could come up with more precise definitions than these, but I am deliberately keeping things simple):

> **train** [trAn]
>> noun   (1) set of railway carriages making a scheduled journey
>>   (*I'll miss my train*)
>>   (2) part of bride's dress
>> verb   to acquire a skill through practice

This entry uses variation of type and layout in order to show how the different parts of the entry fit into a logical structure in which different elements serve different functions. That logical structure might be spelled out in the form of a labelled tree shape, as in Figure 10.1. For instance, the fact that 'I'll miss my train' is an *example* rather than a *definition* is shown in the printed entry by setting it in italics and between a pair of brackets.

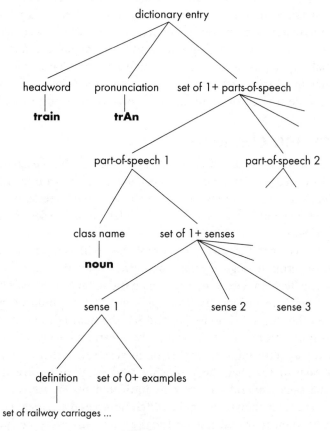

Figure 10.1

Figure 10.1 is intended to suggest not just the structure of the specific entry for 'train', but the full range of allowable entry structures for words in this dictionary. For instance, the word 'train' can be interpreted as either of two 'parts of speech' – it can be a noun ('a train') or a verb ('to train thoroughly') – but, in general, an entry may contain subentries for any number of different parts of speech from one upwards; some English words represent three or more parts of speech. Each entry must have at least one part-of-speech subentry: an entry which consisted just of a headword with a pronunciation but nothing more would be senseless. On the other hand, definitions may be accompanied by any number of examples from zero upwards. It is quite reasonable to quote a definition without giving an example of the word in the respective use, and two of the three definitions in the specimen entry for 'train' have no illustrative examples with them.

In the context of business IT, dictionaries are an unusual category of document. But a dictionary entry makes a good illustration of the ideas underlying markup languages, because dictionary entries contain a fair amount of structure in compact form. Other, more ordinary document types will have their own structures, though the lowest-level structural elements may be long paragraphs of text, so that it is less easy to demonstrate an example within a brief space. A company's range of user manuals, for instance, might each consist of a title, a preface, a table of contents, and one or more chapters each consisting of a chapter title, a summary, and a set of one or more sections each beginning with a subheading (and so forth). Outside the field of publishing, a business document such as a purchase order will similarly have a predictable logical structure, with elements such as delivery address, required to include street name and number, town name, and postcode.

Structures and elements

With SGML, the material dominated by any node in a tree structure such as Figure 10.1 is called an *element*. An element may contain character data (a dictionary definition, for instance, will be a string of characters), or child elements (a *part-of-speech* element contains a *className* element and a set of *sense* elements), or a mixture of both.

It is easy to see that the dictionary publisher will want to store information about words in terms of logical structure rather than in terms of their graphic rendering. In the file from which our specimen dictionary entry was generated, 'I'll miss my train' needs to be labelled 'example', not 'italics'. Italics may well also be used for some other logical function(s); and for the next edition of the dictionary, the book designer might decide it would be clearer or more attractive to mark examples by roman lettering in a smaller point size, say, rather than by italics.

It is also easy to see that the publisher will want to ensure that all entries conform to the same general structure as indicated by Figure 10.1. If the 'train' entry has the structure shown above, in which numbered senses are grouped under parts of speech, then it would not do for the 'try' entry, say, to have a different structure:

try [trI]

    1. <u>noun</u>   an attempt

    2. <u>noun</u>   rugby goal

    3. <u>verb</u>   to attempt

– where different senses are simply listed one after another, with no grouping together of the successive noun senses. That might be a reasonable structure for entries in another dictionary, but any one document or series of related documents should choose one structure and stick to it. People who use complex documents (dictionaries, user manuals, or any other category) need consistency of structure, if they are to avoid confusion. If the documents are large and complex, then that consistency needs to be mechanically enforced. It would be near-impossible for human beings to achieve complete consistency throughout a document as complicated as a dictionary by purely manual means.

Document Type Definitions

The solution to this is called in XML-speak a *Document Type Definition* (DTD). A DTD is a formal specification of what counts as a structurally-valid document of some particular genre. A linguist might call a DTD a 'grammar' for a document-type; it specifies what structural properties a file has to have in order to count as a document of that type.

A dictionary publisher might use a Document Type Definition which specifies that an electronic file representing a dictionary must have a structure like Figure 10.1: it must comprise a series of *entries*, in which each entry contains exactly one *headword*, one *pronunciation*, and one or more *parts-of-speech*; a headword might be specified as any sequence of character data, while a part-of-speech is a *className* followed by one or more *senses*; and so forth.

All this, and further details about the properties a file must have in order to count as a valid dictionary, are stated in a standard format. In the default case, an SGML (or XML) document will be a file that begins with a copy of its own DTD, before going on to include the tree structure of the individual document, coded as a linear sequence of characters. Linearization is done in the way familiar from HTML; a nonterminal node labelled xyz is represented as a pair of 'brackets', <xyz> and </xyz>, surrounding whatever the node dominates. Thus, Figure 10.2 shows part of the character-sequence corresponding to the entry structure of Figure 10.1.

A document does not have to contain the substance of its DTD; in place of that, it may alternatively contain a reference to a file elsewhere which contains that DTD and is assumed to be available to anyone dealing with the document. Either way, someone who receives the document gets the information he needs to check that it is a valid example of the structural class of document which it purports to represent, and he gets a classification of the contents in terms of the meaningful names of the element-types.

```
...  <entry><headword>train</headword><pronunciation>trAn</pronunciation>
<partOfSpeech><className>noun</className>... ... </entry> ...
```

Figure 10.2

A program which checks the conformance of an SGML or XML file to its Document Type Definition is called a *parser*. An SGML parser enables one to check that a document has a valid structure, and to locate elements of interest within a complex file: for instance, one could tell a parser to pick out all the word-pronunciations and print them between square brackets (conventionally used to indicate phonetic notation).

Document Type Definitions and parsers liberate us from the dependence on surface details of file structure that are unavoidable with traditional EDI. Provided the structure of a file as defined by the DTD represents its contents accurately, physical aspects of its format (for instance use of whitespace characters or incidence of linebreaks) are irrelevant. Even the sequencing of elements may often be unimportant: a DTD may say something like 'each employee has an age and a salary, in either order' – an application using such a file will look for the tags it needs, it will not look (as a traditional EDI application might) for 'the three bytes immediately following the surname field', say.

Different kinds of document will contain elements of different types. A dictionary publisher may need to define a pronunciation element; a publisher of cookery books will have no use for that, but may need recipe and ingredient elements, say. Some kinds of element will be very widely useful and will tend to receive standard names: for instance very many document-types include 'paragraph' elements, and conventionally (as in HTML) these are tagged <p> ... </p>. But they do not have to be: nothing would stop some SGML user defining a DTD using <para> ... </para>, if he preferred. Other element-types may be highly specialized and relevant only to one particular organization. SGML does not specify the element-types available to users. A Document Type Definition can be defined to include any kind of elements one chooses to dream up, and SGML simply provides a general framework for defining element-types and the structures of documents containing them.

The flexibility that derives from elements and Document Type Definitions being user-definable meant that in the world of documentation, SGML quickly became a standard, used to encode everything 'from transcriptions of ancient Irish manuscripts to the technical documentation for stealth bombers, and from patients' clinical records to musical notation'.[1] SGML potentially defines a vast family of different document formats, each with its own DTD containing specific element-types relevant to that genre.

SGML versus HTML

HTML might be seen as one member of that SGML family – a member that has element-types such as <a> for 'anchor', <image>, and so forth, which are useful for defining Web pages rather than ancient Irish MSS or stealth bomber construction.

But HTML is a very unrepresentative member of the SGML family, if it is a member at all. In particular, the Document Type Definition concept, which is crucial for SGML, does not apply to HTML. HTML files do not contain DTDs; indeed (for most if not all versions of HTML) there is no DTD which *could* in principle be included in Web page files.

This fact tends to be hidden from the average user by the way HTML manuals are worded. They explain tag usage with remarks along lines such as:

DL element: glossary lists
  Can contain: DT, DD
  Can be inside: BLOCKQUOTE, BODY, DD, FORM, LI

1. Quoted from the XML FAQ, www.ucc.ie/xml/faq.xml

When reading material like this, it is easy to suppose that the remarks for the various elements add up between them to a fully specified Document Type Definition defining the class of all and only those files which count as valid HTML; the only reason why the DTD as a whole is not shown in the manual is that readers absorb it more easily in bite-sized chunks. But in reality there is no Document Type Definition. The definitions of elements are too loose to add up to a precise formal specification; the only definition of 'valid HTML document' (for most HTML versions) is 'any file that an HTML browser succeeds in rendering on screen in the way intended'.

The looseness of HTML is necessary, because Web pages are commonly hand-composed. It is often said that the majority of pages on the Web contain errors of HTML grammar; browsers like Explorer and Netscape are as tolerant as possible. For instance, in principle every open-paragraph tag <p> ought to be balanced by a close-paragraph tag </p>, but browsers happily render files in which the close-paragraph tags are missing; many HTML users routinely leave them out. Because the structure of Web pages is essentially simple, this looseness works. SGML, on the other hand, is designed for use in professional contexts where document structure is so diverse and complex that it would not be practical to tolerate any looseness. An SGML file with one required tag omitted is junk.

Another difference between HTML and SGML has to do with formal versus functional properties of documents. The essence of SGML is about defining the *logical* – or 'functional' – structure of documents, leaving it to publishers and printers on particular occasions to choose how to render the logical properties visually. Early versions of HTML were similar. For instance they contained a tag <em> for 'emphasized' but not a tag <i> for 'italics': most browsers use italics in order to render emphasis, but that is the browser's rather than the HTML writer's choice. When the Web morphed from an academic into a largely commercial tool, this was unsatisfactory to the business community, who demanded the ability to control every detail of the way their companies present themselves to the world – so newer versions of HTML have increasingly come to contain tags referring to physical properties of Web page rendering, defining things such as particular typefaces, type sizes, and colours.

XML versus SGML

SGML has been a universal standard for documentation since the 1980s. The more recent arrival of XML was linked to the realization that documents are not the only bodies of complex data which it would be useful to be able to exchange in a self-defining, self-validating format. XML is used for exchanging business (and other) data files which in many cases never have been and never will be read by human beings.

Arguably, XML should be seen as a relaunched SGML rather than a different system. The formal differences are less far-reaching than the switch in area of application, from documentation in particular to structured data in general.

Some formal differences relate to minor tidying up of SGML syntax. A larger difference is that XML reins back much unnecessary generality in the definition of

SGML. For instance, in SGML angle brackets are no more than default choices for the characters marking the beginning and end of an element tag. The user is free to choose whichever two characters he pleases, and SGML gives him a way of declaring his choices within a Document Type Definition. Only, no-one ever chooses any characters other than the defaults; there is never a reason to do so. Consequently, in XML, tags *must* begin and end with < ... >, and there is no machinery for declaring alternative choices.

More significant than these differences is the fact that XML allows file-validity definitions to be explicit about things that cannot be stated in an SGML Document Type Definition. At the bottom of a tree structure, all that a DTD can say about a leaf node is that it contains character data – in the publishing world from which SGML emerged, that is enough. But XML has a system of 'Schemas' as an alternative to DTDs for defining the properties of valid files, and an XML Schema can specify data-types which leaf elements are required to belong to. For instance, a Schema might define a `<salary>` ... `</salary>` element whose content is required to be, say, a positive number not greater than ten million.

Thus XML has cut the link with the publishing world and, since the late 1990s, it has been the obvious choice of format for defining and exchanging *any* class of structured data, numerical and/or qualitative. Catalogues, accountancy data, orders and billing notification, stock inventories – you name it: any kind of business data is grist to the XML mill. The speed of its adoption has been explosive.

Limitations of XML

Some observers urge caution. David Linthicum (2001: 269) remarks 'The hype around XML threatens to turn us all into wide-eyed kids at a carnival'. The specific point which Linthicum sees as in danger of being overlooked is that the existence of XML as a universally-accepted data format does not in itself solve the problem of linking separate legacy B2B applications whose inputs or outputs were defined independently of one another. In the past, such collections of applications were integrated via middleware systems, drawing on standards such as CORBA – Common Request Broker Architecture. The decision to adopt XML does not magically make the problems solved by middleware vanish:

> You or your vendor must provide the technology to move the XML documents from application to application. You or your vendor must make any necessary changes to your source and target applications so that they can consume and produce XML. (Linthicum 2001: 270–1)

Another drawback of the XML approach is that it massively increases the bulk of a file encoding a given body of data. Traditional EDI often used binary files. With XML, everything is text-based (even a datum which can take only the two values 'yes' or 'no' is represented not as a single bit but, minimally, as a whole byte, perhaps 'y' versus 'n'); and the data themselves are interspersed with numerous markup tags. In consequence, the size of a file can easily be twenty times larger than it would be in a pre-XML environment, or more. In many circumstances, size matters.

There is also a problem that XML assumes that any kind of complex data can logically be structured as a tree. In real life there are cases where an element belongs simultaneously to separate logical hierarchies, and XML provides only kludgy mechanisms to deal with this.

Nevertheless, the advantages of the XML concept are so manifest, and so widely exploitable, that the technology is here to stay even if not perfect. XML may not do the whole job of integrating independent legacy applications; but it is so desirable to be able to move data from application to application in a self-defining and self-validating rather than opaque and ad hoc format, that it will often justify the overhead of translating between XML and applications' native formats. File size does sometimes matter, but as the capacity of computing equipment continues to grow it matters less. And exceptions to the tree-structure assumption are probably marginal in the business context.

In the world of IT, no solutions last for ever. No doubt XML will eventually make way for some superior approach to data encoding. But it seems overwhelmingly likely that this will be a language that evolves out of XML as we know it today, rather than an unrelated system.

The arrival of Web services

The creation of XML has led to a burgeoning of applications that would have been impractical without it. So far as e-business is concerned, the most important of these areas is almost certainly *Web services*.

At the start of 2002, the phrase 'Web services' was little known. By the end of that year, it had moved to the top of the agenda – research by *Computing* magazine (19 Dec 2002) found that Web services was second only to security as a hot issue for IT managers and financial directors. When a buzzword emerges as suddenly as this, the natural suspicion is that we are dealing with hype. This suspicion is reinforced when we notice that commentators find it hard to say exactly what the new phrase means. Laura DiDio, senior analyst with the Yankee Group, remarks 'no-one seems able to come up with a clear definition';[2] according to William Oellermann (2001: 14), 'Depending on whom you ask, you could get any number of answers to the question "What is the definition of a Web service?"' But, though there is hype about (in IT, when is there ever not?), nevertheless the consensus is that Web services really are potentially big, perhaps the Next Big Thing not merely for e-business but for IT in general.

Alan Jebson, IT director for the HSBC banking group, comments 'I'm a technology cynic. I've been in this business long enough to have watched it over-promise and under-deliver for ... years, so I immediately treat any hype as just that'; yet he nevertheless says 'The last great technology breakthrough was the relational database ... Web services could be in the same category. I really do believe it will be revolutionary'.[3]

2. Quoted in *Computing*, 24 Oct 2002.
3. Quoted in *Computing*, 12 Sep 2002.

If there is even a plausible prospect that Web services may turn out to be as significant an innovation as relational database technology, then clearly it merits coverage here. The December 2002 *Computing* survey already referred to found that, at that date, a majority of companies polled were already pursuing a Web services project.

So what is Web services? (Or, 'What are Web services?' – but people are tending to treat the overall topic as a singular, with the separate services representing diverse instances of the topic.) We have heard that no-one can define the concept clearly, but let us try.

Web services defined

At present, the Web is essentially about publishing documents to (human) users. The data moving from site to site across the Web are almost entirely data concerned with graphic presentation of Web pages to human eyeballs. To some extent, website visitors' responses are captured as inputs to site owners' software; downloaded Web pages never function as program input.

The essence of the Web services concept is to use the simple, standardized communication technology of the World Wide Web to allow software programs at unrelated websites to provide input to one another.

Here we see why XML is crucial. The Web as we know it only became possible because HTML offered a universal standard for computers at sites having no prior relationship with one another to exchange documentation in the expectation that it would be rendered as a meaningful display at the other end. Likewise, it is XML – as a universally-recognized format for data that defines its own structure and content – which creates the possibility of computers that 'don't know each other' nevertheless sending one another usable program input.

Oellermann illustrates the potential of the concept by inviting us to imagine a businessman returning to the airport to get home after a work trip; because of unforeseen traffic hold-ups, he begins to realize that he is going to miss his flight. If he carries on regardless, perhaps there will be a later flight available; but perhaps the next flight is tomorrow morning, and he ought instead to focus on finding a hotel room for the night. If so, he would have various special requirements – say, he would need a data line for his work, and he would want a room that is set aside for non-smokers. Sorting all this out would take a number of separate mobile-phone calls – or website visits, assuming he has wireless internet access. Meanwhile, what should he say to the taxi-driver?

How much simpler if he could visit just one website and let its systems sort everything out, with the airline's site negotiating with hotel sites as required. That is the kind of thing that Web services will make possible.

Why is this new?

Is the scenario just outlined not possible already with current technology? Well, even if technically feasible, in practice it is not happening. A crucial step in understanding why people are so excited by the Web services concept is to analyse why the things it promises to do cannot be done by the systems we are familiar with. Oellermann describes how, in 1999, he found himself puzzling out why he was not seeing an explosive rush to B2B automation, comparable to the rush to build company websites that had already occurred. In principle, the economic advantages of B2B automation were manifest. Why was progress so sedate, relative to what happened with the Web?

One barrier was technical. Building a simple initial website requires mainly understanding of HTML, which Oellermann rightly describes as 'one of the easiest technologies for non-technical people to pick up', and visiting a website needs no technical skill at all – whereas B2B automation requires business expertise, to grasp the detailed logic of the transactions to be automated, and also IT expertise, to implement systems in an environment where there were few high-level standards, so every detail had to be decided ad hoc.

But the other, very significant barrier was political. Even when partner organizations are on an equal footing, achieving detailed collaboration and agreement between people working at different sites for separate employers is always massively harder and more time-consuming than when the individuals concerned work in a face to face situation; that is just a fact of life. In this case, perhaps more importantly, the technology was making it hard for B2B partners to relate to one another equally even if they wanted to.

One might think that active collaboration should not be necessary in order to use Web communication infrastructure for providing input to software. The Web does not physically insist that agents accessing it must be human beings. Nothing prevents someone setting up a program which downloads Web pages and uses the information contained in them as software inputs. Nothing, except that it would not work. Web pages are fluid. Their design and contents are frequently changed, in order to make them more appealing or more useful, and they rely on visitors' human intelligence to interpret the graphically-rendered HTML files and pick out the wanted information from places on a page which may well have altered since that individual's last visit. As Oellermann puts it, a program designed to extract data from an airline's website might well find, after the next tweak to the site, that it was receiving information on a flight departing at b>07 rather than 0748.

So it will not work to treat a website set up for presenting information in human-usable form as a source of software input. Of course, an airline website could help visitors find hotel rooms by treating hotel websites as they are designed to be treated: that is, by including links on the airline website that take the visitor to the hotels' sites. But that would not be very satisfactory either for the airline (no company wants to encourage visitors to its site to leave for other sites) or for the visitor – in Oellermann's scenario he would still be making the Web-equivalent of separate phone calls (if his hotel requirements are very specific or the hotels are full, maybe many calls), though with the minor advantage of having each calling partner 'dial the next number' for him. Suppose tomorrow's flight is delayed for some reason: the airline will have no way of sending a message to the traveller's hotel to tell him that he can take longer than planned over breakfast – the airline has no way of knowing whether one of the hotel website links it offered led to a room booking.

The airline could collaborate with a range of local hotels to develop a jointly-owned website. This might solve the problems of the last paragraph, but in a way that the companies would find unappealing. Within such a consortium it is inevitable that content relating to one company's business will often have to reside on a server owned or physically controlled by another consortium member, so updating content in the normal way will involve the large time-and-effort overheads of inter-organization collaboration: the companies will see themselves as surrendering ultimate control over core aspects of their own businesses. And an arrangement like this would be inflexible. Adding another hotel to the airline's offerings could only happen after successful completion of negotiations to admit the new member to the consortium, with its various arrangements for sharing legal, financial, and operating responsibilities. Contrast that with a case where an airline offers benighted travellers a printed list of local hotels: a new hotel advertises its details to all comers, and if the airline wants to add it to the list it just does so, with no hassle. (In practice, an airline might well make a deal with hotels that want to be included on its list – but it does not need to.)

Web gurus may spot other methods that might be adapted to address the airline/hotel problem using standard Web technology, but Oellermann (2001: 7) sees all such methods as 'simply techniques of "faking it" that may meet certain requirements but are not true enablers for application integration'. The Web is a technology invented for one purpose, and there is a limit to how far it can be forced to serve a quite separate purpose.

Machine shall speak unto machine

What Web services offers is an approach to integrating different organizations' applications that exploits those aspects of Web technology which remain relevant to the new goal (the communication channel linking unrelated agents, and the concept of a universally-accepted markup language), but marries them to new technologies, including XML, to handle aspects of the new tasks which go beyond exchange of documentation.

Thus, in the near future, the traveller will visit the airline website and discover that his next available flight is on the following day. The site will offer a hotspot with a legend such as Find me a hotel room; clicking on this will not cause the traveller's browser to move to a hotel's website – instead, it will cause software on the airline's server to exchange XML files over the internet with various hotel servers. After asking the traveller about his specific requirements the airline server will look for a suitable vacancy, make a reservation when one is found, and report back to the traveller accordingly. Airline and hotel both know about the transaction; if the next day's flight is delayed, it is a simple matter for the airline's system to ask the hotel's system to pass a message to the traveller. When a new hotel opens for business, it will add details about its Web-based reservation system to the public Web services register. Airlines will be free to add it to the list of sites that their site negotiates with when someone clicks the Find me a room button.

The public register – the 'phone book for Web services' – is already being developed, by an industry-wide consortium called UDDI, *Universal Description,*

Discovery and Integration.[4] UDDI was launched in 2001; it is developing an electronic resource which companies looking for trading partners can search, as one uses Google or AltaVista to search the Web. What the UDDI register returns, though, will not be a list of URLs related in relevant or irrelevant ways to the user's search terms. It will be a list of entries constructed in a standard format by companies offering Web services, including elements such as business names and contact details intended for human consumption, but also metadata specifying the interfaces of resources intended for access by machine.

The airline/hotel scenario is just an example, but it hardly makes sense to ask in general what range of tasks Web services could be used to address. That would be like asking what a computer can be programmed to do: the answer is 'anything that can be stated as a well-defined algorithm'. A markup language that allows data files to define their own structure and content introduces the possibility of migrating this degree of application diversity from the level of processes executed within single organizations, to the level of processes executed jointly by organizations that need not have a prior relationship with one another.

XML does not magically eliminate every problem of inter-organization application integration. But it does reduce these problems to proportions that look manageable by players which would previously have been daunted at the prospect of getting involved in B2B automation.

Standards and security

Agreeing to use XML as the data definition format is only a small part of the spectrum of agreements on standards that need to be in place before Web services becomes a routine reality. Standards are one of the chief problems at present for this technology. A Web Services Interoperability Organization ('WS-I') was established by a consortium of major software companies in February 2002 to address the standards area; seven months later, it had identified 200 issues to be resolved.

For instance, Web services needs an agreed object-sharing protocol – a system sitting between HTTP (Hypertext Transfer Protocol) as a low-level communication protocol, and the XML objects themselves which are to be accessed by different organizations' processes. The solution which is emerging (see for example, Coyle 2002: 124ff.) is SOAP (Simple Object Access Protocol). SOAP decouples Web services from particular communication software: a SOAP packet may be delivered via HTTP, but it may equally be delivered to a file system via FTP, or to a mailbox via SMTP. The specification for SOAP 1.0 was released in 1998, and (after more companies joined the consortium developing it) SOAP 1.1 was published as a Note by the World Wide Web Consortium in 2000. In August 2003 specifications for SOAP, UDDI, and other necessary elements were launched as a unified package of standards under the name WS-I Basic Profile 1.0.

The other big problem about Web services is security. This scarcely needs spelling out. Putting it bluntly: if unrelated organizations' computers are going to be interacting and running each other's software with their own inputs, then who

---

4. See the *UDDI Executive White Paper*, 14 Nov 2001, epilicae.notlong.com

knows what they may be saying or doing to one another? The fact that SOAP is text-based (unlike the corresponding protocols for earlier enterprise application integration techniques such as CORBA, which were binary) is an advantage with respect to security: text-based communication is more humanly-transparent and hence easier to control. Nevertheless, security must be a major concern in any real-life deployment of Web services.

J2EE and .Net

The WWW, XML, and SOAP provide the infrastructure for the communications aspect of Web services. Before this communications infrastructure can be exploited for serious industrial applications, platforms must be available to the participants for managing their dealings with the environment of other participants. Such a platform needs to support 'the four pillars of Web-based e-business: messaging, transactions, security, and identity' (Coyle 2002: 12).

At present there are two solutions available: J2EE (Java 2 Enterprise Edition), developed by a consortium including Sun, IBM, Hewlett-Packard, Oracle, and others; and Microsoft's .Net ('dot-Net'). J2EE is a specification for constructing enterprise applications, which can be implemented somewhat differently by different vendors (it was originally created for traditional websites, and has been extended to support Web services). On the other hand .Net is more of a finished product: a complete enterprise architecture designed for compatibility with the Windows operating system.

Whether J2EE and .Net should be seen as rivals competing for dominance in the new field is open to question. Many do see them in that light, and in Britain currently rather more Web services projects are using J2EE than .Net. But quite a number of projects are using a mixture of both. James Hall (global managing partner for technology, Accenture) sees J2EE and .Net as complementary rather than in competition, with different features suitable for different tasks. According to Hall, 'There is only one architecture for Web services and that is to use both J2EE and .Net'. [5]

Conclusion

In 2003, the e-business world is poised on the brink. The infrastructure elements are all (just about) in place; it looks as though industrial-strength engagement with the potential of Web services is about to begin. It seems safe to predict that the face of e-business will change dramatically as a result. But it would be a foolish writer who tried to predict just what the changes will be, or how soon they will arrive.

---

5. Quoted by Colin Barker, 'IT managers start to wake up to Web services', *Computing* 19 Dec 2002.

11

Websites

A lost decade?

Many areas of technology discussed in this book will have been unfamiliar to a proportion of readers; but not websites. Everyone knows what a website is, and most readers will know at least something of HTML and the other technologies involved. (For a full survey of technical aspects of website construction, an excellent reference is Niederst 2001.) No-one needs persuading that in the context of e-business, websites matter.

One might imagine, then, that what makes a good website should be well established by now. That is far from true.

Jakob Nielsen is at present probably the world's best known expert on Web usability. He feels strongly about the poor quality of many business websites:

> We are emerging from a lost decade of user interface design. From 1993 to 2002 ... [p]ublic websites were often designed to be actively user-hostile and were dominated by self-serving messages and bloated fluff that made it very difficult for customers to find the answers to their questions. (Nielsen 2002: 6)

Nielsen sees this situation as beginning to improve, but with a long way to go. Commentators are sometimes surprised at how much less care companies take to project a favourable image on the Web relative to traditional channels. Adrian Porter, introducing a report published in January 2003 surveying the home pages of the UK's top hundred companies (the FTSE 100), found it

> staggering to see how fastidiously they protect their image in every way possible – from the cut of the CEO's suit, to the car he drives, to the hundreds of thousands they spend on their corporate literature, to the millions they spend on their corporate headquarters. Yet, when it comes to the Web, the way the world sees them, they seem happy to squander all that hard-earned benefit on an ill-thought-out, ill-designed and ill-executed mess.[1]

---

1. 'FTSE-100's Web sites are still "wallowing in mediocrity"', 5 Jan 2003, almulumb.notlong.com

The report assigns percentage scores to FTSE-100 home pages, ranging from 86.0 per cent for the National Grid down to 26.75 per cent for the clothing chain Next.

In assessing comments like Nielsen's and Porter's, we need to bear in mind that their authors earn their living through website consultancy. They have an interest in stressing the shortcomings of present-day corporate use of the Web. But these are not unsupported rants. They are overall conclusions based on painstaking, fact-filled surveys. Although websites have been so much more in the spotlight than any other aspect of e-business, ever since the internet was commercialized, we are only starting to learn what is needed for a website to function well.

Jakob Nielsen and Adrian Porter both referred to website 'design', but this word is ambiguous. Design can refer specifically to the graphic appearance of a site, but Nielsen would be the first to agree that there is a great deal more to constructing a good website than getting the look of it right. I shall use the term *website construction* to refer to all aspects of putting together a complex site which serves its intended purposes successfully. I shall reserve the word *design* for the visual, aesthetic properties of a site; design in this sense is one aspect of website construction, but not the only aspect.

The internet is a two-way communication channel. Most company sites ought not to limit themselves to displaying information; they should be portals through which customers and potential customers may be drawn into relationships to which both sides contribute. Jim Sterne (2000) offers an insightful survey of how the internet can be exploited as a customer service medium. This chapter will focus on the use of websites for communication from site owner to visitor, which is where the questions are specific to website technology rather than general business issues.

The state of the art

At the most basic level, because the Web is new there are still sometimes business problems that boil down to companies not genuinely seeing their websites as integral parts of their overall organization. The IT journalist David Neal has an entertaining anecdote of booking a package holiday online and finding, when he reached the resort and the booking proved problematic, that the tour rep did not perceive this as the company's responsibility.

> It was almost as though the Web site was a radical splinter group, an army of assorted, peeved package holidays that had banded together to mess people around. 'Oh, we've had problems with the Web site before,' he said, as though that would in some way explain the situation.[2]

A story like this is not unique. But by now it is probably an issue that is on the way out. A much more acute problem is companies that are anxious to embrace the new communication medium, but are going about it in ways that do not work very well.

That does not mean that this chapter will lay down rules for constructing good websites. As with most areas of business, there is no algorithm for success. The

---

2. David Neal, 'Postcard to Web site operators', *IT Week* 15 Jul 2002.

consultant Steve Krug writes 'I've been at this for ... long enough to know that there is no one "right" way to design Web sites' (Krug 2000: 7). But one can look at what works and what does not work on existing sites, and distil at least a range of considerations that are worth taking into account.

The numerical scores assigned to FTSE-100 home pages in the report quoted above were based on a series of criteria widely agreed to be significant. Ideally, one would like to find an objective, scientific basis for deciding what properties of a site are in fact most important, and checking automatically how far a given site embodies them. That will probably never be realistic.

It is easy to automate the checking of trivial issues such as broken links. A techie web expert might think of rating sites in terms of the extent to which they exploit the range of technical possibilities currently available – but there is general agreement among observers of e-commerce that the technical features of a site are among the least significant considerations in practice. Cutler and Sterne (2000) discuss a range of measures to assess the way that visitors interact with e-commerce sites. And there are interesting software offerings (for example, the WebEffective system from Keynote Systems, or various packages discussed by Sterne 2001) that aim to give deeper insight into site performance – for instance, by generating statistics on the tracks taken by site visitors. But, overall, website quality is too subjective an issue to quantify without drawing on human judgement.

Nevertheless, there are techniques for processing subjective judgements so as to derive quantitative measures which are more reliable than a random assortment of individuals' off-the-cuff reactions.

The WebQual technique

Particularly interesting is the WebQual technique developed by Stuart Barnes and Richard Vidgen.

The WebQual approach (for example, Barnes and Vidgen 2002) begins by using focus groups to brainstorm criteria that participants see as desirable in an e-commerce site. Respondents then use the resulting long list of qualities to score sites, and they score the criteria themselves for relative importance.

The raw results are then converted into more meaningful form through the statistical technique of *factor analysis*, which shows how far questionnaire items correlate with one another. Factor analysis uncovers a small number of *principal components* or factors which are real for the respondents; individual questionnaire items are shown to be close or less-close proxies for these underlying factors.

WebQual applied to online bookshops

Barnes and Vidgen illustrate the technique by using it to compare the sites of the three leading British online bookshops: Amazon.co.uk (launched in 1998 as the UK subsidiary of Amazon.com); the Internet Bookshop, owned by W. H. Smith and launched in 1993 – hence the oldest-established of the three; and Bertelsmann Online, launched in 1999 following acquisition by the German-based Bertelsmann media company of a 50 per cent share in BarnesandNoble.com.

The 22-item questionnaire derived from focus-group input was administered to 376 respondents, who were experienced internet users and book purchasers. One of the three sites was assigned at random to each respondent, who was asked to use it to find details on a particular book, and then to score it on the 22 scales. Factor analysis extracted five principal components from the scores for the 22 criteria. For instance, the four criteria 'It feels safe to complete transactions', 'My personal information feels secure', 'I feel confident that goods/services will be delivered as promised', and 'Has a good reputation' turned out all to be proxies (in decreasing order of closeness) for a single underlying factor, which Barnes and Vidgen call Trust. (Another type of statistical analysis established the inter-respondent reliability of the ratings.)

Figure 11.1 shows the spidergram (Barnes and Vidgen call it a 'radar chart') displaying the scores of the three sites on the five factors which emerged from factor analysis. (For the sake of legibility, the spidergram includes only the 0.4 to 1.0 section of the scales.)

The overall verdict is very clear in this case. The Internet Bookshop and Bertelsmann score similarly to each other; Amazon beats the other two on all factors, but in particular it outranks them head and shoulders on the Trust factor.

This is specially significant, since the data also show that respondents rank Trust as the most important of the five factors. The importance scores, expressed as percentages of the maximum possible score, are:[3]

Trust	83.2
Usability	82.8
Information	78.0
Design	60.5
Empathy	44.0

The lowest-ranked factor, Empathy, relates to criteria such as 'Conveys a sense of community' and 'Creates a sense of personalization'.

It is noteworthy that Design (in the narrow sense, i.e. graphic appearance) is ranked a good deal lower than the first three factors. Design is often seen as crucial by companies concerned with website construction. But there are two ways of visiting websites. Respondents in the WebQual experiment were actually *using* bookshop sites in order to execute tasks; they were not just 'surfing'. As Jared Spool put it in a classic study of website usability, 'When users surf, they are just browsing, clicking whatever looks most interesting or "cool," ... When looking for information, users are much more focused' (Spool et al. 1999: 12–13).

In the early years of the Web, 'Eyeballs ruled the day, and it didn't matter much whether users could actually accomplish anything' (Nielsen 2000: 7) – that is, businesses thought that what mattered about their site was simply attracting a high

---

3. For each of the five factors, the score shown is the weighted average of the mean importance scores assigned to the separate questionnaire items contributing to that factor. Barnes and Vidgen do not include this computation, but it is easy to carry out on the data they do include.

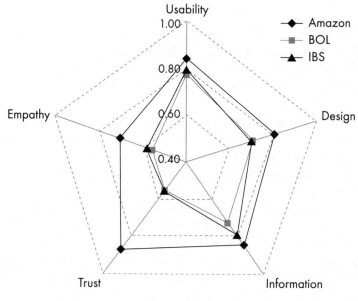

Figure 11.1

number of visitors. Various studies have suggested that attracting surfers, and attracting serious visitors, are not just distinct but actually conflicting goals. Mere surfers are not much use to a business. Relative to the visitors a business really wants to attract, Design is not the top priority.

Intertwined factors

The 2002 online-bookshop study is only an example. There is no guarantee that WebQual applied to a different domain would yield the same five factors with the same importance ranking. But the factors and their ranks emerged from the raw data, rather than being inserted into the data by the experimental design, so it is reasonable to hope that the outcome of another experiment might not be too different.

The principal factors identified in this case are of course closely intertwined. Graphic design may contribute to the trustworthy or untrustworthy impression created by a site; the way information is organized will be highly relevant to the usability of a site. But we cannot discuss everything at once; Barnes and Vidgen's five factors make a good list of headings for analysing what mankind has learned to date about good and bad practice in website construction. The Empathy factor relates to issues that were discussed in Chapter 8; the strikingly low importance value for this factor calls into question the ideas surveyed there about the business significance of 'virtual communities'. Remaining sections of this chapter will deal with various aspects of Trust, Usability, Information, and Design.

Trust

The single leading factor that emerged from the WebQual experiment was Trust. We have already discussed this topic at length in Chapter 4. There, though, we were concerned with the general topic of trust in e-business. There are more specific points to be made about how a website can promote or discourage trust between buyers and sellers.

At a basic level, the English must be impeccable. Young computer science students are often people lacking strong feelings for the niceties of their mother tongue; it can sometimes be hard for them to grasp how readily, for the average educated citizen, trust is destroyed by encountering a single spelling mistake or grammatically crippled sentence. Yet it is so. The text of a website is a company's interface with its potential clients; if the company cannot be bothered to get that correct, many Web users instinctively feel, why should we expect them to get right the more significant things that we have no immediate way of checking?

Another point about language which seems obvious but – judging by the wording of many current sites – apparently must not be obvious, is that trust is destroyed by hype. Of course a site owner would like visitors to believe that its offerings are 'stunning', or 'cool'. If you want visitors to believe it, don't say it. People are not stupid: they know words are cheap. If a site's wares really are good it should be possible to make objective, factual statements which carry an implication of good quality but leave it to the visitor to draw the implication. Factual statements, because they are so easy to challenge if false, are more believable.

A Web page is not an advertisement. Adverts are forced to 'shout' at potential viewers because they have to compete for attention with other adverts in a newspaper or magazine, or with their surroundings in the case of a poster. Someone who sees a Web page has made an active decision to visit it, if only through the minimal action of clicking on a link. In an open-air market, stallholders may shout their wares to attract passers-by, but after a potential customer has arrived the shouting changes to more normal talk. Hypey language in a Web page is like a stallholder who shouts at a customer who has already found his way to the stall.

Jakob Nielsen believes that websites foster trust through making available documentation which visitors rarely read, but want to know they *could* read. 'Even though you might think users care only about what your site can do for them and not about your company itself, experience shows that providing information about the company is one of the most trust-enhancing elements you can add' (Nielsen and Tahir 2002: 46). This includes information about the company's physical location and telephone number: the website may be intended to channel users towards making contact via e-mail, because it is cheaper for the company to respond to that than post or phone, but it is crucial that website visitors see that they *could* use those more physical and direct means of communication if need be.

Ultimately there is only so much one can give in terms of rules of thumb for making websites trustworthy, because the issue is not mainly about specific website features: it is about human character. If it were possible for a cynical businessman to say 'We've got our site functioning, now here is *N* thousand to spend on adding trustworthiness to it', what kind of trustworthiness would that be? Trust is something that emerges when those responsible for a site share an ethos of honest dealing. If the ethos is there, the website is likely to contain small, subtle clues to it which visitors may subconsciously pick up. But, paradoxically, the more well-defined these clues are, the less effective they will be – because they will be too easy to feign. Trustworthiness may be the most important single property of an e-commerce site, but it is also, necessarily, the least definable.

Usability: scope for improvement

The chief purpose of a corporate website is normally to enable visitors to find the answers to questions about the organization, its offerings, and whatever related topics it chooses to include. Many sites do not achieve this well. Jared Spool's classic website usability study of nine prominent websites found that

> Searching for information on web sites is an intensely frustrating experience. Throughout our study, we were amazed by the time and effort it took users to answer even simple questions. And repeatedly, users gave up without ever finding what they were looking for. Even in the smaller web sites, we watched users get lost or wander off the site without being aware of it. (Spool et al. 1999: 6–7)

It is not easy to quantify the return on putting effort into improving site usability, but Jakob Nielsen has attempted to do this, in a report co-authored with Shuli Gilutz released in January 2003. Nielsen and Gilutz examined 42 case studies of sites that were redesigned to make them more usable. The 'before' and 'after' versions of the sites were compared on a series of objective metrics: *conversion rate* (i.e. visitor becoming purchaser), visitor count, user performance/productivity, and use of specific (desired) features. Nielsen and Gilutz found that redesign led to average usability improvements ranging from 100 per cent for conversion rate to 202 per cent for use of specific features. They also found (from a far larger study) that current best practice is to spend only about ten per cent of a website development budget on usability. Nielsen infers that it would be worth spending much higher proportions.

The logic here is indirect. Nevertheless, Nielsen's findings do seem to imply that the usability aspects of website construction must be seen as more than an optional extra, which it is nice to get right if time is left over after the technical functioning of the site has been implemented.

Disagreements on usability

Unlike trust, usability sounds like an area where it should be possible to get reliable answers through objective experimentation. There have been many Web usability experiments; the Spool study was only one of the earliest well-known examples. Often, experiments have yielded surprising findings. One of Spool's findings, for instance, related to an important difference between assessing websites and assessing software packages – the latter being a longer-established art. With software, the packages users like best will be the packages they are capable of using most successfully. With websites, there is little correlation between likeability and usability. Spool's subjects said 'things like "I liked Disney, it seemed more interesting," even if they had gotten completely lost and failed to complete any of the tasks'.

However, experts who are aware of the experimental literature sometimes flatly disagree with one another about the value of basic website features.

Should a home page include a 'search this site' button, for instance? Nielsen (2000: 224) has examined the search behaviour of different users and feels that the answer is a clear yes. For him it seems 'Unbelievabl[e]' (Nielsen and Tahir 2002: 41) that 14 per cent of corporate home pages surveyed lack the feature. Louis Rosenfeld and Peter Morville (1998: 99–100), by contrast, urge that you should 'think twice before you make your site searchable', arguing that search engines are often 'bandages for sites with poorly designed *browsing* systems'.

Again, many writers stress the importance of using simple, succinct language. Nielsen (2000: 101) urges 'Write for scannability. Don't require users to read long continuous blocks of text; instead, use short paragraphs, subheadings, and bulleted lists'. But Spool measured text readability in terms of standard metrics that educationists have worked out to assess the difficulty level of documents. Startlingly, the *less* 'readable' a site was, the *more* usable it was for test subjects in practice, and the more useful, satisfying, clear, and authoritative they perceived it as being. Equally counterintuitively, the *more* whitespace in a site, the *less* successful users were at extracting information from it, and the lower ratings they gave it on criteria such as ease of use and overall appearance. (Spool concludes: 'When people are hunting for information, they benefit by covering a lot of ground quickly. Whitespace spreads out the information and slows the hunt.')

Test early and often

If experts can disagree as fundamentally as this, it seems unlikely that any set of general axioms will be adequate to guide website construction. There is no alternative to testing specific pages and sites and tuning them, or radically reorganizing them, in the light of test subjects' reactions. Fortunately, the testing process does not need to be elaborate. Steve Krug (2000) describes an informal régime of usability testing which can be carried out easily and cheaply and which delivers valuable results with tiny numbers of subjects. Tom Landauer and Jakob Nielsen (1993) have claimed that in practice it is not worth using more than five test subjects – though this is controversial: cf. Woolrych and Cockton (2001). Krug sees it as far more worthwhile to do repeated light-touch usability testing at an early stage in site construction, when test findings have the best chance of influencing the development of the site, than to do more formal tests at a later stage.

Areas of agreement

While there are surprising disagreements on some usability issues, there are also important areas of consensus.

One of the most important relates to what Nielsen somewhat immodestly calls 'Jakob's Law': 'users spend most of their time on *other* sites than your site' (Nielsen and Tahir 2002: 37). The implication is that, whenever conventions on navigation or page layout have emerged, they should be followed – 'users say different is bad, so only do new things if they are going to be substantially better.'[4] A departure from convention might in some cases seem to permit a better, more logical page structure, and in the abstract it might indeed be better; but visitors have no time to learn special routines for using individual sites, so the abstract gain in logical structure would have to be huge to justify departing from an existing convention.

Steve Krug (2000) and Nielsen and Tahir (2002: 52–3) give handy checklists of conventions which have emerged to date, for example, where on the home page to place a Help button (top right, but only if it is really needed).

Naturally, since the Web is so new, potential conventions have not finished jelling. Writing a few years ago, Krug believed he had detected an emerging convention to make the company logo on each page clickable as a link to the home page; that could be a useful convention, but in 2003 it is not clear that it has been accepted as such.

Another consensus recommendation is to avoid using the most up-to-the-minute technical features, or features which only work well in a particular browser or browser version. As Peter Kent (1998: 163) puts it, 'In the Web-design world, stay a couple of steps behind'. One often sees a notice telling visitors that a site is 'Best Viewed with XXX Version X': Kent describes these as 'a little rude and very foolish, like a store that makes you change your shoes before you enter'. For the moment, Internet Explorer has a very large share of the action, but it is not probable that any one browser will have such a dominant position in future, and many Web users work with long out-of-date browser versions.

A related area of consensus is the question of animation and audio material. On animation and moving elements in general (for instance, HTML <blink> tags), the agreement is overwhelming: avoid. Any movement in a Web page draws the eye so strongly that the page becomes effectively unusable – the Spool study described test subjects using their hands to cover an animated element decorating a company home page in order to be able to read the text. Peter Kent (1998: 161) hits the nail on the head: 'The Internet is not a multimedia system'.

There are special cases where a content-oriented page makes valid use of animation to illustrate some 3-D object or changing process that cannot be adequately grasped from still pictures. And the Internet may become more of a multimedia channel if the day comes when most users worldwide have broadband connexions. But for the near future, for the vast majority of cases, the Web is best treated as 'text, with a few static images thrown in for good measure' (Kent 1998: 162).

Likewise, usability experts concur that including facilities because they are technically feasible is a bad habit of webmasters. Among the first things seen by visitors to one university computer science department's home page is a link to download a current weather forecast. Would anyone think of such a site as a good

---

4. Quoted in David Neal, 'Good online design pays off', *IT Week* 18 Nov 2002.

place to go to check the weather? Is the weather relevant to any of the normal reasons for visiting the site? No, and no. What looks like a minor benefit offered to the visitor is really a disbenefit: it is a distraction from the aims he is actually pursuing. Space on Web pages, and particularly home pages, is so scarce, and visitors' page-scanning time so short, that nothing should be included which will not give genuine benefit to visitors, to the organization that owns the site, or preferably to both.

Information architecture

A key concept for successful website construction is Louis Rosenfeld and Peter Morville's concept of *information architecture* (Rosenfeld and Morville 1998). Website construction is not at all the same thing, they point out, as Web page construction. Producing a good Web page requires technical skills with HTML and JavaScript, together with a sensitivity to graphic design. Constructing a useful large website requires skills that are almost wholly disjoint from these. They have more in common with librarianship skills; but in several ways the information architect's task is more challenging than a librarian's.

One challenge for a large website is ensuring that the masses of information it contains are kept consistent and up to date, with clear allocation of responsibility for updating different areas. Books, once acquired, do not change their contents; Web pages do and must. This is the sphere of *content management* software – a leading name is Documentum.

However, information architecture is about not just ensuring the validity of the materials but finding useful ways to present them. Librarianship is to a great extent about labelling, classifying, and cataloguing units of information. The classification task is not trivial. Even if we have a good scheme of subject classification, there will be many ambiguities about how to fit particular books into it. Should a biography of Elizabeth I be classified under Biographies? under Tudor History? perhaps under Famous Women? Each choice may be reasonable, depending what perspective a typical reader brings to the library; but libraries can often make broad predictions about their readers' perspectives. A small-town public library whose borrowers read mainly for pleasure is likely to shelve the Elizabeth I book under Biographies. The library of a leading research university is more likely to file it under Tudor History – though if the university has a strong Women's Studies department then Famous Women might be an alternative choice.

Visitors to a website are probably more diverse than the users of any library. But in addition, the items which need to be classified in organizing a large website are much more diverse than in the case of a library, where with minor exceptions they are all books. As Rosenfeld and Morville put it:

> First, web sites often provide access to documents and their components at varying levels of *granularity*. A web site might present articles and journals and journal databases side by side. Links might lead to pages, sections of pages, or to other web sites. Second, web sites typically provide access to documents in *multiple formats*. You

might find financial news, product descriptions, employee home pages, image archives, and software files. Dynamic news content shares space with static human resources information. Textual information shares space with video, audio, and interactive applications. (Rosenfeld and Morville 1998: 24–5)

Hierarchy versus hypertext

Any large website will be organized hierarchically: pages will group into sections, which will in turn be partitioned into subsections, and the hierarchical structure will be reflected in the links between pages: the home page will contain links to introductory pages for the top-level sections of the site, these will in turn direct users to lower-order subsections, and so on. (Rosenfeld and Morville use the term *navigation page* for the home page and the introductory pages to sections, subsections, etc., as opposed to *destination page* for the bottom-level pages containing information which visitors are actually trying to find.) Logically, a website forms a tree structure, with the home page as the root.

It is worth taking a moment to consider how radical a departure this is from the original concept of *hypertext* which the World Wide Web was created to implement – HTML stands for 'Hypertext Markup Language'. The hypertext concept was invented by Ted Nelson in the 1960s, and it involved no tree structure. Documents would contain links to other documents, which might be in the same or some distant and unrelated ownership, but the universe of documents would all be on the same logical level. A person reading one document would follow up a link from a topic of interest to a document covering that topic more fully, and from there would take another link again, pursuing unpredictable paths.

This was an academic vision of the pursuit of pure knowledge for its own sake; it was necessarily abandoned as the Web came to be used as a practical business tool – hypertext supports surfing rather than focused work. (Nelson's vision comprised an intellectual kind of surfing, compared to the connotations of the word today – nobody in the 1960s foresaw the commercial glitz or the amateurish frivolity that have come to be hallmarks of the Web; but it was surfing, nevertheless.) For a large website to enable people to carry out serious tasks efficiently, hierarchical organization turns out to be quite necessary. There may be some use of hypertext links, taking visitors from one destination page to another destination page in a distant section of the site or in another site entirely; but it is recognized nowadays that these will be subsidiary to the main structure of links which provide hierarchical paths connecting destination pages into a tree of navigation pages. (Ted Nelson repudiates what his brainchild has turned into, saying angrily 'The Web isn't hypertext, it's *decorated directories!*'[5])

It may be that tree structure is necessary less because that is the only way users can navigate, than because it is the only way that people can develop a large site successfully. Complex software can only be developed by dividing tasks into modules and submodules whose workings are hidden from one another, and

5. luguerte.notlong.com

modern structured programming languages ban the GOTO statements which used to allow the flow of control to hop between unrelated modules. In the same way, the process of website development may need to be modular. One reason for doubting whether tree structure is imposed by user needs is that users typically do not seem to exploit that structure. Jared Spool's study found that few users would use their browser Back button to return more than one or two levels up a site hierarchy when the path they had followed did not lead to what they were seeking; some users never used the Back button. In general, Spool comments:

> We expected that users of web sites would ... form a mental map of how the site is laid out and how the information is organized. ... none of our users did this. When they got lost, they went forward from where they were, navigating 'in the moment.' ... Users apparently don't think about site structure at all. (Spool et al. 1999: 20)

On the other hand, one could argue the other way that this propensity on the part of users to keep moving forward until either they reach what they are looking for or they give up in frustration makes it all the more important for a site to provide mainly or only hierarchically-organized links, in order to reduce the chances of visitors getting lost on random walks through cyberspace.

Broad or deep trees?

If hierarchical website structure is inevitable, whether because of the producers' or the consumers' needs, another general question is what shape of tree is best. Should it be bushy and flat (i.e. many links in each navigation page, so that the maximum number of levels between home page and destination pages can be few), or tall and thin (few links at each node, long home-page-to-destination-page paths)? Flat, bushy site structures allow the visitor to reach any page with a few clicks from the home page, but the cost is that the home page, and other navigation pages, have to be relatively complex. Tall thin trees permit simple menus but require a lot of clicking, which users may find almost as frustrating as the button-pressing required to get a result from a company's telephone call-centre.

Rosenfeld and Morville argue (1998: 38) that *both* breadth and depth should be limited. For navigation pages to avoid confusing users, they suggest the maximum number of links they contain should be about seven (they refer to the psychologist George Miller's famous finding about human information-processing capacity entitled 'The magical number seven, plus or minus two' (Miller 1956)); and they argue that it is unwise to require users to click more than four or five levels from home to destination page.

It is not clear how seriously they intend these two limits, though, because taken together they mathematically entail an absolute limit on site size: no site could have more than a few thousand pages. (Seven to the fourth power is 2401. Seven to the fifth power is over 16,000, but that size could be reached only if *every* navigation page at each level had a full seven downward links, which is implausible.) A few thousand pages is a large site, but there are plenty larger. Nielsen defined 'very large' sites in 2000 as having over 10,000 pages, and many will have grown since. So it is desirable to establish a priority as between the breadth limit and the depth limit.

The consensus is that greater breadth is preferable to greater depth. For one thing, companies invest heavily in the look and feel of their home page and other top-level pages; putting plenty of links on these pages to begin with reduces the risk of having to redesign them as the site develops – it creates more headroom to allow adaptation to occur at lower levels of the site, where navigation-page appearance is less crucial to brand image. And visitors find it less frustrating to search through a page for what they need, even if the page is complex, than to wait for successive pages to load.

Company perspective versus user perspectives

The next question is how the totality of material which an organization wants to publish on its site is to be divided up hierarchically.

Here there is a trap which it is difficult for any large organization to avoid. The obvious solution is to let the website hierarchy mirror the organization's internal operating structure. This is easy because it provides a natural mechanism for sharing out responsibility for constructing (or at least providing content for) the sections of the site: top-level sections can be farmed out to division heads, who pass on responsibility for subsections to their subordinates, and so on. But also, it solves the problem that any *other* organization for the website is likely to be politically inflammatory. If the main units of the organization do not all see themselves appearing alongside one another on the home page, the less-visible units will perceive themselves as downgraded.

However, it is essential to structure a complex site in terms of the users' perspectives. Content is gathered from a company's organizational units, but it must be digested and reorganized to cater to site users.

This is all the more difficult because website visitors are so diverse. They will certainly have a greater variety of perspectives than, say, readers in a university library. Steve Krug puts it in extreme terms: 'there is no Average User ... all of the time I've spent watching people use the Web has led me to the opposite conclusion: all Web users are unique, and all Web use is basically idiosyncratic' (Krug 2000: 136). Nevertheless, one simply must find some kind of compromise between the most frequent visitor perspectives, resisting the temptation to fall back on the 'safe' choice of modelling website on company organization.

Because website structure has large consequences for how an organization is seen and how it sees itself, the role of information architect is unavoidably politically sensitive. As Rosenfeld and Morville say, there is no possibility of avoiding political problems; the most one can hope for is that, knowing in advance that problems will occur, one may be able to steer a reasonable course which avoids unnecessary battles while standing firm on issues that are crucial to the success of the website.

Steve Krug points out that politics is another reason why early testing is a very good idea: it provides an objective device for resolving company-internal political disagreements. It can do this even if the test does not produce knock-down evidence showing that one side of the argument is indisputably correct. People who may be unwilling to climb down while a debate is just opinion against opinion will often yield a point if they can see themselves as yielding to some sort of evidence, rather than to their human opponent.

Labelling

Planning the structure of a complex website involves not only deciding how pages of content are to be grouped into sections and subsections, but also deciding how links should be labelled – at the point in a navigation page where the link occurs, as a heading at the top of the page linked to, and as an HTML <title> in that page. Clearly labels in these different places should be consistent, in wording, use of capitals, etc., but they also need to be well chosen. For a small site, choosing wording to label site sections and destination pages may be a trivial matter. With a large site it must be handled systematically, like every other aspect of site organization. Wording is crucial; another finding from the Spool study is that, even when icons are used to make links graphically distinctive, users prefer to navigate by reading text.

Again, the first issue is that wording needs to reflect website users' perceptions – not the company's internal perceptions. Many companies have their own internal jargon for functions or facilities that are known by other names in the wider world. Jared Spool gives an example relating to the financial services company Fidelity, which uses the term 'global' in a special way. Instead of being a synonym for 'international', in Fidelity-speak 'global' relates specifically to its network of subsidiaries in countries outside the USA. Because this private usage spilled into the Fidelity website, when Spool's experimental subjects were asked to research international investment opportunities (which could be done on the American parent company's site) they often found themselves looking at Web pages in foreign languages, without understanding where they had gone wrong.

Using internal jargon on the company website not only makes it unnecessarily difficult for visitors to find what they are looking for: worse, it tacitly tells visitors 'We care more about our own agenda than about helping potential customers to fulfil theirs'.

Resolving to use generally-understood terminology rather than private jargon is only the beginning. The English language is rich and full of near-synonyms; how to choose wording that will be most widely understood?

If the website includes a search facility, analysing the log of user queries may be a good way of identifying terminology that is natural to users and hence suitable for a revamped labelling scheme. Also, Rosenfeld and Morville point out that for some areas there exist standard controlled vocabularies. For instance, the US Library of Congress publishes a Legislative Indexing Vocabulary of words and phrases relevant for searching databases of federal legislation, containing both recommended terms and common alternatives (for example, 'Domestic animals: *use* Livestock'). Resources like this may provide useful guidelines for a standardized labelling scheme.

Design

With design, we reach an area where any hope of finding objectively 'correct answers' has to be abandoned: tastes differ. This is made almost laughably obvious by Amazon reader reviews for leading books on design for the Web. For instance, Patrick Lynch and Sarah Horton's *Web Style Guide* (Lynch and Horton 2002) is described by one reviewer as 'the Bible of digital style ... wonderful', while another reviewer comments 'What a horrible, horrible book ... terrible!'

Furthermore, the aesthetic considerations that designers care about can conflict with Web usability considerations, rather than helping to support them. The Spool usability study looked at a large number of graphic variables and concluded that the vast majority of them did not affect usability, but there was one exception: the colours used for visited and unvisited links. Sites which allowed browsers to use their default colours were more usable than sites which imposed their own choice of colour. For Rosenfeld and Morville (1998: 49), overriding browser-default link colours in order to achieve pleasing colour co-ordination in a site is 'like putting up a green stop sign at a road intersection because it matches the color of a nearby building.' On the other hand, the graphic designer David Siegel specifies visited/unvisited link colours which, to him, are the 'right choice' irrespective of browser. He supplies readers with an HTML file header to impose these colours, and says 'I hope you will use this formula on your pages, unless you have good reason to do otherwise ... It's much nicer to surf with these colors' (Siegel 1997: 288). There is not likely to be an easy meeting of minds, if a graphic designer can assert an aesthetic preference as if it were a matter of fact, while a usability expert thinks in terms of objective measurement of user success in navigation and information retrieval.

We saw, earlier, that website projects involve unavoidable political tensions between different divisions of an organization, which all want to see themselves recognized at a high level in the site. Here we have a different but equally unavoidable kind of political tension, between the different skills involved in constructing a site.

The Spool study seemed to show that design features are almost wholly irrelevant to usability, so one might think that design is a low-priority issue. If the graphic designer's needs or preferences conflict with those of the information architect or with what the technical member of the team sees as feasible, then too bad for the designer.

But that won't do, because websites are about more than enabling visitors to retrieve information. For the visitors, this is their function; but for the owner organizations they are also about creating a favourable brand image. Graphic design may be crucial there. So there is no easy answer to designer-versus-usability-expert tensions. As with other continuing political differences, the most one can hope for is that awareness of their existence will enable managers to steer debates towards acceptable compromises rather than getting lost in unproductive bickering.

Whatever visual style is favoured by a website designer, it needs to be balanced against other requirements for a successful website. So long as that is recognized, a variety of visual personalities on the Web is very much to be welcomed.

12

The open source movement

Naïve or world-changing?

Since IT has become crucial to business, the production of software has standardly been treated like the production of other necessary business supplies. Just as a company needing to install a piece of apparatus or machinery to carry out some physical process will either get it built by its own technicians or engineers, or else will purchase it from an outside manufacturer, so when software is needed either programmers employed by the company will write it, or a standard package will be licensed from a software house.

Software is an unusual kind of business supply, though. Some people believe that buying and selling it like capital equipment or consumable supplies is the wrong economic model: software is not that kind of thing at all. Society will get substantially less benefit from computer technology than it should, while people persist in this false perception of how software fits into the economic structure.

For many years, advocates of 'free software' were seen by the sober business community as naïvely impractical and somewhat wild-eyed idealists. This may have been a fair characterization of some of them. More recently, though, the case has been argued in hard-nosed terms that make sense to economists and businesspeople, and free software has been colonizing economic niches that were previously occupied by paid-for systems developed by Microsoft and other orthodox players. A point of view which seemed naïve if not plain silly is being taken seriously.

Some even see the open source movement as potentially world-changing. Eric Raymond's *The Cathedral and the Bazaar* (Raymond 2001), the leading statement of the open-source thesis, is described on its cover by Guy Kawasaki as 'The most important book about technology today'.

A parting of the ways

Thirty-odd years ago, the concept of software as a tradable commodity scarcely existed. Computer hardware was manufactured and sold; companies that wanted to computerize bought the hardware and employed programmers to make it do what they wanted (the tasks commonly being specific to the particular organization). Hardware manufacturers such as IBM supplied operating-system software and languages bundled with their machines, but these were not treated as separate marketable packages – they were things you had to have to make the machine do anything. (IBM first unbundled software from hardware in 1969, under threat of anti-trust litigation.) Individuals with access to computers through their work had fun writing hobby programs which they swapped freely with other enthusiasts.

The split between contrasting views of software as property is graphically described in Steven Levy's *Hackers* (Levy 1984). 'Hackers' in the original sense were youngsters who became passionate about mastering the workings of computers, in days when tiny memories and lack of modern user interfaces meant that getting the machines to do anything interesting required a lot of abstruse technical know-how. (The alternative sense of hackers as people who intrude into and damage other people's systems had not yet emerged – some writers still reserve 'hacker' for the former sense and distinguish the bad guys as 'crackers', though this term has not caught on so widely.)

Levy describes the communities of geeky enthusiasts who coalesced at places like MIT and Berkeley, California, as evolving a 'hacker ethic' whose axioms included 'Mistrust authority', 'Access to computing ... should be unlimited', 'All information should be free'. Within that cultural background, when in 1975 a group of these youngsters who had purchased one of the earliest home computers (the Altair) went to a meeting which demonstrated a high-level language (Basic) running on it, it seemed unobjectionable to 'borrow' one of the paper tapes containing the code and duplicate it for club members' benefit. The person who had (with a friend) coded Altair Basic and sold it to the manufacturer was a teenage college dropout called Bill Gates. To him this was straightforward theft. He published an open letter in hacker newsletters:

> most of you steal your software ... Who can afford to do professional work for nothing? What hobbyist can put three man-years into programming, finding all the bugs, documenting his product and distributing for free?

To a professional economist, Bill Gates's point here seems an obvious truism. The idea that software, or any other useful good that takes intense effort to produce, should be given away without charge might sound charming, but it cannot work. If those responsible for producing the good are not paid by those who consume it, then very little will be produced. Hobbyists may generate a certain amount of software for the fun of it, just as a gardener might raise a few apple trees and give the fruit away to friends for the pleasure of interacting with Nature – but there is no way that the total appetite of society for apples could be satisfied in that fashion: far fewer apples will be produced voluntarily than people would be glad to pay for.

If software is not treated as property to be sold for money, then programmers will lose out, because they are not paid for their labour, but would-be users of software will lose out too, because software that ought to be written never will be. This is basic economics: 'there ain't no such thing as a free lunch'.

To most of the hacker community, on the other hand, Gates's letter was inflammatory. He received a storm of protest letters. A local computer club threatened to sue him for calling its members thieves.

The Free Software Foundation

Gates and the hackers went their separate ways. No reader needs to be told that Gates made a good thing out of his proprietary approach to software. The hobbyists continued to work in the style that pleased them, and in due course they produced a champion for their approach: Richard Stallman.

Stallman developed an editor, Emacs, in 1975, which in a later version is probably still the most widely-used editor program in the scientific community. In the mid-1980s he produced a C compiler, gcc, which again remains a staple tool in academic computing. In 1984 he initiated the GNU Project, a collaborative hacker enterprise which aimed to emulate all the functions and facilities of the Unix operating system within free software. In 1985 Stallman formed the Free Software Foundation as a vehicle to manage this massive undertaking.

These were large achievements, but the most significant thing about Stallman is the ideology underpinning his work. For Stallman the concept of *free software* is not a convenience for hobbyists but a moral imperative. Stallman is an intense man – he has been described as an 'implacable Old Testament prophet' (Moody 2002: 29), living on a shoestring, wearing his hair down to his shoulders, and he believes passionately that in a modern society the hacker ethic is an essential component of political freedom.

This attitude, while perhaps admirable in the abstract, is not likely to impress the average businessman. Until recently the business world, if it even knew about open-source software or the GNU Project, took for granted that these were things that hobbyists and academics might have fun with but which could have little relevance to the world of industry and commerce. The name 'open source' was coined in 1998 for the movement which the hacker approach has morphed into, as a deliberate attempt to distance this movement from the anti-business connotations of Stallman's term 'free software'.

Nevertheless, developments in the last few years have begun to suggest that even in sober economic terms, leaving politics aside, the future may lie with Stallman and the hackers, more than with Bill Gates.

'Open source', 'proprietary', 'free'

Before examining Eric Raymond's arguments for the economic rationality of open source, let me define some terms. The opposition *open source* versus *proprietary* covers several separate distinctions. Software is 'open source' if it is released as source code, which users can read, modify, and adapt to their purposes, rather than as opaque compiled object code which has to be accepted and used as is. Code is 'proprietary' if its owners actively enforce their copyright in it to prevent others using it without payment. (GNU software, by contrast, is released under a form of licence which positively requires any new software based on it to be freely available.) Stallman often insists that the phrase 'free software' relates to 'free as in freedom, not as in beer' – he did not himself give away products such as Emacs; but he sold them for nominal prices which covered modest individual living expenses without amounting to the foundation of a commercial empire.

In practice, it has made sense to contrast 'open source' with 'proprietary', because most software has either been proprietary and distributed as object code for whatever price the market will bear, or else has been distributed as source code, freely or cheaply, under the GNU Public Licence or otherwise unencumbered by copyright restrictions. (If programs are distributed as source code which is easy to copy and modify, it is difficult to maintain copyright and hence to charge significant prices – though companies do sometimes choose to distribute software free of charge but in object-code form, as Microsoft does with its Explorer browser.) The reader should bear in mind that 'open source' v. 'proprietary' is a broad rather than logically clearcut contrast. In due course we shall see that it is blurring.

Technical and economic issues

Eric Raymond's *The Cathedral and the Bazaar*, first published as a series of essays on the Web beginning in 1996, argues for two surprising points of view: one technical, the other economic.

The technical claim (in the essay with the same title as the book) is that it is possible for large-scale, high-quality software to be produced by a loosely-organized community of free agents – by the kind of social set-up that he sees as typical of a bazaar. People previously supposed that a tightly-knit, carefully co-ordinated organization was crucial – as it is for building a cathedral, where intricate architectural structures composed of massive masonry make careful planning essential.

The economic claim (argued in a sister essay, 'The Magic Cauldron') is that the hacker-style approach provides the right structure of incentives for software development to be well matched with society's software needs.

Technical feasibility

Raymond illustrates the technical argument largely by reference to *Linux*, the operating-system kernel whose development was initiated by the Swedish-Finn Linus Torvalds in 1991. (Linux is part of, and depends on other parts of, the GNU Project, and the complete operating system is properly known as 'GNU/Linux'. The term 'Linux' is commonly used as shorthand for the entire system; I shall follow that familiar usage here for convenience, without any wish to undervalue the non-Linux components of the whole.) Linux is by now a serious threat to the hegemony of Microsoft's Windows, but Linux was built in a very un-cathedral-like way:

From nearly the beginning, it was rather casually hacked on by huge numbers of volunteers coordinating only through the Internet. Quality was maintained not by rigid standards or autocracy but by the naïvely simple strategy of releasing every week and getting feedback from hundreds of users within days, creating a sort of rapid Darwinian selection on the mutations introduced by developers. To the amazement of almost everyone, this worked quite well. (Raymond 2001: 16)

Raymond argues that the traditional approach to software development leads to a mistaken perception of software bugs:

In the cathedral-builder view of programming, bugs and development problems are tricky, insidious, deep phenomena. It takes months of scrutiny by a dedicated few to develop confidence that you've winkled them all out. Thus the long release intervals, and the inevitable disappointment when long-awaited releases are not perfect. (p. 31)

The bazaar approach, on the other hand, leads one to see the bug problem in terms of what Raymond calls Linus's Law: 'given enough eyeballs, all bugs are shallow'. In the bazaar model, 'you release often in order to get more corrections [at one stage, Torvalds was releasing updated versions of Linux every few days], and as a beneficial side effect you have less to lose if an occasional botch gets out the door' – because you only need to wind back a short way to return to the last non-botched version.

What does proprietary buy us?

If software as complex as an operating system can be produced in the bazaar style, Raymond says, then we have to ask ourselves

what, if anything, the tremendous overhead of conventionally managed development is actually buying us.

Whatever it is certainly doesn't include reliable execution by deadline, or on budget, or to all features of the specification; it's a rare managed project that meets even one of these goals, let alone all three. It also does not appear to be ability to adapt to changes in technology and economic context during the project lifetime, either; the open-source community has proven *far* more effective on that score ... (p. 56)

This last point coincides with points made by Larry McVoy in a famous document of 1993 (the 'Sourceware White Paper', McVoy 1993) which predicted that turning Unix into a closed-source, proprietary product would lead to its stagnation:

A great deal of the early development of Unix was done by researchers because of Unix's ready accessibility. ... Almost every good feature in computer operating systems today, including most features in DOS,

Windows, and Windows/NT, came from the mind of one hacker or another. Typically, the work was not commissioned by a company, it was done as a research project and then productized. Without these people, we make no forward progress.

Another advantage in buying from an established company, in the case of simpler products, is that it gives the customer a legal recourse if the products prove unsatisfactory. But that is not a reason to prefer proprietary software, because software licences standardly exclude virtually all responsibility for product quality (they have to, because of the impossibility of ensuring that software is bug-free).

Raymond identifies various other reasons why a software purchaser might think it worth paying the costs of conventional commercial project management. In each case he argues that they are illusory.

Manufacture or service?

Technically, then, Raymond believes that the bazaar approach *can* produce software. But, economically, why *will* it? An economist would suppose that it will not, or at least not enough software will be developed: people need incentives to produce anything.

In discussing the economic issue, Raymond is careful to explain that he is *not* saying that closed-source software development is morally objectionable, that there ought not to be copyright in software, or that there is an obligation on programmers to share their output altruistically. He is not advocating the open-source approach on idealistic, hacker-ethic grounds. He believes that approach makes practical sense as a means of providing society with a good choice of high-quality software.

In the first place, Raymond argues, 'software is largely a service industry operating under the ... delusion that it is a manufacturing industry' (Raymond 2001: 120). The great majority of all code written by professional programmers is written for in-house use rather than sale, and most of what programmers do is maintenance rather than creation of novel programs. What serious software consumers are willing to pay for a package relates to the expected value of future 'service' (in a broad sense, including consultancy and training, upgrades, and so forth), more than to the intrinsic properties of the package itself: if you doubt that, look at the rock-bottom prices put on remaindered copies of discontinued software lines (which, physically, still work as well as when the line was new). Computer games are an exception which really should be classed as products, not services; but games are a special case.

If we accept that business software is really a service industry, then logically consumers should not pay mainly through an up-front purchase price but through payments which continue as the service continues, for instance via annual subscriptions or repeated fees for support and maintenance. Even if the vendor owns copyright in the software package, it could make commercial sense for it to give copies away, in order to encourage a market for its paid-for support services. In that case, whether the software is in fact proprietary or not becomes fairly irrelevant to the economics of the situation.

Writing in 1996, Raymond noted that this pattern was already visible with the largest-scale business software, such as enterprise resource planning systems, where development costs are so massive that they could not realistically be recouped through one-off purchase fees; companies such as PeopleSoft who sell ERP systems derive their income chiefly from after-sales consultancy payments. Raymond predicted that as the software industry matured, most of it would move in that same direction. And broadly speaking this is how companies that distribute Linux, such as Red Hat (founded in 1993), are operating.

Consequences of manufacture delusion

As Raymond sees it, the pricing model encouraged by 'manufacture delusion' has serious negative effects. It encourages developers to produce *shelfware* – packages that can be marketed well enough to sell, but which deliver little value in practice – and to put less effort into after-sales support than users need. It encourages developers to discontinue good lines prematurely in order to reap profits from newer packages. And it makes it difficult for good second-place products to compete against market leaders, stimulating excellence in both.

Although Raymond believes that much of the software development industry is destined to move onto the open-source model, he also believes that there are cases which will always be more rationally treated as products for sale. Raymond lists a series of considerations which push a specific software project in one direction or the other; for instance, the open-source model is specially attractive in cases where correctness of design and implementation are hard to assess other than by independent peer review, or where the package serves a business-critical function for the consumer (so that the consumer does not want to be tied to a single commercial supplier). Raymond's example of a package which fails most of the tests, so that economic rationality implies that it ought to be sold as a closed-source product, is software for sawmills which calculates optimal cutting patterns for extracting the most valuable configuration of planks from a given log. It is straightforward to evaluate the performance of such a system objectively; and it is not business-critical – sawyers can do the task reasonably well manually, if they have to. But, according to Raymond, cases like this which should remain closed-source are exceptions, not the norm.

Where software *is* business-critical, Raymond believes, user companies will come to realize that closed source is simply not acceptable as a strategic business risk.

> The brutal truth is this: when your key business processes are executed by opaque blocks of bits that you can't even see inside (let alone modify), *you have lost control of your business*. You need your supplier more than your supplier needs you – and you will pay, and pay, and pay again for that power imbalance. (p. 152)

Programming for money or love

Still this does not answer the incentive question: why will people devote time and effort to developing software packages if they are distributed for little or no money?

In some cases, Raymond says, the programmers will be employed by software houses as programmers are now, to create packages which the company can then earn its living by supporting, rather than selling. And in other cases companies may derive other kinds of benefit through employing people to develop software that is given away. Raymond cites a case where the network equipment manufacturer Cisco assigned two of its programmers to write a complex distributed print-spooling system, and made it open-source in order to stimulate the growth of a community of outside users and co-developers who would between them ensure that maintenance was available into the future. If the system had been closed-source and the two programmers had left the company, it would have been hard for someone new coming to the code to learn enough to maintain it.

But other open-source software will continue to be produced by unpaid volunteers, according to Raymond, in the same way that Linux has been. Furthermore the volunteers do not necessarily need to be motivated by the intrinsic pleasure of hacking, or by peer esteem. Hackers are people with software needs of their own, which they will often want to solve for themselves rather than waiting an indefinite time until someone else happens to do the job – and, when a hacker has produced code that meets a specific need, it pays him to document it and contribute it to the community, rather than keep it to himself, because in that way the ongoing effort of maintaining the code is taken over by the community.

Still, Raymond makes clear that he believes the pure joy of hacking is and will continue to be one of the main driving forces behind the production of useful software.

To a businessperson, this is a very strange idea. In an academic context, though, it should be easy to understand the idea that good work depends on self-motivation and peer esteem more than on an employer/employee relationship: this is essentially how academic research functions. The fact that we know as much as we do about every subject under the sun, from the structure of the atom to the structure of government under the Plantagenets, is because researchers have chosen for themselves topics to work on and pursued them in the gaps of time between teaching and other duties, motivated by a mixture of love of study and the admiration of their fellow specialists. Nowadays there are mechanisms such as national Research Assessment Exercises which give universities a financial motive to press their staff to do good research, but in Britain these innovations are quite recent and it is questionable how far they have altered the quality of research.

Pure academic research might sound a far cry from software development, but in fact there are strong analogies. In particular, the fact that a complex software system is virtually never perfect (the 'last bug' is never found) makes it similar to academic research, where the last word is never said on any subject and there is always room for reinterpretation and further discovery. If software were rejected for a single flaw, we would have to do without computers altogether; so a software system must be evaluated in broader and less clearcut terms. And because of the complexity of software, the people involved in developing it are far better placed to do this than users, even users who have a general background in IT – just as members of the public who take an interest in advances in human knowledge, for instance by watching science or history programmes on television, have to rely on the professionals to sieve the sensible ideas from the dross.

One could imagine that, alongside the world of particle physicists or Plantagenet historians publishing academic papers and books, finding shortcomings in one another's theories, and arguing publicly for revisions, there might be companies containing paid researchers who did not read others' work or publish their own, but who would sell to commercial clients for their private use their own scientific or historical theories, backed with the company's authority. In real life such companies do not exist, because (even if accurate knowledge of Plantagenet history were a marketable commodity) we all recognize that this is not the way to produce reliable knowledge. It is a recipe for generating one-sided, eccentric systems of ideas whose flaws go undetected for lack of publicity. Advocates of open-source – and, by now, many neutral commentators – see the proprietary model of software development as suffering from a similar disadvantage.

The breakthrough happens

When Eric Raymond was writing in the late 1990s, he was making a prediction: the economic logic of open-source, he argued, meant that it was bound in due course to spread through the business computing environment.

From about 2002 onwards, it has been rather clear that Raymond's prediction is coming true. We cannot yet foresee where the boundaries will ultimately fall between functions where open source will predominate and functions that will continue to be executed largely by proprietary systems, but nobody any longer could see open source software as an impractical phenomenon associated with unrealistic hacker culture. A decisive breakthrough to business credibility has occurred.

Linux is the clearest example. Michael Dell (chief executive of Dell Computers) argued in November 2002 that 'Linux is the new Unix', and indeed that Linux is now superior to Unix.[1] A report, *Fear the Penguin*, from the investment bank Goldman Sachs in January 2003 judged that Linux has now 'evolved into an enterprise-class operating system'.

But open-source was shouldering proprietary aside in other functions too. A September 2002 survey by the research company Netcraft found that the open-source scripting language PHP was overtaking Microsoft's ASP in popularity as a server-side Web scripting technology – and that almost two thirds of all internet sites used the open-source and free Apache web server software, while the Microsoft equivalent, IIS, was used by only one site in four.

1. Quoted by Paul Krill, 'OracleWorld: Sun's Gage urges community participation in security', *InfoWorld* 14 Nov 2002, bunycrub.notlong.com

The chief locus of active opposition to the open source movement has naturally been Microsoft, which has campaigned against it in various ways. One example was a page posted on the Microsoft website in October 2000 documenting a series of so-called 'Linux Myths'. Microsoft claimed that much of the buzz which Linux was starting to attract represented hype rather than reality, arguing that Linux fell down relative to proprietary operating systems with respect to considerations such as reliability (for example, preservation of data in cases of system failure) and security, as well as shortage of available applications. More recently, Microsoft has argued that the apparent cost saving with open source is illusory, once consultancy fees are taken into account, and that for industrial-strength computing infrastructures it is actually cheaper overall to license Microsoft solutions. Likewise Jonathan Schwartz of Sun: 'Linux is like a puppy – in the beginning it's great, but you also have to take care of it'.[2]

One can debate how fair the 'Linux Myths' arguments were at the time, or just how fully they have ceased to be fair with later developments in Linux. Open-source enthusiasts pointed out that the very decision by Microsoft to mount this type of campaign was itself a tacit admission that open-source had become a serious alternative to Microsoft's business model. But any remaining inclination to see open-source as just a hobbyist's plaything was decisively exploded in February 2003 by David Stutz, who had until then led Microsoft's anti-open-source strategy. A few days after he retired, Stutz used his new freedom to announce publicly that Linux is now becoming a legitimate alternative to Windows, and that Microsoft would need to be more creative in developing new products if it hopes to maintain its market position.

Meanwhile, Microsoft's quarterly filing with the US Securities and Exchange Commission in the same month envisaged having to reduce its prices to compete against open source in future. Steve Ballmer, chief executive of Microsoft, says that Linux is the development he most fears.

The second of Stutz's points chimes with Larry McVoy's 1993 comment about closed-source software leading to stagnation. *The Economist* suggested in November 2002 that the Microsoft anti-trust trial may have been near-pointless, because the lack of innovation resulting from its closed-source business model ensured that the company would fall behind:

> What is striking is how little innovation there has been in the bits of the market that Microsoft dominates, and how much where it has little influence. Operating systems, web browsers and word-processing software all look much as they did five years ago. But not many people are using five-year-old mobile phones, handheld computers or music-sharing software.[3]

2. Quoted in 'The ponytail versus the penguin', *The Economist* 24 May 2003.
3. 'Giving the invisible hand a helping hand', *The Economist* 9 Nov 2002.

Open source in government computing

Perhaps surprisingly, many early indications that open source is becoming a credible option have come not from private-sector companies but from governments, which are the largest consumers of software of all.

This might seem unexpected, for two reasons. In the first place, one does not normally associate governments and civil servants with innovative, radical developments. Secondly, the cheapness of open-source software is less of an issue for governments, which are financed through taxation, than it is for companies which need to control costs in order to stay in profit.

But governments care deeply about retaining control over their domains. Eric Raymond's warning that closed-source software implies losing control of one's business would sound even more chilling to a mayor who translated it into losing control of his city, or to a prime minister who translated it into losing control of his country.

Furthermore, security against loss of confidentiality and against malicious hacker ('cracker') attacks is often even more vital for government departments than for business – and one aspect of Microsoft's 'Linux Myths' which has been very widely criticized is the suggestion that open-source software is inherently insecure. Many commentators believe that security flaws have a better chance of being detected and eliminated under the 'democratic' code-review process characteristic of open-source development. Paul Cormier, executive vice-president of engineering at Red Hat, has put it this way: 'There are all of these eyeballs ... who have no agenda other than doing the right thing. The closed[-source] community relies on a small group of developers, and most of their vulnerabilities are found by the bad guys.'[4] A supremely security-conscious application area is cryptography, whose whole purpose is to defeat attacks by crackers; the cryptography expert Bruce Schneier wrote in 1999 that 'In the cryptography world, we consider open source necessary for good security; we have for decades.'[5]

Otto Schily, German Interior Minister, quoted worries about Microsoft's security record, and the wish to avoid dependence on a private foreign company, as leading motives when in July 2002 he announced a plan for German federal and *Land* governments to switch from Windows to Linux – though the plan also aimed at cost reductions. Gilbert Robert and Frédéric Schütz (2001: 17) reported a similar trend in France. Several North and South American governments had by 2002 adopted policies which formally discourage use of proprietary software in public projects.

The British government has not yet gone that far in embracing the logic of Raymond's argument. At the time of writing, it makes hardly any use of open-source software – its first major open-source-based application was the Purchase and Pay project that went live at the Department for Work and Pensions in February 2003. But change seems to be on the way. A July 2002 Cabinet Office report urged that government departments should in future consider open-source alternatives to proprietary systems, in order to 'avoid lock-in to proprietary IT

4. Quoted by Dennis Fisher, 'Red Hat profits from fear', *IT Week* 11 Nov 2002.
5. Quoted by Moody (2002: 285).

products and services' as well as to obtain value for money. After Sun announced in September 2002 that it will be marketing a range of desktop machines based on Linux and the StarOffice office-productivity suite, *Computing* magazine reported that the Inland Revenue had been talking to Sun about migrating its 70,000 desktops from Windows/Microsoft Office to this solution. In February 2003 the Office of Government Commerce announced that it may use open-source for a new interdepartmental government purchasing-information system which it is about to commission.

Another way in which governments have been pushing software business practice in the open-source direction has been to insist that they themselves should be given confidential access to otherwise closed-source code. In January 2003 the Russian and British governments, and NATO, secured agreements with Microsoft along these lines relating to Windows 2000 and other systems. How far this will lead to modifications in software-development practice that benefit other, non-government users remains to be seen.

Breakthrough in the private sector

In the economically-harsh opening years of the new century, private-sector businesses are focusing on cost-cutting before all else: the priority has been simple survival rather than possibly advantageous but risky innovation. However, the cheapness of open-source systems makes them appealing from that point of view too – though partisans of open source would argue that cheapness ought not to be the main motive for switching. 2003 seems to be the year in which open source is making the breakthrough to acceptance in the business world.

Thus, in January 2003 Unilever announced a plan to move its global IT infrastructure from Unix onto Linux – for an expected saving of £66m over three years, but also in order to achieve infrastructure simplification. In February 2003, Reuters released a version of its Market Data System software on Linux, claiming this as the first major example of open-source use in the area of financial services; Reuters said that the Linux-based version gave a large performance improvement over a Unix-based alternative.

At the desktop end of the market Windows remains dominant at the time of writing. But already in December 2002 the European arm of the largest South American bank, Banco do Brasil, announced plans to migrate the whole of its computing infrastructure, desktops included, from Windows to Linux. It had begun to make the switch at the server level, and claimed to be achieving greater productivity and reliability as well as cost savings.

Of course, senior managers commonly do not know in detail just how their IT departments are operating. One thing that has been happening a lot is managers discovering that their subordinates have quietly been running open-source systems in specific areas for some time past. The difference now is that the senior people are giving this their blessing, publicizing it, and adopting explicit open source policies at division-wide or company-wide levels.

The other point of view

From the discussion so far, readers may have concluded that open-source versus proprietary is a one-sided debate. It was appropriate to give the arguments in favour of open source a very full hearing, because they are so counterintuitive in terms of ordinary economic assumptions – and there seems little doubt that Raymond is right to argue that some of the 'obvious' economic reasons why the open source model 'cannot work' are far weaker than they seem at first.

Nevertheless, there are also downsides to the open-source model, and we need to look at these.

How good a precedent is Linux?

The first issue is theoretical. We have seen that Raymond's case is partly technical – software *can* be produced through 'bazaar' methods – and partly economic – if it can be, sufficient software *will* be produced that way. Raymond's argument for the economic logic of open-source is reasonably persuasive, but the technical side of the case seems weaker.

The idea that successful, complex software can emerge from a disorganized 'bazaar' contradicts longstanding axioms about software engineering. Frederick Brooks's IT classic *The Mythical Man-Month* (Brooks 1975) pointed out that the more programmers are assigned to a project, the slower development becomes, because of the increasing possibilities of hidden inconsistencies between separate individuals' work. The discipline of software engineering has evolved to cope with this problem through strong co-ordinating and planning mechanisms – that is, by enforcing a cathedral-building rather than bazaar-like working method. Glyn Moody (2002: 151) claims that 'Linus's Law' offers a solution to the problem identified by Brooks; but what *is* the solution? On the face of it, Linus's Law merely denies that the problem is real.

Clearly, Linux demonstrates that some complex software can be produced by loose networks of free agents; but Linux may be a special case. Unix, the system it set out to emulate, consists largely of numerous independent utilities which interact with one another in a standardized way by exchanging sequential files. This minimizes the danger that work on one part of the system might inadvertently interfere with the way another part operates, so it is an ideal case for the bazaar approach to development. But there is no way that (say) an efficient word-processing program could be designed with a similar architecture.

Possibly, the success of Linux in particular is being taken to mean more than it really does.

Bugs emerge

The second point is practical. Many people have been persuaded by the argument that democratic, many-eyeballs software development yields code with fewer bugs and security vulnerabilities. Now that open-source software is being more widely deployed, experience is beginning to call this into question. According to a November 2002 report by the analysts Aberdeen Group, 'Open-source software …

is now the major source of elevated security vulnerabilities',[6] having overtaken Microsoft in that role. More than twice as many alerts issued by the American computer security advisory body Cert related to open-source or Linux products as to Microsoft software in the first ten months of 2002.

Matching effort to needs

Even if the open-source approach does on balance yield higher-quality software, with a more satisfactory maintenance/support model, than the proprietary approach, it seems that nothing in the open-source approach can guarantee that the range of functions for which software is produced offers a good match to the functions which need to be served.

We saw in Chapter 5, for instance, that commercial websites in Europe will soon be required by law to be accessible to disabled users. Linux is behind Windows in developing the features needed to support this. One can surmise (so far as I know the issue has not been studied) that this may be a consequence of the interests and preferences of the open-source developer community. They are enthusiastic about coding packages which they might want to use themselves, but hackers tend to be bright young people who surely suffer from proportionately fewer disabilities than the general population. In consequence it may be that they have little natural understanding of what the new law requires, and little spontaneous interest in providing it. A traditional software company, on the other hand, can simply assign a task to a group of employees because it is a commercial imperative.

The analogy with academic research is again relevant, but this time in a negative sense. Probably everyone agrees that the best way to get at the truth about a pure academic topic, whether scientific or humanistic, is through open, voluntary research and debate by members of a global academic community. But at the same time, governments and taxpayers often suggest nowadays that this system yields an imperfect distribution of effort across the different research areas. They may feel, for instance, that mediaeval history, or literary theory, get more attention than the public really require, while some applied topics which may be intellectually less exciting, but potentially highly relevant for the prosperity of UK plc, are relatively neglected. Many policies have been introduced to try to marry the academic balance of efforts with the public interest. With open-source software it is not clear what mechanisms could possibly get the analogous distribution of efforts well matched to society's needs.

Leadership and organization

There are also issues, which are only beginning to become visible now that the open source movement is maturing and its products are being used in more 'serious' contexts, about leadership and organizational coherence. The ideologists of open-source sometimes portray the movement as if it were an example of

6. Quoted by Dennis Fisher and Madeline Bennett, 'Open-source flaws multiply', *IT Week* 2 Dec 2002.

successful anarchy, in which individuals come forward to do what is needed without being subordinate to any central control. But at the same time, in the case of Linux, writer after writer attests to the crucial role of Linus Torvalds in guiding its development through the force of his engaging personality. Linux does demonstrate that complex software can be developed without legal employer/ employee relationships, but it does not demonstrate that the leadership role is redundant. Leaders who can persuade people to accept their guidance purely voluntarily may be even harder to find than managers who can lead successfully with the help of legal authority to reinforce their personal charisma.

Dealing with program code, like mathematical research, is a young man's activity: the current generation of open-source project leaders will not fill their current roles for ever. For Linux, Glyn Moody (2002: 322-3) claims that this will not be a problem, because Torvalds has been so successful at creating a 'distributed-leadership' model that no single individual will be needed to succeed him. Clearly this is a large claim, which remains to be tested. But even Moody notes that Richard Stallman 'says despairingly, "I'm going to keep working on the free-software movement because I don't see who's going to replace me."' Moody names an individual who, he believes, may turn out to be a worthy successor to Stallman, but in the open-source model it seems to be largely a matter of chance whether or not such a person appears when needed.

Now that Linux in particular is becoming a crucial technology, it is increasingly coming under the control of a formal organization, the Open Source Development Labs (OSDL), which is a non-profit entity supported by a consortium of technology companies – Torvalds recently joined OSDL. This is probably a good way forward, but it is a far cry from Raymond's bazaar model.

One thing that legally-constituted organizations such as companies are good at is ensuring that there are no responsibility gaps. All necessary functions, the boring ones as well as the interesting ones, are covered, and there is always an identifiable person in charge of each function, with new people slotted in as previous incumbents move on. On the face of it, there seems to be a risk that after businesses and governments have made the shift to reliance on open-source systems (for the positive reasons already discussed), they could find that support and development for these systems melt away, because the kind of people who currently enjoy hacking open-source might find it cooler in a few years' time to do something entirely different.

Advocates of the open-source approach might reply that guaranteeing absence of responsibility gaps is only an apparent advantage, not a real one. In the first place, private-sector companies can go out of business; one of the benefits of open-source is that continuity of support does not depend on survival of individual companies. But also, think of the analogy with academic research: there is nobody whose job it is to kick ass if our understanding of Plantagenet history stagnates, but would it help to have someone with a job like that? Probably not: good historical research is so subtle an activity that if potential historians were to lose the taste for it, it would not happen however many butts were kicked. People might put up smokescreens and go through the motions, but real advances in knowledge can emerge only from real enthusiasm. It may be that developing complex software is equally unamenable to traditional employment disciplines – implying that companies such as Microsoft can succeed in producing proprietary systems only because their employees get some of the same satisfactions from their work as open-source hackers get.

If that is correct, the risk that business or government software users might find themselves marooned in ten or twenty years' time remains a real one, but open-source versus proprietary would not be a relevant variable.

The danger of splits

Another potential problem with the open-source model is splitting into divergent development streams. In the 1980s the leading operating system was Unix, and most onlookers at the time probably expected it to predominate as business made increasing use of computing. Unix still has a significant role, but there are large areas of business computing where it was thoroughly shouldered aside in the 1990s by Windows. A main reason is that the original Unix developed by Ken Thompson and Dennis Ritchie at AT&T Bell Labs in 1969 split into rival, incompatible variants, such as Sun's Solaris and IBM's AIX. Disunity led to weakness.

The open-source movement lacks any formal mechanism to guard against splits. The beginnings of what might be such a split in Linux emerged in May 2002, when the UnitedLinux consortium for developing a common Linux core was formed by a number of Linux-related companies (the leading European player, SuSE; the SCO Group; Conectiva; and TurboLinux), but the most successful Linux distribution company of all, Red Hat, remained aloof from this consortium and announced a collaborative deal with Dell and Oracle.

But again defenders of open-source would surely reply that the proprietary model offers no real defence against splits either. After all, the Unix fractionation of the 1990s came about through rival companies creating separate versions. In the hacker community, there is no legally-binding guarantee against splits, only cultural resistance to 'forking code' – but although this cultural taboo has occasionally been violated (for example, with Emacs in 1993), it is clearly powerful in practice.

Indeed, Larry McVoy seems to believe that the fractionation of Unix was not so much a consequence of commercial pressures on management as of the fact that working for private-sector companies on closed-source systems released talented software developers from this social taboo:

> ... there was this pool of O[perating] S[ystem] engineering talent, and these guys would encourage their managers to do this sort of [duplication]. Because ... they liked being the kings of the heap, being the kernel jocks. They kind of liked this situation where every OS vendor was doing their own version of Unix ... (quoted by Moody 2002: 142).

Perhaps the most judicious conclusion is that, with a human activity as complex and subtle as software development, the institutional framework within which programmers work is less significant than it seems. Nominally, employees of private-sector companies execute the commands of their superiors, but the nature of the software they actually produce will be determined as much by the attitudes and interests of the community of programmers as by companies' commercial strategies. The open-source movement is making obvious what is largely true anyway.

Not whether, but what

Whether the conclusion of the last paragraph is correct or not, there seems little doubt now that open-source software is here to stay in the business computing world. We are even beginning to see companies outside the IT industry becoming sufficiently convinced of the benefits of 'many eyeballs' to release the source code of software developed in-house. In July 2002 it was reported that the merchant bank Dresdner Kleinwort Wasserstein has released the source code for the middleware it uses to link the firm's different systems.

One consequence of the increasing take-up of open source by the business world is that the sharp contrast between software that is written by volunteers and distributed freely or for nominal charges as source code, and software produced by paid employees and distributed at high prices as object code, is blurring. The economic slump has hit open-source-related companies at least as hard as other technology companies, and one survival strategy some of them are adopting is to get involved with proprietary code: in January 2002, Red Hat released a high-end Linux version which is not wholly open-source. Conversely, Linux development is no longer wholly in the hands of hackers, now that large companies have been persuaded of its virtues. Computer manufacturers such as Hewlett-Packard, and business software firms such as Oracle and SAP, are investing heavily in making their hardware and software compatible with Linux.

The question now is how large a range of business-computing functions open source is destined to fill.

Early efforts were all at the systems rather than applications end of computing, with editors such as Emacs, MySQL as a relational database system, new languages such as Perl, language compilers such as gcc, and the Linux operating system kernel. For a while it seemed that open-source might be good for systems programming but applications would remain a proprietary sphere.

More recently, open-source efforts have been spreading into the applications area. The office-productivity suite OpenOffice has evolved as a free spin-off from Sun's (open-source, but proprietary and paid-for) StarOffice. (Sun donated its source code in October 2000, and the first OpenOffice.org conference was held, in Hamburg, in March 2003. For Sun, one advantage of sponsoring OpenOffice is that the hackers who develop it are producing innovations which Sun can incorporate back into StarOffice, which is bought by customers who need the 24/7 support and training that the hacker community cannot provide.) The SourceForge site was founded in January 2000 as a central repository for open-source applications, many of which are business oriented. In March 2003 SourceForge was hosting over 50,000 projects – its current 'project of the month', TUTOS, was a team-organization package for managing events and calendars, addresses, teams, projects, tasks, and so forth, which had received over 150,000 downloads to date. The GNU Project was advancing well with the development of GNUe (GNU Enterprise, see for example, Tiffin and Müller 2001), intended as an open-source competitor to proprietary ERP systems.

Unless one is ideologically driven, there is no reason to hold that proprietary software should, or can, be replaced in every application domain. But there no longer seems much doubt that open source will be a factor – possibly a very large factor – in the future business computing scene.

13

E-business and small firms

Small firms are big business

Most discussion of e-business focuses on two cases: companies which are set up to implement an IT-based business idea; and large going concerns that find new ways of using IT to carry out functions better or more cheaply.

What this leaves out is the world of smaller existing companies, whose business may have nothing intrinsically to do with computing, but which cannot just ignore the new technology if they want to remain competitive. For small firms, coming to terms with IT is specially problematic. A household-name company can easily afford to second several workers for a year or two to an IT-based business process re-engineering project – if it does not work out, the money spent will scarcely affect overall company profitability, and the project will be a useful learning experience for the firm. Small firms have not normally got this level of slack in the system. It takes virtually all their resources to carry out their daily tasks of producing and selling whatever goods or services they deal in. Planning and implementing a radical operating innovation requires almost as much thinking time in a 50-person company as it does in a 5000-person company, but the 50-person company may find it hard to release the thinker from his other duties. So there is a real danger that the e-business revolution will drive many existing small companies to the wall.

Some readers might instinctively respond 'So what? It's bad luck for the little fish, but (except to themselves) they don't matter very much anyway.' That would be an error. The fate of any one small company may not be of great significance to society as a whole, but there are a very large number of small companies, so that collectively they matter a lot to all of us.

Precise figures obviously depend on how small we count as 'small'. A 1994 report found that if the threshold is 500 employees, in Europe 99.9 per cent of all businesses are smaller than that, and they accounted between them for 70 per cent of all jobs. 500 employees is quite a lot; governments discuss statistics in terms of *small and medium-sized enterprises* – 'SMEs' – and the European Commission defines an SME as employing fewer than 250 people. But the collective figures are still impressive when one goes much lower than that. In Britain, in 1995, businesses employing fewer than *fifty* people accounted for almost half (47.9 per cent) of all private-sector jobs. Figures for the USA are comparable. A US Small Business Administration factsheet in 2002 showed that the 25 million small businesses in the USA represent 99.7 per cent of all employers and more than half of private-sector output and jobs. (The Small Business Administration uses a complex definition of 'small business' which depends on industry sector, for instance in wholesale trade a small business is one with fewer than 100 employees, in manufacturing and mining fewer than 500.)

Small firms have special roles

Simple numbers understate the significance of small firms for a national economy. It is widely accepted that small firms are qualitatively important also, as the principal sources of innovation – and a nation that fails to foster innovation in the 21st century is unlikely to enjoy a bright future. If a new business idea is implemented by creating a new company, then it will obviously begin small. But apart from that, the culture of small organizations tends to be more open to change than that of large organizations. When a company grows really large, it is hard for it not to succumb to a culture in which rules and precedents become more influential than intuition and original thought in responding to the changing business environment. Good managers of large organizations strive to prevent them from developing that way, but the pressure is hard to resist.

That is one reason why 'the top is a slippery place', and the industrial giants of one generation often disappear or lose their lustre a generation later. In Britain in the decades following the Second World War, there was an idea in the air that large companies enjoyed a dominance which made them unassailable – but that was never really true, and to the extent that it was more true then than at other periods this was because government intervention artificially protected the big boys against small innovative competitors (Jewkes 1977). That was also an era when Britain found it difficult to earn its living in the world. Since the political transformation of the 1980s which has turned the UK into one of the world's most vibrant economies, it has become evident that big companies can and often do lose their way and collapse, unless governments prop them up or they manage against the odds to keep reinventing themselves.

One concrete index of the relatively innovative nature of the small-business sector is that it plays a disproportionate role both in creating new jobs and in giving new workers their first foothold on the ladder of employment. In the USA, the Small Business Administration factsheet already quoted reports that small businesses are providing about three-quarters of net new jobs added to the economy, and about two-thirds of individuals' first jobs. Both of these fractions are considerably higher than the overall share of employment attributable to small businesses.

Consequently, if computerization is damaging to the small business sector in general, this is not something that any of us can afford to take lightly. We have seen why one might expect such damage. Small-company ethos may be receptive to the idea that the way things were done in the past need not be the way they are done in future; but ethos in itself does not create man-hours for planning radical business-process revamps, or capital to spend on equipment.

Difficulties for small firms

There are pointers which hint that this problem may be real. The figure quoted earlier of 47.9 per cent of British private-sector jobs being located in small companies in 1995 represented the high point of an increase that had continued since about 1970 (for 1980 the corresponding figure was only 35.6 per cent). But since that high point the trend has gone into reverse and is now falling precipitately. The figures for the years 2000 and 2001 were 43.6 per cent and 30 per cent respectively. The reversal seems to have happened at very roughly the same period when computers were ceasing to be merely an auxiliary tool and were starting to transform business processes.

It would be rash to assume that the two things were necessarily linked, though. The reversal also, for instance, coincided to within a couple of years with the change of governing party in Britain, which entailed many consequences for the business régime that could well have impacted differentially on small and large companies. It is obviously difficult to be sure of any one explanation for statistics like these.

Possibly more telling was a finding in December 2002 that the number of British SMEs trading on line had actually fallen by almost ten per cent over the previous year. It is hard to see this other than as a case of small firms trying to adopt techniques which are proving in practice to be beyond their grasp, though perhaps other explanations are possible (for most small firms that are selling online, their websites are profitable).

This is not to say that small firms are remaining aloof from all aspects of computerization. Even in the retail sector, in August 2002, 71 per cent of all British firms were using e-mail, and 53 per cent had websites. This could be close to saturation, since there will always be many small enterprises to which the technology really is of marginal use. (People who live close to a little corner grocery know it is there without going online; someone who lives further away is hardly going to make the trip even if it has a website offering a few pence off baked beans.) E-mail, and websites that advertise a firm's activities without providing for much or any input in the other direction from customers, are the aspects of computerization which do not stretch even a small-scale operation. E-business functions such as ordering from suppliers via electronic data interchange are in principle as relevant to small firms as to large, but these are areas which require serious reorganization and steep learning curves; small companies are tending to leave them alone.

Amelia Baldwin, Andrew Lymer, and Roland Johnson (2001: 105) quote a report by IBM Australia dating back to 1998, that found that most small companies which were adopting e-commerce at that time were doing so in order to reduce costs –

rather than, for instance, in order to open up new business opportunities. Baldwin et al. see this (surely rightly) as an unstable situation. A local food retailer may have little possibility of creating new markets through a website; his customer base is tightly limited geographically. But many small companies deal in goods that can be delivered by post or courier, or are of high enough value for deliveries by the company to be commercially viable.

As Baldwin et al. point out, traditionally a strength of small companies relative to large competitors has been quality of service; and the internet makes relationships between traders and customers more direct, so that there is greater opportunity for the customer to experience superior service. Logically, then, a small company which adopts e-commerce ought to play to its strength by cultivating the kind of personal relationships with far-flung customers that it has previously maintained with customers close at hand; and it will need to seek out a new customer base in that way, because the internet is simultaneously giving distant competitors the chance to develop close relationships with customers based in the first company's vicinity. The logic of the internet pushes SMEs towards specializing in narrow niches within wide, perhaps global markets – whereas they have been used to serving broader sections of local markets.

Broadening the customer base geographically, though, particularly if it means selling across national boundaries for the first time, requires a company to develop expertise in and put effort into unfamiliar activities apart from IT. Exporting involves dealing with language barriers, customs procedures, foreign currencies and international payment systems, unfamiliar shipping and insurance procedures, and perhaps legal requirements of alien jurisdictions. Furthermore, a more far-flung customer base creates problems of brand recognition which are disproportionately difficult for small companies to address. Quoting the British government's 'e-Envoy' Andrew Pinder, 'the real issue is where people are unsure of the supplier and don't recognize the brand, which sometimes counts against small businesses'.[1]

For a small company, these things add up to another large hurdle blocking access to the potential benefits of e-commerce. It does not seem at all surprising if small companies continue to be reluctant to take advantage of the possibilities which, in theory, the new technology makes available.

A classification of internet impacts

Baldwin et al. try to develop a precise picture of the impact of the internet on small companies by defining a matrix model classifying impacts on two dimensions – 'categories of impact' and 'levels of impact' – and by analysing a series of case studies in terms of this matrix. Their two-dimensional analytic framework is perhaps over-elaborate, relative to the unavoidable fuzziness of many of the distinctions drawn. But Baldwin et al.'s 'categories of impact' dimension does offer an interesting classification scheme, even if it is possibly neater than the reality it aims to describe. They classify potential internet impacts under five headings:

---

1. Quoted in Emma Nash, 'Ebusiness players fight the fear factor', *Computing* 31 Oct 2002.

productivity; *information retrieval*; *communication*; *knowledge management*; and *environment*.

Communication here refers both to exchanges within a company, and to information transmitted from the company to the outside world. Knowledge management is a category whose significance relates to the idea – discussed in Chapter 9 – that the essence of a company is the knowledge built up by its staff. For those who accept this as a useful way of thinking about business, maintaining and improving these collective knowledge repositories must be one of the crucial tasks for companies; and the internet has a potential role as an educational tool, upgrading individual workers' expertise and hence the collective knowledge of their firms as wholes. ('Information retrieval' refers to locating particular data which are needed momentarily and, commonly, forgotten as soon as they have been used; the internet as educational tool refers to people acquiring general concepts or skills which, once learned, are available for use over long periods.)

The 'environment' category refers to possible internet impacts on an admittedly vague but important range of matters such as the way staff and office space are deployed, office 'culture' and human relationships, choices between working on the employer's premises v. homeworking, and even the labour market from which the company recruits.

A three-company sample

Baldwin et al. use this scheme to examine the nature of internet impacts on a small sample of SMEs.

It would be inappropriate here to recount in detail Baldwin et al.'s various findings under the five impact headings. For the US cut-flower importer Hosa Inc. of Miami, with 32 employees, benefits were being achieved under all five headings when Baldwin et al. researched the firm. Some of these were general, but under the 'communication' heading there was one activity that is highly specific to Hosa's line of business. If a consignment of flowers has wilted by the time it reaches Hosa's client, there would be no point in sending it back even for verification purposes (if the flowers were acceptable when they reached the client, they certainly would not be when they returned to Miami). So Hosa was developing a system under which clients uploaded digital photographs of unsatisfactory flowers for checking by Hosa staff.

Baldwin et al.'s second case study was a high-quality English confectionery shop, Sweet Seductions of Leamington Spa. For Sweet Seductions, which had been retailing confectionery over the counter and by mail order, the consequences of including the Web as a sales channel were different from what the firm had expected. It had seen the Web chiefly as a means of fostering increased loyalty among existing customers, but in reality many Web sales were to new customers.

One reaction is that this ought to be the natural consequence of a B2C website. Companies have many ways of promoting loyalty among customers they already know; consumption of good confectionery will surely do more to encourage repeat purchases than any amount of pictures or write-ups on computer screens. It is the potential customers a company does not know about who could not previously be reached with such rich information, so cheaply and conveniently, as the Web makes possible.

Nevertheless, the fact that the Web apparently works as a tool for finding new customers for this company's products is not trivial. It runs counter to one plausible point of view about which kinds of goods are and which are not suitable candidates for e-tailing. Stan Liebowitz (2002: 58–86) argues that, among others, *experience products* (ones where the detailed look and feel are specially important to the consumer), and 'products providing instant gratification', are unlikely to sell well via electronic channels. I would have predicted, for instance, that original paintings will normally sell only to customers who can get physically close to them. Surely someone buying an expensive work of art wants to be able to look at each brushstroke directly, unmediated by pixel rasters and palette code conventions? Furthermore, at the upper end of the market one would imagine that part of what the customer is 'buying' is association with the dignified, opulent tradition embodied in the Bond Street galleries and auction rooms in which such pictures are commonly sold. High-quality confectionery is not just an 'experience product' but, unlike paintings, it is an 'instant gratification' product too. (At least, it is the latter when the customer buys it for his own consumption. Sweet Seductions' headcount varies seasonally between three and fifteen; this large variation may imply that most of their ouput is bought as presents, in which case this point would be less true.)

Liebowitz should predict, it seems, that marketing this product to new customers via the Web would be a real non-runner; but the Sweet Seductions case suggests that things are less simple. Likewise – surprisingly, to me – some art firms seem to be succeeding quite well in selling paintings over the Web, partly because the quiet dignity of traditional galleries is actually offputting to some younger, modern-minded clients. The question of which categories of goods are suitable for e-tailing remains unresolved, and the indications are that the range of suitable candidates may be broader than one would expect a priori.

The smallest firm in Baldwin et al.'s sample, CPR Works, was a Birmingham public relations company serving the heating and energy industries. CPR Works had three fulltime employees when the authors studied it, together with relationships with various self-employed workers to whom it farmed work out; annual turnover was about £200,000. For CPR Works, the experience of becoming an e-company was not wholly positive. Public relations is an area where fast responses are critical (if a damage limitation exercise is called for, for instance, it needs to be initiated straight away, not after the weekend); so, in principle, the speed of the internet might seem to offer large benefits to a company like CPR Works. However, Baldwin et al. find that for this company internet speed proved to be a two-edged sword. The fact that prompt responses become technically easy to achieve creates an expectation that they will happen, yet in a tiny company it is very hard to guarantee that a suitable person will always be available to generate a response.

Furthermore, for this company, the internet had evidently been disappointing as an information retrieval tool. Such a company needs to keep up to date with the activities of other companies. It needs to know what its clients' competitors are up to, so that it can help the clients respond to rival marketing campaigns and the like; and it needs to know about initiatives by its clients' partner companies, so that it can help the clients to co-ordinate with them. In principle, access to the Web seems to offer the possibility of achieving this kind of intelligence gathering faster and more conveniently; but in practice CPR Works staff often cannot find time for the amount of surfing that would be needed. Many of us, surely, will recognize the problem that although the Web is amazingly comprehensive, it tends to be a very time-consuming means of locating information. A traditional library or filing system can offer a quick and efficient route to finding a specific fact, *if* the fact in question is contained there in a logical place; overall the Web may offer a better chance of finding a fact, given time, but it often takes a great deal of time.

Common features

Baldwin et al.'s three specimen SMEs are a diverse but tiny sample, perhaps too tiny to give rise to any general conclusions. But there are common threads to their different experiences of internet use, and it seems plausible that in this respect the sample may be fairly representative of the small-company sector, at the time when Baldwin et al. looked at it and indeed still today. In terms of Baldwin et al.'s five categories, the new technology seems on the whole to have had a significant impact on the sample SMEs in terms of productivity, information retrieval, and communication, but much less so under the knowledge management and environment headings. A more general way of putting this might be that the SMEs were still in the main using IT as a new tool for executing some of their existing tasks more efficiently or cheaply, but they had hardly begun to exploit IT to change the nature of the functions executed.

Admittedly, at the period of Baldwin et al.'s research, large companies too had moved less far in the latter direction than they have since. Even at that period, though, a comparable survey of larger companies might have been expected to show more developments in terms of business process re-engineering. Although small organizations are often seen as nimbler than large ones, in terms of exploiting the potential benefits of business computing they probably are lagging – whether because they cannot afford to release people from day-to-day operations in order to plan radical business process re-engineering, or because they cannot afford the capital cost of investing in complex systems (or, conceivably, because the nature of operations within small companies, with relatively direct contacts among staff, means that the new systems genuinely have less to offer them).

Utility computing and web-enabled applications

In view of what was said earlier in this chapter about the importance of small companies as creators of new jobs and first jobs, it is disquieting to find that e-business technology may be tending to leave them behind. However, there are developments within the technology itself which offer some prospects of levelling the playing field.

One is the advent of *utility computing*. A problem for small companies in adopting e-business techniques at present is that the entry cost is often too high. A company has to invest in expensive commercial software, in machines suitable for running it, and in recruiting staff who understand it, in order to execute functions which, in a small concern, may not need to run continuously, and even when they are run may use only a small fraction of the power inherent in the hardware and software. It is as if any suburban householder who wanted to light his house with electricity had to buy and maintain his own industrial-strength generator. 'Utility computing' or 'pay-as-you-go computing' – IBM use the term 'ebusiness on demand' for the utility computing strategy it launched in November 2002 – promises to turn the supply of business computing facilities into an operation more akin to modern electricity supply. To quote an analogy expressed by IBM's Michel Teyssedre, 'You don't ring your local power company to tell them you're going to use a toaster. In future you won't need to phone your IT supplier in advance to say you need more computing power.'[2]

One underlying technology making utility computing possible is *grids*: systems emerging from recent academic research which allow many high-performance computers networked together to share and balance a complex workload among them automatically. Another is *autonomic computing*, which is beginning to lead to computing systems that have abilities to configure themselves, heal themselves when elements break down, and optimize themselves in response to changing demands – rather as a person's bodily organs take charge of their own functioning, protecting themselves and recovering from injury without conscious intervention by the body's owner.[3] A company which used autonomic computing systems would still need staff who understood what the systems were good for, but it might no longer need staff who could mend them when they crashed – a large part of the daily activity of computing support staff at present.

These things, and utility computing in general, are only beginning to move from the research stage into commercial reality, so there is no telling yet how far hopes will be realized; and they are not being developed to solve the problems of small companies in particular. Utility computing is likely to be exploited by large companies whose workloads involve occasional high peaks of processing demand – Bryan Glick gives as examples 'petroleum companies looking at seismic simulation applications, banks with risk analysis'.[4] But if utility computing does succeed in developing as currently envisaged, the possibility it offers of being able to draw on and pay for just as much processing as you need, when you happen to need it, and have it manage itself rather than having to actively manage it, should be a help to small companies trying to exploit e-business technology without excessively draining their resources.

The other technical development which is beginning to make it easier for small companies to exploit e-business applications is the migration of many of them to

2. Quoted in Bryan Glick, 'Extra computing power at the flick of a switch', *Computing* 14 Nov 2002.
3. On autonomic computing, see e.g. www-3.ibm.com/autonomic/, and John Teresko, 'Autonomic computing: the next e-business step', *IndustryWeek.com* 1 Jan 2003, tenpophe.notlong.com
4. See note 2.

the Web. For a small company, an enterprise resource planning system such as SAP's R/3, for instance, was perceived as too complex to get involved with, under the client-server architecture for which it was originally designed. But, as we saw in Chapter 7, the software is now beng converted to run in Web browsers, so that it ceases to daunt potential small-company clients. Increasingly, e-business applications are being Web-enabled. The consequence is a lower requirement for computing support expertise among users, which must be helpful to small companies.

So it is reasonable to hope that the small-company sector may manage to weather the e-business revolution. But at present the signs are that it is struggling. This is being treated as a matter for serious concern by government, at UK and European levels. It should concern us all.

14
Into the future

A speculative conclusion

The preceding chapters have recounted 'the story so far'. It seems right to round things off with a few pages of speculation about what will happen to e-business next. Needless to say, this can be no more than rash guesswork. Phrases like 'I think', 'I believe' will loom large, and anything said here may turn out to look very silly indeed in a few years' time.

That said, two developments are coming over the horizon. Some people expect both to be revolutionary. In one case I believe they are correct.

Mobile computing

Many commentators see the Next Big Thing for e-business as lying in the possibilities of mobile computing using wireless network connexions – what some are beginning to call *m-business* or *m-commerce*.

Ravi Kalakota was co-author of one of the earliest, classic books on e-commerce and of the standard current e-business reference work (Kalakota and Whinston 1996, Kalakota and Robinson 2001). He certainly sees this as the way we are going. In his newest book Kalakota makes large claims for the significance of wireless technology, saying:

> As new technologies and trends slowly shift the center of gravity from tethered to untethered models, a change-wave is unfolding. The companies anticipating this change-wave are moving quickly to reinvent themselves. (Kalakota and Robinson 2002: 2)

Many other commentators have described the trend towards wireless networking in similarly dramatic terms. Johan Hjelm (2000: 2) sees us 'facing a wireless revolution' comparable in significance to the internet revolution. Peter Keen and Ron Mackintosh (2001: 5) see m-commerce as inaugurating 'a new era in business'. Some even see the wireless revolution as a phenomenon that will change our philosophies of society as well as business. Tsugio Makimoto and David Manners foresee people's working lives becoming compatible with unrestricted travel, so that they have a choice between settling or becoming 'global nomads' (Makimoto and Manners 1997). Even that staid and judicious magazine *The Economist* made mobile computing a cover story in November 2002. There is a weight of opinion here that cannot be dismissed lightly.

The chief way in which mobile computing is already beginning to modify business practice relates to supporting maintenance engineers and sales representatives, and keeping them in touch with head office while they are on customers' sites or travelling. A company salesman can arrive at a customer's premises forearmed with up-to-the-minute information about recent interactions between the respective companies – has there been a query or complaint about a previous order, for instance? As maintenance work and negotiations proceed, the representative can retrieve data that unpredictably become relevant, at the time the data are required, rather than having to say that he will check back, with much consequent toing-and-froing and delay. An order once placed can be fed into the supplier's system immediately rather than only after the salesman gets back from his trip, speeding up the overall business process. Travelling time can be used productively rather than just wasted on getting from A to B.

Another key trend foreseen by Kalakota and Robinson is 'queue-busting': customers of service-providing firms such as car rental or hotels will be able to communicate their needs before they arrive, reducing the time they have to spend waiting in line when they finally turn up at the reception desk.

If mobile computing does take off it will have a large impact on the balance of power between users, network operators, and traders. To quote Tom Standage (2001: 279–80):

> On the fixed Internet, the network access provider acts as a '[mindless] pipe' between the user's PC and, say, an online bookstore or travel agent. The access provider will not know how the connection has been used, and there is no question of claiming a commission. Mobile network operators ... are in a far more powerful position. 'Wireless is a smarter pipe,' says Chris Matthiasson of BT Cellnet.

Undoubtedly, mobile computing will have other kinds of effect on business too. But nobody really knows what they will be. In the same breath as they tell us that 'the mobile economy is inevitable', Kalakota and Robinson (2002: 30) go on to admit the impossibility of 'predict[ing] the shape and form of mobile innovation ... the future cannot be foreseen'.

Less than meets the eye

I shall stick my neck out here, at risk of perhaps looking very foolish in five years' time, and say that to my mind there is less to m-business than meets the eye. Keen and Mackintosh believe 'it's impossible to over-hype the potential of M-commerce', but it seems all too easy to me.

Giving a travelling salesforce the possibility of interacting in the field with head office systems and databases is a real business advantage, but a limited advantage. I cannot see wireless networking as destined to 'revolutionize' business (or society) in the same sense as the effects of the internet have been revolutionary. Even the business consequences of the internet have been rather less dramatic than people were imagining in the gold-rush days of the late 1990s, but nevertheless, in the case of the internet, the word 'revolution' does arguably apply. In the case of wireless computing, my personal belief is that it never will. I do not doubt that a lot of wirelessly networked, handheld computers are going to be sold – both for computer manufacturers and for the mobile-phone industry this currently looks like the direction with best prospects of escaping from a mature, flat market into renewed growth; but I do not see pocket computers changing the shape of business.

Possibly my judgement is affected by idiosyncratic personal tastes. I share the preferences of the technology marketing expert Geoffrey Moore, who writes 'I do not carry a PalmPilot, preferring a pocket size notebook and a pen. ... In general, I hate "being connected," which I associate with being either interrupted or confused, not with being in touch' (Moore 1999: 45). But there is more to it than individual tastes, I believe.

After all, if someone truly believes that mobile computing is going to liberate people from the need to be in any particular place to do their work, then why does that commentator also think that business will still be relying on travelling representatives? Physically, it is already possible for the kinds of communication and negotation which a visiting salesman engages in to be conducted remotely, between individuals sitting in their respective company offices. In reality, suppliers' representatives travel to their customers, because there is a chemistry in people talking face to face in the same room which matters deeply for business dynamics: this is a fact about human beings, not about computing technology. (If you are sceptical and think that, some time soon, the technology will be able to reproduce everything including the chemistry in virtual form, then logically you ought to see little future in m-business, because, soon, few businesspeople would need to travel.) Businesses need to send people to talk to customers because of complex human factors which are too subtle to define easily but are nonetheless very significant in practice. And other subtle facts about human beings probably imply that many employees regularly need to be physically present on their company's premises, interacting face to face with colleagues, to work effectively – even if each specific work activity could be supported by mobile computing facilities. I doubt whether a society of business and industrial employees could ever be a society of global nomads, even supposing that the nomadic life appealed to them.

Clearly, if sales representatives are expected by their employers to keep in touch via wireless devices while away from base, they will do so. But I question how much extra value overall will be generated for the employers by this style of working. It becomes possible for the representative to download data into his employer's system while riding on a train, or in a hotel room; but in the past these will often have been welcome periods of enforced relaxation after stressful hours spent in demanding negotiations. People are people, and their bodies and minds can take only so much punishment; if relaxation time is converted by mobile computing into working time, then there will be a tradeoff somewhere – perhaps the overall quality of work will be somewhat degraded. If companies are wise, they will understand that they need to compensate for insisting on immediate communication of new business data by actively giving extra time off at other periods. The outcome could be a net advantage to the employers, but not, surely, one that merits the term 'revolution'?

Indeed, as mobile computing becomes a reality, some are beginning to see it as positively dangerous. Alan Thompson, head of Toshiba Information Systems, commented in February 2003 'When you're young you sleep when you collapse – as you get older, it's different. We don't want to push people over the edge into mental illness. ... We want to say that it's fine to be switched off and away from your work.'[1] Toshiba is considering giving its employees an explicit charter to protect them against the dangers of 'always-on' working.

Technical possibilities and human limitations

The emerging technical possibilities, and the human factors which may limit their practical potential, are both well illustrated by a scenario that Kalakota and Robinson (2002: 237) offer to exemplify the uses of mixed-mode messaging:

> Barb has dropped off her son, Joey, at soccer practice. Practice ends early, so Joey takes out his cell phone and calls his mom. 'Mom,' he says, 'my practice is over. Please come and get me.' However, Barb, a senior VP at a Fortune 50 firm, is sitting in a meeting with her notebook PC opened in front of her. It's wirelessly enabled, and her cell phone is on meeting mode. Barb wants messages received during meetings to be handled in a unified-messaging 'store and forward' fashion. Using a speech-to-text translation feature, she gets an instant message from Joey on her laptop. She looks at it and says, 'I can't deal with this right now.' She forwards it to her husband and writes, 'Jim, I can't get Joey for another two hours. Can you please pick him up?' Jim is driving home from work in a car equipped with telematics capability. He gets the message from Barb on the dashboard with an attachment (message from Joey) and the soccer practice location. Jim clicks on the location link and gets the navigational information he needs to go and pick up his son.

What immediately strikes me about this is that, for meetings to be successful, it is important in my experience that those present should *not* be subject to the distraction of external messages. Standardly, incoming phone calls are intercepted, so that the expensive time of the meeting participants is not dissipated. In emergencies such filters are overridden: if someone's child phones because he is in trouble, a secretary will fetch the parent out of the meeting – but the purposes of business meetings are advanced only if families develop strategies for dealing in other ways with non-crisis happenings.

1. Quoted in *IT Week* 3 Feb 2003.

What is more, when I am in traffic I would prefer the drivers of other cars not to be decoding children's requests translated by speech recognition software onto dashboard screens.

In expressing scepticism about the significance of 'm-business', I am perhaps merely revealing my own lack of vision. But while m-business gurus show such limited interest in relevant human considerations, I feel entitled to predict that these will constrain the possibilities more tightly than the gurus suppose.

The impact of Web services

What about the other Next Big Thing – Web services? Is the fuss currently being made about Web services just yet another example of IT hype?

I believe not – though no more than anyone else can I foresee what specific business or social changes are going to emerge as Web services are deployed. Large changes of one kind or another there will surely be, though. The idea of software program being able to talk to software program across boundaries of physical distance, separate ownership, and lack of longstanding relationships between the people responsible for the software, is a real innovation of great generality. Unlike the case of mobile computing, exploiting this new possibility does not run up against any immediate, obvious problems stemming from human nature or behaviour. (No doubt there will be some potential applications of Web services that involve human-factors problems, but with mobile computing it is hard to think of applications that do not.)

Students on software engineering courses have it drummed into them that a key to successful software development is modularity: complex programs must be built up from routines which each know as little as possible about the internal workings of the other routines. Now, Web services are about to take modularity to a new level. The separate software packages co-operating to achieve some common task will be running on separate machines, and designed by people who may never hear one another's names.

Doubtless the science-fiction concept which we encountered on p. 118, of computers interacting to evolve valuable new configurations of products or services never imagined by the people who set the mechanical systems up, is destined to remain just that – science fiction. There is no particular difficulty in arranging for computers to use randomizing routines to generate unforeseen output configurations, but to be interesting in the context of e-business these would have to serve some business or consumer need better than what already exists. Generating and assessing new business ideas is so difficult for human beings that it seems inconceivable that machines might be able to do it unaided.

But even though it will be people who choose the tasks to which Web services are harnessed, the new technology should hugely change the chances of getting complex tasks achieved successfully in practice by machines. Web services technology seems likely to transform the nature of the relationship between technology-based industry and the software on which its operations ultimately depend.

The end of the software project?

One way of envisaging the impact of Web services — and this relates to industrial computing in general, not just to e-business applications — is that they may mean the end of the traditional 'software project'.

Up to now, a company needing to achieve a new goal through IT has assembled a little army of programmers who have worked up specifications and hacked out code to fit them, following more or less closely as a team one or other of the methodologies advocated in software engineering textbooks. The company requiring the package will often buy it in rather than developing it in-house, but the team of hackers will exist somewhere, if not necessarily at the company which uses its output. Within the project as a whole, there will be many individual components that do in effect the same thing as components within many other software packages developed elsewhere as parts of other applications. But in practice, except for some special cases such as sophisticated mathematical routines, the work is duplicated rather than re-used. There would be no way to locate relevant modules within other companies' systems, and even if one somehow realized that module X in package Y developed by company Z would meet one's current need, and got permission to copy it, the fact that it was developed in a different computing and business environment would probably mean that adapting it would take more effort than writing equivalent code from scratch.

In the world of Web services, there will be little difficulty in locating software modules to execute given functions. Their owners will advertise them and will be only too happy to let others use them for a mutually agreeable fee. Code modules will be written in order to be used over the Web, so they will be as free as possible of any local business-environment assumptions. Differences among computing environments will be irrelevant, because code modules will be run in the environment for which they were written — only inputs and outputs, not copies of the code itself, will be exchanged between companies.

A business may be offering a product or service which as a whole is novel, or may be instituting a novel internal way of working; but the software needed to implement the innovation will be decomposable into generic components. University computer-science research may involve getting machines to do genuinely new and unexpected things, but industrial computing is not like that: it is about assembling standard operations into different configurations to suit varying circumstances. In the world of Web services, a company needing a new software system can be sure of finding virtually every component it needs already written by someone, somewhere, and ready to run.

Thus the role of organizing a software project may change from a man-manager who encourages and enables a team of people to produce sections of code that are compatible with each other and fit together to achieve the overall goal, into a kind of editor, who finds the required code modules wherever in the world they exist, and uses Web-services technology to meld them together. The teams of hackers will melt away; far fewer people in total will be employed to write code.

Conclusion

I said in Chapter 1 that e-business must be thought of as business that happens to use computing technology, not as a branch of IT which happens to be applied in business. If this picture of the future of Web services proves to be broadly accurate, then that principle will be even more valid in time to come than it is already.

So far as business computing is concerned, the day of the techies may be drawing towards its close.

References

Ammann, J., J. M. González-Barahona, and P. de las Heras Quirós, eds. (2001). *Free Software/Open Source: towards maturity.* Special issue of *Upgrade*, vol. 2, part 6, www.upgrade-cepis.org

Baldwin, Amelia, A. Lymer, and R. Johnson (2001). 'Business impacts of the Internet for small and medium-sized enterprises'. In Barnes and Hunt (2001).

Barnes, S. and B. Hunt, eds. (2001). *E-Commerce and V-Business: business models for global success.* Butterworth-Heinemann.

Barnes, S. and R. Vidgen (2002). 'An integrative approach to the assessment of e-commerce quality'. *Journal of Electronic Commerce Research* 3.114–27, bauhemal.notlong.com

Brin, D. (1998). *The Transparent Society: will technology force us to choose between privacy and freedom?* Perseus Books.

Brooks, F. P. (1975). *The Mythical Man-Month: essays on software engineering.* Addison-Wesley.

Chircu, Alina N. and R. J. Kauffman (2001). 'Digital intermediation in electronic commerce: the eBay model'. In Barnes and Hunt (2001).

Coase, R. H. (1937). 'The nature of the firm'. *Economica* n.s. 4.386–405; reprinted in R. H. Coase, *The Firm the Market and the Law*, University of Chicago Press, 1988, and in Williamson and Winter (1993).

Cooper, R. and W. B. Chew (1996). 'Control tomorrow's costs through today's designs'. *Harvard Business Review* Jan–Feb 1996, 88–97.

Cox, B. J. (1996). *Superdistribution: objects as property on the electronic frontier.* Addison-Wesley.

Coyle, F. P. (2002). *XML, Web Services, and the Data Revolution.* Addison-Wesley.

Cringeley, R. X. (1996). *Accidental Empires: how the boys of Silicon Valley make their millions, battle foreign competition, and still can't get a date*, new edn. Penguin.

Cutler, M. and J. Sterne (2000). *E-Metrics: business metrics for the new economy*. NetGenesis, www.emetrics.org/articles/emetrics.pdf

Davenport, T. H. (1998). 'Putting the enterprise into the enterprise system'. *Harvard Business Review* Jul–Aug 1998, 121–31.

Drucker, P. E. (1968). *The Practice of Management*. Pan Books.

Easterly, W. and R. Levine (2002). 'Tropics, germs, and crops: how endowments influence economic development'. Working Paper 9106. National Bureau of Economic Research, www.nber.org/papers/w9106

Friedman, Batya, P. H. Kahn, and D. C. Howe (2000). 'Trust online'. *Communications of the ACM* Dec 2000, 35–40.

Fukuyama, F. (1995). *Trust: the social virtues and the creation of prosperity*. Free Press.

Gelbord, B. (2000). 'Signing your 011001010'. *Communications of the ACM* Dec 2000, 27–8.

Gloor, P. (2000). *Making the e-Business Transformation*. Springer.

Goldfarb, C. F. (1990). *The SGML Handbook*. Clarendon Press.

Goldfinger, C. (1997). 'Intangible economy and its implications for statistics and statisticians'. *International Statistical Review* 65.191–220.

Hagel, J. and A. G. Armstrong (1997). *Net Gain: expanding markets through virtual communities*. Harvard Business School Press.

Harvey-Jones, J. (1988). *Making It Happen: reflections on leadership*. Fontana/Collins.

Hjelm, J. (2000). *Designing Wireless Information Services*. Wiley.

Jewkes, J. (1977). 'Delusions of dominance: a critique of the theory of large-scale industrial dominance and of the pretence of government to "restructure" British industry'. Hobart Paper 76. Institute of Economic Affairs.

Johnston, R. B., H. C. Mak, and Sherah Kurnia (2001). 'The contribution of Internet electronic commerce to advanced supply chain reform – a case study'. In Barnes and Hunt (2001).

Kalakota, R. and Marcia Robinson (2001). *E-Business 2.0: roadmap for success*. Addison-Wesley.

Kalakota, R. and Marcia Robinson (2002). *M-Business: the race to mobility*. McGraw-Hill.

Kalakota, R. and A. B. Whinston (1996). *Frontiers of Electronic Commerce*. Addison-Wesley.

Kannan, P. K., Ai-Mei Chang, and A. B. Whinston (2001). 'E-business and the intermediary role of virtual communities'. In Barnes and Hunt (2001).

Keen, P. G. W. and R. Mackintosh (2001). *The Freedom Economy: gaining the mcommerce edge in the era of the wireless internet*. Osborne/McGraw-Hill.

Kent, P. (1998). *Poor Richard's Web Site: geek-free, commonsense advice on building a low-cost Web site*. Top Floor.

Keser, Claudia, J. Leland, J. Shachat, and H. Huang (2002). 'Trust, the internet, and the digital divide'. IBM Research Report RC22511 (W0207-024), subvolle.notlong.com

Krug, S. (2000). *Don't Make Me Think! A common sense approach to Web usability*. New Riders.

Landauer, T. K. (1995). *The Trouble with Computers: usefulness, usability, and productivity*. MIT Press.

Landauer, T. K. and J. Nielsen (1993). 'A mathematical model of the finding of usability problems'. *Proceedings of the ACM INTERCHI'93 Conference*, Amsterdam, 24–9 Apr 1993, 206–13.

Lessig, L. (1999). *Code: and other laws of cyberspace*. Basic Books.

Lessig, L. (2002). *The Future of Ideas: the fate of the commons in a connected world*. Vintage Books.

Levitt, T. (1960). 'Marketing myopia'. Reprinted with 'Retrospective commentary' in *Harvard Business Review* Sep–Oct 1975, 26–44 and 173–81.

Levy, S. (1984). *Hackers: heroes of the computer revolution*. Dell.

Levy, S. (2000). *Crypto: secrecy and privacy in the new code war*. Allen Lane.

Lewis, M. (2001). *The Future Just Happened*. Hodder & Stoughton.

Li, F. and H. Williams (2001). 'Interorganizational systems to support strategic collaboration between firms'. In Barnes and Hunt (2001).

Liebowitz, S. J. (2002). *Re-Thinking the Network Economy: the true forces that drive the digital marketplace*. Amacom.

Linthicum, D. S. (2001). *B2B Application Integration: e-business–enable your enterprise*. Addison-Wesley.

Lipnack, Jessica and J. Stamps (1998). 'Why virtual teams?' In P. Lloyd and Paula Boyle, eds., *Web-Weaving: intranets, extranets and strategic alliances*, Butterworth-Heinemann.

Loebbecke, Claudia (2001). 'Online delivered content: concept and business potential'. In Barnes and Hunt (2001).

Lynch, P. J. and Sarah Horton (2002). *Web Style Guide: basic design principles for creating Web sites*, 2nd edn. Yale University Press.

McVoy, L. (1993). 'The sourceware operating system proposal'. Revision 1.8 of 9 Nov 1997 online at milquerz.notlong.com

Makimoto, T. and D. Manners (1997). *Digital Nomad*. Wiley.

Malone, T. W., JoAnne Yates, and R. I. Benjamin (1987). 'Electronic markets and electronic hierarchies'. *Communications of the ACM* Jun 1987, 484–97.

Manasian, D. (2003). 'Digital dilemmas: a survey of the internet society'. Supplement to *The Economist* 25 Jan 2003.

Marshall, P., Judy McKay, and Janice Burn (2001). 'Structure, strategy and success factors for the virtual organization'. In Barnes and Hunt (2001).

Miller, G. A. (1956). 'The magical number seven, plus or minus two: some limits on our capacity for processing information'. *Psychological Review* 63.81–97.

Moody, G. (2002). *Rebel Code: Linux and the open source revolution*, new edn. Penguin.

Moore, G. A. (1999). *Crossing the Chasm: marketing and selling technology products to mainstream customers*, 2nd edn. Capstone.

Mougayar, W. (1998). *Opening Digital Markets: battle plans and business strategies for internet commerce*, 2nd edn. McGraw-Hill.

Needle, D. (2000). *Business in Context: an introduction to business and its environment*, 3rd edn. Business Press.

Niederst, Jennifer (2001). *Web Design in a Nutshell: a desktop quick reference*, 2nd edn. O'Reilly.

Nielsen, J. (2002). *Designing Web Usability: the practice of simplicity*, 7th printing. New Riders.

Nielsen, J. and Marie Tahir (2002). *Homepage Usability: 50 websites deconstructed*. New Riders.

Norris, G., J. R. Hurley, K. M. Hartley, J. R. Dunleavy, and J. D. Balls (2000). *E-Business and ERP: transforming the enterprise*. Wiley.

Oellermann, W. L. (2001). *Architecting Web Services*. Apress.

O'Neill, Onora (2002). *A Question of Trust: the BBC Reith Lectures 2002*. Cambridge University Press.

Piercy, N. F. (2002). *Market-Led Strategic Change: transforming the process of going to market*, 3rd edn. Butterworth-Heinemann.

Raymond, E. S. (2001). *The Cathedral and the Bazaar: musings on Linux and open source by an accidental revolutionary*, revised edn. O'Reilly. Online at catb.org/~esr/writings/

Reid, R. H. (1997). *Architects of the Web: 1,000 days that built the future of business.* Wiley.

Resnick, P., R. Zeckhauser, E. Friedman, and K. Kuwabara (2000). 'Reputation systems'. *Communications of the ACM* Dec 2000, 45–8.

Rheingold, H. (1993). *The Virtual Community: homesteading on the electronic frontier.* Addison-Wesley.

Robert, G. and F. Schütz (2001). 'Should business adopt free software?' In Ammann et al. (2001).

Rosenfeld, L. and P. Morville (1998). *Information Architecture for the World Wide Web: designing large-scale Web sites.* O'Reilly.

Schoder, D., R. Strauss, and P. Welchering (1998). *Electronic Commerce Enquête 1997/98: survey on the business uses of electronic commerce for companies in the German speaking world.* Konradin-Verlag.

Schumpeter, J. A. (1943). *Capitalism, Socialism and Democracy.* Allen & Unwin.

Shirky, C. (2000). 'The case against micropayments'. *O'Reilly Network* 19 Dec 2000, eluersha.notlong.com

Siegel, D. (1997). *Creating Killer Web Sites* (2nd edn). Macmillan.

Smith, A. (1776). *An Inquiry into the Nature and Causes of the Wealth of Nations.* Glasgow edition, ed. by R. H. Campbell and A. S. Skinner, 2 vols., Clarendon Press, 1976.

Spector, R. (2000). *Amazon.com: Get Big Fast: inside the revolutionary business model that changed the world.* Random House.

Spool, J. M., Tara Scanlon, W. Schroeder, Carolyn Snyder, and Terri DeAngelo (1999). *Web Site Usability: a designer's guide.* Morgan Kaufmann.

Stallman, R. (2001). 'Harm from the Hague'. In Ammann et al. (2001) and at www.fsf.org/philosophy/hague.html

Standage, T. (2001). 'Mobile telecoms'. In *E-Trends, The Economist* in association with Profile Books.

Sterne, J. (2000). *Customer Service on the Internet: building relationships, increasing loyalty, and staying competitive*, 2nd edn. Wiley.

Sterne, J. (2001). *World Wide Web Marketing: integrating the Web into your marketing strategy*, 3rd edn. Wiley.

Tiffin, N. and R. Müller (2001). 'GNU enterprise application software'. In Ammann et al. (2001).

Wallis, J. J. and D. C. North (1988). 'Measuring the transaction sector in the American economy'. In S. Engerman and R. Gallman, eds., *Long Term Factors in American Economic Growth*, University of Chicago Press.

Weintraut, J. N. (1997). Introduction to Reid (1997).

Williamson, O. E. and S. G. Winter, eds. (1993). *The Nature of the Firm: origins, evolution, and development*. Oxford University Press, paperback edn.

Winter, S. G. (1993). 'On Coase, competence, and the corporation'. In Williamson and Winter (1993).

Wishart, A. and Regula Bochsler (2002). *Leaving Reality Behind: the battle for the soul of the internet*. Fourth Estate.

Woodall, Pam (2002). 'Survey: the world economy'. Supplement to *The Economist* 26 Sep 2002.

Woolrych, A. and G. Cockton (2001). 'Why and when five test users aren't enough'. J. Vanderdonckt, A. Blandford, and A. Derycke, eds., *Proceedings of the IHM-HCI 2001 Conference, Toulouse*, Editions Cépaduès, 2.105–8, subvioan.notlong.com

Index

Frequently-used technical terms are indexed only for passages that define them.